Voices *of*
Insight

BOOKS BY SHARON SALZBERG

A Heart As Wide As the World: Stories on the Path of Lovingkindness

Lovingkindness: The Revolutionary Art of Happiness

Voices of Insight

VOICES *of* INSIGHT

EDITED BY

Sharon Salzberg

SHAMBHALA
Boston & London
2001

Shambhala Publications, Inc.
Horticultural Hall
300 Massachusetts Avenue
Boston, Massachusetts 02115
www.shambhala.com

9 8 7 6 5 4 3 2

Printed in the United States of America
⊗ This edition is printed on acid-free paper that meets
the American National Standards Institute z39.48 Standard.
♻ Shambhala Publications makes every effort to print on recycled paper.
For more information please visit us at www.shambhala.com.

Distributed in the United States by Random House, Inc.,
and in Canada by Random House of Canada Ltd

The Library of Congress catalogues the previous edition of this book as
follows:
Voices of insight/edited by Sharon Salzberg.
    p.   cm.
  ISBN 978-1-57062-398-1
  ISBN 978-1-57062-769-9 (pbk.)
  1. Vipaśyanā (Buddhism)   2. Compassion (Buddhism)
  3. Theravāda Buddhism.   I. Salzberg, Sharon.
  BQ5630.V5V64   1999   99-23692
  294.3'444—dc21   CIP

CONTENTS

DEDICATION

T H E I D E A of compiling an anthology of writings by teachers who lead retreats at the Insight Meditation Society (IMS) first arose many years ago but somehow never came to fruition. Then, one day in 1998, Peter Turner, my editor at Shambhala Publications, called to ask if I would be interested in putting together an insight meditation reader. I explained that this possibility had been under discussion for many years and then added, "I think this kind of project only works if no one makes any money from it."

The next day, while I was meditating, the thought came, "Ram Dass . . . the royalties could go to him." Ram Dass, who had been an inspiration and support for many of us at IMS, had recently suffered a severe stroke and was faced with mounting medical bills and other expenses. I called Peter and said I would be delighted to do the book.

And so this book is dedicated to Ram Dass in gratitude for his pioneering spirit, his love of the Dharma, and his gift of service—and to his teacher, Neem Karoli Baba, whose unconditional love has lit up the path for countless spiritual seekers. All royalties from the sales of *Voices of Insight* will be donated to a special fund for Ram Dass's care.

SHARON SALZBERG

GRATEFUL
ACKNOWLEDGMENTS

EVERYONE WHO teaches at IMS was tremendously supportive of the effort to create this anthology. Unfortunately, not
all the teachers of IMS could be represented here. They are
all nonetheless present in the generosity and lovingkindness they
exemplify, which manifests so clearly in their teaching. The teachers
who did contribute chapters to this book extended a great deal of
time and effort in a remarkable spirit of service.

IMS itself has flourished since 1976 because of those who have
taken retreats there, and because of the staff, administration, bene-
factors and members of the Board of Directors, as well as the teachers. In a similar way, this anthology came into being through the
concerted efforts of many. Martha Ley, Hal Ross, Carolyn Ross, and
Shoshana Alexander edited various chapters on behalf of particular
contributors. Jack Kornfield created the overall organization. David
Berman, in a flash of inspiration, gave us the title. Mirabai Bush, in a
very busy life, generously wrote the foreword. Peter Turner of Shambhala Publications began the whole process and was tremendously
supportive throughout. Kendra Crossen Burroughs brought it all to
completion with skill, insight, and a real sense of humor.

This book would never have happened without Julie Tato and Eric

McCord, who together kept the vision of the project alive. Julie listened to hours of tapes to search out the particular passion and gift of each teacher. She also managed a large amount of the communications mandated by the project, and offered valuable perspectives on the different chapters. Eric worked with the majority of the chapters from the very roughest stage, and in a wonderful way enabled each teacher to create structure and clarity while preserving his or her own unique voice. He also refined several later versions of the entire manuscript, so that his editing skills are manifested everywhere. Eric worked on the book with sincerity and grace from the time it was conceived until it was concluded.

I want to thank the publishers who generously waived or reduced permissions fees in the spirit of this offering: Maypop Books, Parallax Press, Rider, Shambhala Publications, Weatherhill, and Wisdom Publications.

My role in editing this book coincided with an exceptional time in my life spent in New York City, created by the generosity of Amy Gross, and the open minds and hearts of Jennifer Greenfield, Cathy and Salva Trentalancia, Nena Thurman, and Jonathan Cott. In addition, I'd especially like to thank Jonathan for teaching me a thing or two about faith.

FOREWORD

Mirabai Bush

MEDITATION IS NOTHING NEW. But for many years in the West only monastics, mystics, poets, and Asian Americans practiced it. Now this path of observing life simply and directly has made its way into the mainstream. Partly because of the wise and direct words of the teachers in this book, an American meditation tradition has taken root. Buddhism has brought its jewel, the practice of learning by looking within, to a society in need of wisdom to navigate into the next century.

Sometimes now, sitting among corporate scientists and listening to Steven Smith lead a lovingkindess meditation for all species, or watching Joseph Goldstein answer a Yale Law student's question about readiness to learn mindfulness practice, I actually forget that meditation is such a recent arrival in mainstream life. But reminders are everywhere: *Time* magazine lists addresses and websites for Dens of Dharma, and environmental leaders at annual meetings spend their mornings in sitting practice and their afternoons discussing climate change. At a recent conference on the future, meditation sessions were followed by inner city youths rapping their insight (It must be my karma / to get into the Dharma). In a Bryn Mawr classroom, students meditate before studying the Holocaust, slavery, and apartheid; according to their professor, it helps them "keep the encounter with shared human horror from becoming a kind of vicarious intellectual voyeurism."

In this Buddhist tradition, people who teach the meditation practice are called guides or "spiritual friends." They teach, encourage, and struggle to embody the teachings themselves. The teachers who are represented in this anthology have patiently "translated" what the Buddha taught to skeptical, cautious, searching, and grateful students. It is a meditation hall between covers. It is a companion on the journey, a friend to read when you want to be guided a little closer to true home. And it is dedicated to one of the early meditation pioneers and a spiritual friend of IMS, Ram Dass.

Since 1970, when we met in Bodhgaya, the Indian village where the Buddha was enlightened, I have known Ram Dass as a fellow pilgrim on the path of the heart. We often lived together with other friends, in Berkeley and Cambridge and Boulder and Martha's Vineyard and New York; we taught retreats, journeyed in the East, wrote a book, listened to gospel music in New Orleans, and learned the struggles of Mayan Indian friends in Guatemala through our work for the Seva Foundation. Ram Dass was godfather to my son and other children in the extended family.

The unbroken thread of all those years was that he held life as a journey, a process of discovery, a dance of impermanence, the only dance there is. When we were apart, especially if either of us had been investigating some new practice or teacher or sacred place, we would compare notes about what we had learned, how it had changed what we had thought to be true. What was sitting in Burma with U Pandita like? How was it to fast for three weeks in the Alps? What about childbirth?

Then, in 1997, Ram Dass, while writing the last chapter of a book on aging, experienced what many of us have thought we'd experience when writing a final chapter. He had a massive stroke. It changed his life.

When I visited him a few weeks later at the Kaiser rehab hospital in Vallejo, California, he was lying in a hospital bed, paralyzed on one side, pale, looking at a picture of his guru, Neem Karoli Baba, Maharaji, and a batik wall hanging of Hanuman, the Hindu son of the Wind God, the spirit of breath. After a long silence together, he looked at me, trying hard to speak, moving his hand as if he were about to speak, pointing to his paralyzed side, and then trying to express something that he wanted me to hear. It felt very familiar, even in that sterile room through my tears. Then he moved his fingers down his arm, like in the Yellow Pages ads: they were walking. It was the path, the journey. "Learning," he said. Long silence. "Learning . . . patience. Patience." Then he closed his eyes and rested.

Over the years, Ram Dass encouraged thousands of friends and students to do the basic work of spiritual awakening at IMS—learning to see deeply, open their hearts more fully, act with clarity and compassion, be more fully in the moment. In some ways he was an unlikely guide to Buddhism. Born a Jew ("only on my parents' side"), he is devoted to his Hindu guru, Neem Karoli Baba, Maharaji, whose essential teaching is *"Sub ek"*—All paths are one. At Ram Dass's great gatherings of the tribe, which happened everywhere from Hawaii to New Hampshire from the sixties till the nineties, there was often a wide range of eclectic practices. Hindu chanting predominated, but Buddhist practice was a steady presence, returning us all to the breath and the present moment.

So I am pleased that this book, by those who have taught at IMS, has been dedicated to Ram Dass—this book about sacred journey, sacred friendship, right effort, suffering and the end of suffering, unconditional acceptance, the power of silence and stillness, all of what is contained in the practice of being here now. It is offered with great gratitude, by so many people, in the spirit of our interconnection. May it inspire many to deepen their wisdom and compassion and work to relieve the suffering of all beings. In-breath, out-breath . . .

VOICES *of*
INSIGHT

INTRODUCTION

Sharon Salzberg

FROM THE TIME of the Buddha's enlightenment in India twenty-five hundred years ago, the teachings known as Buddhism have spread throughout the world, adapting to the needs of different peoples and cultural settings. Wherever the universal human longing for spiritual freedom has been felt, the Dharma—the Buddha's Teaching—has found a home. Over the past several decades this message of freedom has spread widely in the Western world, where people have been especially drawn to the various techniques of Buddhist meditation. The teachings in this book are centered on two of these practices as taught at the Insight Meditation Society (IMS) in Barre, Massachusetts: insight meditation (*vipassana*) is the observation of the mind/body process with clear and focused awareness, leading to a deepening of wisdom and equanimity; and lovingkindness (*metta*) is the systematic exploration of the ability to love, leading to a deepening of concentration and connection.

The Insight Meditation Society was founded in 1976 by a group of friends; we had all been to Asia, where our lives were fundamentally and radically changed by having encountered the Buddha's teachings and the practice of meditation. On Valentine's Day 1976 we moved into the property in Barre and began operating a retreat center devoted to intensive, teacher-led silent retreats, where anyone interested could learn to practice insight and lovingkindness.

I remember many of the late-night meetings that marked our early years: "Will we be able to survive financially?" we wondered. "Will anybody at all come to practice? Since we are not asking anyone to subscribe to a religion, should we have Buddha statues around or not?" And, most profoundly, "What does it mean to take a tradition steeped in the imagery and metaphor of Asia, to try to find its unchanging essence, and then express that essence in the imagery of our time and place?"

When the Buddha sent off the first group of his disciples to teach "for the good of the many, for the welfare of the many . . . out of compassion for all beings," he instructed them to teach the people they came upon in an idiom that was most accessible and most meaningful. The ancient allegory of a spiritual journey is being re-told today in our own idiom. We are unfolding a tradition that speaks of our current challenges, our own triumphs, and our unique lessons. We are discovering new metaphors—in our own time and place, in our own families and communities and institutions—that connect us to a reality and a teaching that is timeless and universal. This is a wonderful and important step in making the Dharma our own. It is a significant step in the transmission of a living truth.

So far we have survived financially, many thousands of people have come, we don't ask anyone to subscribe to a religion, and there are many Buddha statues about the building and grounds. And the work of transplanting a teaching from one culture to another continues to be our deepest creative effort, offering many challenges in integrity, compassion, discriminating wisdom, and the ability to let go and start anew when we've made a mistake.

Although most of the teachers who lead retreats at IMS are laypeople from the West, throughout the year both Western and Asian teachers, ordained and lay, come to offer the Dharma. There is a wide variety of expression offered at IMS, but all of the teachers are grounded in the same tradition of Theravada Buddhism. The foundation of this tradition is an ever-deepening awareness of the three refuges: the Buddha, Dharma, and Sangha. This book is laid out as an exploration of these three refuges, offering both classical and contemporary understandings. In the end, the crucial understanding is one's own, for the tradition is kept alive through the commitment to insight, moral integrity, and compassion of all who practice it. The voices in this book, though varied and distinct, each remind us of this essential truth: we can all free our minds of habitual clinging, anger, and confusion if we honestly make that commitment and sincerely practice the path of insight.

PART ONE

The Buddha and the
Lineage of Teachers

Introduction
To Part One

W E BEGIN MEDITATION RETREATS by taking refuge in the Three Jewels of Buddhism, the first of which is the Buddha himself. By taking refuge in the Buddha, we recognize the possibility he symbolizes a human being with boundless compassion and an awakened mind. That possibility exists within each of us. As we practice meditation to bring this potential to life, teachers often serve as a bridge between the power of the Buddha's example and our own direct experience.

This section is about such teachers, and about the friendship between teachers and students. It explores what an intricate, profound, blessed, complicated thing it is to have a teacher, and ultimately how we must learn to trust ourselves as the teacher. From the Buddha and his disciples twenty-five hundred years ago, to the teachers of today, Dharma practice has survived through a series of friendships. As Stephen Batchelor says in his book *Buddhism without Beliefs*, "Dharma practice flourishes only when such friendships flourish. It has no other means of transmission."

The particular kind of friendship that is spiritual friendship—often the relationship of student to teacher—causes us to question many of our habitual assumptions, and ultimately brings forth our deepest empowerment, worthiness, and unconditional love. A major strength of these friendships is that they remind us of what we are capable of. When we are mirrored by a spiritual friend, we renew our belief in ourselves, moving beyond our conditioned and limited views of our own abilities.

Spiritual teachers, mentors, and friends remind us again and again: "Freedom is possible. Love is possible. Deep compassion is possible. It is possible for real people. It is possible for you." We rely on a teacher only to learn to rely on ourselves, and ultimately to rely on the personal truth we discover as we see more clearly.

Some of the chapters in this section reflect the experience of Westerners working with Asian teachers, others of householders working with those who have ordained, and one of finding important relationships with women who lived long ago, in the time of the Buddha. Whether we are inspired by the Buddha and his lineage of teachings, have a teacher who guides us face to face, or recognize the impact of an overheard conversation or a poem written in another time, we are simultaneously challenged and embraced by spiritual friendship. Our challenge is to personally and directly embody spiritual teachings rather than simply admire them in others. Many times we are only able to do this because of someone's unshakable and loving conviction that we, each one of us, can wake up.

THE BUDDHA'S
SACRED JOURNEY

Joseph Goldstein

SIDDHARTHA GOTAMA, Prince of the Shakyas, awakened to Buddhahood more than twenty-five hundred years ago. What does that extraordinary event mean for us now, all these centuries later? Does his life and enlightenment have relevance for our own lives, for our own spiritual journeys? In hearing the story of Prince Siddhartha, of how he became a Buddha, we can consider different levels of meaning and significance.

The most familiar level is the Buddha as a particular person in history. He lived in a small kingdom near what is now the border of Nepal and India in the fifth and sixth centuries BC. At the age of thirty-five he had a remarkable spiritual awakening. When we know the elements of his life story, we relate in a very human way, understanding his struggles, his quest, and his enlightenment, from the perspective of one human being to another.

On another level, we can view the Buddha as a fundamental archetype of humanity, an expression of the fully awakened mind, exemplifying the potential for enlightenment that is in us all. On this archetypal level, the Buddha's life is not simply the strivings and realization of a particular individual, but rather the unfolding of a great mythological journey. "Mythological" here does not mean unreal or imaginary. The power of myth universalizes the personal and so helps us view our own life experiences in a larger and more profound context. Through understanding the Buddha's journey, we connect with our own deepest aspirations. We may have begun to follow the same path, motivated by the same questions: What is the true nature of our lives? What is the root cause of our suffering? Can we be free?

In his book *Hero with a Thousand Faces*, Joseph Campbell, the great scholar of world myths, speaks of four stages in the journey of the archetypal hero or heroine. His discussion of the Buddha's life in terms of these four stages is a wonderful interweaving of the Buddha's personal history with the universal principles they embody.

Campbell calls the first stage of the heroic journey the Call to Destiny. In the Buddhist tradition we might term it the Call to Awakening. It arises when something occurs that makes us question deeply how we are living, what our lives are about. It happens when we realize that worldly, conventional understanding no longer satisfies us.

At Siddhartha's birth, a sage predicted that either he would become a world monarch or he would renounce the world and become a Buddha, an Awakened One. The Bodhisattva's father (*Bodhisattva* is the word for a being destined for perfect enlightenment; this is how the Buddha is referred to prior to his awakening), wishing for his son to become a worldly ruler like himself, surrounded Siddhartha with all the pleasures of the senses, occupying him entirely with the delights of the world. The king provided the young prince with different palaces for each of the seasons, with musicians, dancers, and beautiful companions to entertain him. The king did everything within his power to banish all unpleasantness from Siddhartha's life.

At the age of twenty-nine, the prince decided to leave the palace grounds and explore the life of the city around him. Remembering the early prophecy, the king worried that Siddhartha might encounter something disturbing and thus be prompted to question his life of luxury, so he ordered all unpleasant sights to be removed. He had the buildings freshly painted, flowers and incense placed all about, and everyone who was suffering hidden away. But the Bodhisattva's calling was not so easily denied.

It is said that heavenly messengers, celestial beings, appeared to him as he rode throughout the city. The first of these messengers appeared as an old person, stricken with infirmities. The second messenger appeared as a person suffering greatly with disease. The third appeared as a corpse. The prince was startled at each encounter, because in his protected young life he had never come into contact with old age, sickness, or death. Seeing these aspects of life for the first time touched him deeply. He questioned his charioteer about what he was seeing and whether everyone was subject to this fate. The charioteer replied that it is inevitable for all who take birth to grow older, to get sick, and to die. The last of the heavenly messengers appeared to the prince as a wandering monk. Questioned again, the charioteer answered that this was someone who had renounced the world in order to seek enlightenment and liberation.

These four heavenly messengers awakened within the Bodhisattva the energy of countless lifetimes of practice; they awakened within him both the deep sense of inquiry about the sufferings of life and the recognition that freedom is possible. Siddhartha reflected, "Why should I, who am subject to decay and death, also seek that which is subject to decay and death? What is it that's born? What is it that dies?"

These are basic questions confronting us all. Why should we, being subject to decay and death, endlessly seek those things that are also going to disappear, to change, to decay and die? It raises questions for each one of us, just as it did for the Bodhisattva: What are we doing with our lives? What is truly of value? What choices are we making? Although many of us have these passing thoughts, they often get lost as we re-immerse ourselves in the busyness of our lives.

What *is* the nature of birth and death? What is it that is not born and so never dies? The Call to Awakening—the initial stage of the journey that opens us to other possibilities and leads us to read and study about the spiritual path—can happen in many ways. Do we recognize the heavenly messengers in our own lives? What was the impetus for our own beginning practice? Each of us, like the Buddha, has a story. We have all heard some call to awaken.

There are three contemplations that help arouse us from the complacency of conventional, worldly understanding. The first is reflecting on the inevitability of death. It's amazing how the mind can know and understand that everyone dies, and yet how rarely do we internalize this understanding and know deeply and fully that death will also happen to us? It's always *other* people who seem to be dying. We don't often consider our own deaths or those of people close to us until the heavenly messenger pays us a personal visit.

The second reflection is on the uncertainty of the time of death. Even if we somehow have understood that death will inevitably come, it's certainly not tonight, and probably not tomorrow. But, in fact, we don't know when death will come. Can we imagine ourselves, right now, on our deathbeds? What would that be like? What would we most hold on to? Is it our bodies, our possessions, our relationships? Are we ready now to face the inevitable end of life?

The third reflection that awakens spiritual ardency, that helps arouse this Call to Awakening, reminds us that at the time of death it is only our Dharma practice, only the qualities of wisdom, compassion, love, and equanimity, that are our real refuge. Because these are the things that will be of value at the time of death, we need to arouse a sense of urgency to practice and cultivate them now.

Campbell calls the next stage of the hero's journey the Great Renunciation. In order to awaken to the often hidden possibilities of life, we need to be willing to give up our habitual ways of seeing and relating to the world. Things are often not what they seem to be, and if we stay satisfied with superficial perceptions, we often end up living in ignorance and delusion.

There are some striking examples of this in the world of science. Using the Hubbell telescope, astronomers were taking pictures of space in an area around the Big Dipper. It was in a part of the sky where they had previously thought that not much was to be found. But in looking through this new, more powerful telescope, they discovered millions of new galaxies, each with hundreds of millions of stars. We find the same situation when we turn our attention to the microscopic level. A book on discoveries in quantum physics says, "In very round terms, the quantum world operates on a scale as much smaller than a sugar cube, as a sugar cube is compared with the entire observable universe." Might we be also missing something in our own lives?

When we apply the power of an open mind and keen investigation to consciousness itself, we begin to free ourselves from the limitations of conventional understandings, largely expressed through the verb "to have." I *have* possessions, I *have* a body, I *have* relationships, I *have* a mind. Erich Fromm, the well-known psychologist, said we live with the understanding that "I am what I have." When we look at our experience and our ordinary way of viewing things, we find this to be true. But there is a serious problem with this way of living. Because things are always changing, whatever we have we will also lose, whether it's external possessions, relationships, or even things we most identify with, like our bodies and minds. Consequently, in this world of having, there is always an underlying sense of unease, anxiety, or incompleteness.

The Great Renunciation is really the renunciation of the paradigm of "having" as our deepest value. This allows us to turn our attention to the nature of the mind itself, to the quality of being. We begin to see that the quality of our minds has much more to do with our happiness than anything we might have or possess. And, most important, we begin to see that how we are is up to us, that there is the potential to open the heart and awaken the mind.

Renunciation is the ability to let go of those things that no longer serve us. It's not only about giving up excessive attachment to external things; can we also let go of the habits of endless discursive thought, or the various afflictive emotions, those emotions and mindstates that cause us suffering? As long as we don't renounce that "having," we get lost, immersed in the various mind-worlds of proliferating thoughts. Can we actually renounce this habit of *having*, of claiming everything as a possession, as being "me" or "mine"?

After encountering the four heavenly messengers, the Bodhisattva left the palace with all its pleasures and comforts in order to seek liberation. Siddhartha first went to different teachers of concentration meditation and mastered all the levels of meditative absorption. Yet even after attaining the highest levels of concentration, he realized he was still not free. He saw that even the highest of these states was not the Unconditioned, that which is beyond birth and death.

He then spent six years practicing various kinds of austerities and ascetic disciplines, mortifying the body in an effort to subdue the ego. For long periods, it is said, he ate only one grain of rice a day, becoming so emaciated that when he tried to touch his belly, his hand would grasp his backbone. So extreme was his asceticism that he would collapse from fatigue and hunger. After six years of such practice, he realized that this was not the path to freedom, to the end of suffering. Siddhartha gave up this extreme ascetic discipline and, taking some food, nourished himself for the third great event in the sacred journey.

The third event is called the Great Struggle. Having regained his strength, the Bodhisattva sat beneath the Bodhi Tree with the resolve that he would not get up until he had attained supreme enlightenment. As he sat there with unwavering resolve and determination, all the forces of Mara, of illusion and ignorance, assailed his mind. Joseph Campbell describes this encounter in powerful mythopoetic language, vividly conveying the energy involved in the Bodhisattva's commitment to truth:

"The Bodhisattva placed himself, with a firm resolve, beneath the Bodhi Tree, on the Immovable Spot, and straightaway was approached by Kama-Mara, the god of love and death. The dangerous god appeared mounted on an elephant carrying weapons in his thousand hands. He was surrounded by his army, which extended twelve leagues before him, twelve to the right, twelve to the left, and in the rear as far as to the confines of the world; it was nine leagues high. The protecting deities of the universe took flight, but the future Buddha remained unmoved beneath the Tree. And the god then assailed him, seeking to break his concentration.

"Whirlwind, rocks, thunder and flame, smoking weapons with keen edges, burning coals, hot ashes, boiling mud, blistering sands and fourfold darkness, the Antagonist hurled against the Savior, but the missiles were all transformed into celestial flowers and ointments by the power of Gautama's ten perfections. Mara then deployed his daughters, Desire, Pining, and Lust, surrounded by voluptuous attendants, but the mind of the Great Being was not distracted. The god finally challenged his right to be sitting on the Immovable Spot, flung his razor-sharp discus angrily, and bid the towering host of the army to let fly at him with mountain crags. But the Future Buddha only moved his hand to touch the ground with his fingertips, and thus bid the goddess Earth bear witness to his right to be sitting where he was. She did so with a hundred, a thousand, a hundred thousand roars, so that the elephant of the Antagonist fell upon its knees in obeisance to the Future Buddha. The army was immediately dispersed, and the gods of all the worlds scattered garlands."*

This is a wonderful rendering of the Bodhisattva's struggle with Mara; and in a very real way, each one of us also sits under the Bodhi Tree every time we strongly resolve to be aware, to be mindful. Mara may assail the mind with desire and anger, with restlessness and fears, with all the same forces personified in the imagery of myth. It is the same struggle, the same commitment, and the same process of becoming free. This effort resonates in an arena beyond just our immediate experience; at that time we are expressing the determination and courage of the hero and heroine.

Thomas Merton highlighted this stage of the spiritual path when he wrote, "Prayer and love are learned in the hour when prayer becomes impossible and the heart has turned to stone." This is true of meditation as well. It is the real meaning of courageous effort—the willingness to open to it all, to explore all the hidden and difficult aspects of our experience.

Great care is also needed. Effort, when it is wrongly understood, can get confused with expectation, with ambition, with tension, resulting in pride or discouragement. But the quality of effort can be understood very differently—that is, effort as a "courageous heart." It is the courage that doesn't give up in the face of difficulties. Some-

---

*Joseph Campbell, *Hero with a Thousand Faces* (New York: World Publishing Co., 1971), p. 32.

times we may need to retreat a bit to find balance, but courage in practice is that quality of heart that is always seeking to understand.

At this stage of our journey, the Great Struggle, the question for us is whether we can generate this courage, this courageous heart, not from some external model of how we should be, but from within ourselves—from our own interest, our own willingness, our own passion for freedom. It is this courage that allows us to keep playing at the edge of exploration, the edge of discovery, even when it's uncomfortable, when we don't want to be there. When we're at the edge of what is known, new possibilities emerge.

A few years after the founding of the Insight Meditation Society, I sat a Zen *sesshin* (intensive meditation retreat) with Sasaki Roshi, a fierce old Zen master. The retreat was quite intense, with formal group practice from before dawn till late into the evening. In that tradition of Zen, we did *koan* practice, a koan being a question that demands a response of intuitive wisdom rather than one of intellectual understanding. We saw Roshi four times a day to present our responses. For the first few days of the retreat, in every interview, Roshi would respond gruffly to my answers with comments like, "Oh, very stupid," or, "Good answer, but not Zen." As this continued, four times a day, I was getting more and more tense, dreading the times I would have to see him.

Finally, perhaps out of compassion for my increasing difficulties, he gave me an easier koan: "How do you manifest Buddha-nature while chanting a sutra?" It was clear that I needed to go in and chant a few lines of one of the sutras. What I don't think he knew (or perhaps he did) is that this koan touched one of my deepest conditioned fears, going back to a third-grade singing teacher's saying, "Goldstein, just mouth the words." Of course, many friends over the years have continued to reinforce that suggestion. So there I was, already distressed by the intensity of the sesshin, by my seeming inability to get anything right, and then needing to go in and "sing" something.

Through all the next meditation sessions I practiced the chants to myself, repeating them hundreds of times. Finally, the bell for the interviews rang. I delayed for as long as I could, but in the end I found myself in Roshi's room, doing the customary bows and telling him my koan. I started to chant and within the first few words proceeded to get everything wrong—the words, the melody, the rhythm. I felt completely naked and exposed, as if every emotional protective covering had been stripped away. And then something quite remarkable happened. He looked directly in my eyes and said, "Very good."

It was an amazing moment. Because I was in such an open and vulnerable space, his words touched my heart deeply. There was no barrier there to keep them out. In that moment of openness there was a transmission of love.

The last stage in our account of the Buddha's journey to enlightenment is called the Great Awakening. After the hosts of Mara were dispersed, the Bodhisattva spent the three watches of the night contemplating various aspects of the Dharma. With his power of concentration, he surveyed the succession of his innumerable past lives and understood their insubstantiality—the endlessness of being born in a particular situation, having all kinds of experiences, growing old, dying, and being reborn, over and over again.

Just think how our own perspective would change if we could see the endlessness of life and death and rebirth. But even if we can't see into our past lives, we can get a taste of that perspective when we look at our past experiences in this life. All the things we have seen, and felt, and thought—where are they now? However intense or wonderful or difficult they might have been, they have all passed away. This flow of change is happening from moment to moment. There is nothing we can hold on to.

In the second watch of the night, the Bodhisattva contemplated the law of karma. He saw the destinies of beings, and how, because of their own actions, they are reborn either in various happy planes of existence or in planes of suffering. Compassion arose in the Bodhisattva when he saw that all beings desire happiness and yet, out of ignorance, often do the very things that cause suffering. Can we see this in our own lives as well?

In the third watch of the night he saw how the mind becomes attached, and how through attachment there is suffering. He understood the possibility of deconditioning that attachment and coming to a place of freedom. And just at the moment of dawn, when the morning star appeared in the sky, his mind realized the deepest, most complete illumination. After attaining the great enlightenment, the Buddha expressed this verse in his heart (*Dhammapada*, verses 153–54):

I wandered through the rounds of countless births,
Seeking but not finding the builder of this house.
Sorrowful indeed is birth again and again.
Oh, housebuilder! You have now been seen.
You shall build the house no longer.
All your rafters have been broken,
Your ridgepole shattered.
My mind has attained to unconditioned freedom.
Achieved is the end of craving.

The Buddha saw that in this world of *samsara*, of constant appearing and disappearing, being born and dying, there is great suffering. Craving, the builder of this house of suffering (the mind and body), was discovered; the defilements of mind, the rafters, were broken; the force of ignorance, the ridgepole, was shattered; and thus the Bodhisattva realized *nirvana*, the unconditioned. In attaining the great enlightenment, he experienced the completion and fulfillment of his long journey, a fulfillment of the potential shared by all human beings. He had become the Buddha, the Awakened One. He then spent the next seven weeks in the area of the Bodhi Tree, contemplating different aspects of the truth. Having completed his own journey of liberation, he now wondered whether it was possible to share with others the profound Dharma he had realized.

According to legend, a celestial being, a Brahma god, came down from the highest heaven realm and urged the Buddha to teach the Dharma for the welfare of all beings, out of compassion for all beings. He asked the Buddha to survey the world with his eye of wisdom, stating that there were many beings with but little dust in their eyes who would be able to hear and understand the truth. The Buddha did as the Brahma god asked, and out of deep compassion for the suffering of beings he began to teach.

He first traveled to a place outside of Benares called Sarnath, where the five ascetics with whom he had previously practiced were living in a deer park. The Buddha gave his first sermon to these five ascetics, thereby setting in motion the Great Wheel of the Dharma. In this sermon he spoke of the Four Noble Truths and the Middle Way, that path between the extremes of sensory indulgence and self-mortification, thus laying the foundation for the next forty-five years of his teaching.

When his first sixty disciples were fully enlightened, he instructed them in a way that is very significant. He said, "Go forth, O *bhikkus* [monks] for the good of the many, for the happiness of the many, out of compassion for the world, for the good, benefit, and happiness of people and *devas* (celestial beings). Let not two go by one way. Teach the Dharma, excellent in the beginning, excellent in the middle, excellent in the end. Proclaim the noble life, altogether perfect and pure. Work for the good of others, you who have accomplished your duties." And so, from the very beginning of our own practice, we understand that we are not doing this for ourselves alone, that our practice can be for the benefit and welfare of all.

There are many stories in the Buddha's life illustrating his wisdom and skill in helping others to liberation. Every morning he would survey the world with his unhindered eye of wisdom, encompassing all beings in his net of compassion. With the ability to penetrate hidden tendencies, he would recognize all those who were ripe for awakening, and he would appear to them, offering the exact teaching they needed to open their hearts and minds.

There is a story of a monk who had been practicing meditation on the unpleasantness of the body, visualizing its parts—internal organs, blood, hair, bone, flesh, sinew, and so forth—as a way of developing dispassion. Although he practiced diligently for several months, he made no progress, and his mind grew agitated and restless. The Buddha came to know of this, and he saw that for this monk that particular practice was not appropriate. Through his psychic power, the Buddha created a golden lotus, which he instructed the monk to contemplate. As the monk contemplated it, the golden lotus began to change and disintegrate, and through contemplating the process of change and decay in the beautiful flower, the monk was enlightened. In telling of this later, the Buddha said that for five hundred consecutive lifetimes this monk had been a goldsmith, working with and fashioning beautiful objects. The monk's mind was so attuned to beauty that he could not relate to unpleasant objects in a balanced way; so contemplation of the impermanence and insubstantiality of beautiful things was his own particular doorway to liberation.

One of my favorite stories is of a monk who was known as the dullard because he couldn't learn or remember anything. His older brother, who was an enlightened monk, tried to teach the dullard a Dharma verse of four lines, but each time he learned a new line, it would push the previous line out of his mind. He worked for a time trying to remember these four lines, but he was unable to do so. His brother thought that there was no hope and suggested that the dullard leave the monkhood and return to a householder's life.

Although he had a slow mind, the dullard had a good and open heart, and this suggestion made him quite sad. He was walking down the road, feeling dejected, and the Buddha, having come to know what had happened, came and stroked his head consolingly. The Buddha then gave him an object of meditation: a white handkerchief. He told the dullard to take the handkerchief and rub it at a time when the sun was high. This was the entire meditation instruction. As the dullard meditated in this way, the handkerchief grew dirty, causing him to understand the impurities coming out of the body. Seeing this led his mind to a state of dispassion, and out of that deep balance of mind, he too became enlightened. The story goes on to say that with his enlightenment came all the various psychic powers and knowledge of all the teachings.

The Buddha had seen that in a past lifetime the dullard had been a great king who had one day gone out in the hot sun bedecked in his lavish finery, which slowly became soiled in the heat. At that time he began to see the unpleasant aspect of the body and to become detached from it. The Buddha touched on that seed that had been planted in him long before, and in a single stroke his mind emerged from its dullness into freedom.

There are innumerable stories of people from all walks of life—beggars, merchants, artisans, courtesans, village people, nobles, kings and queens—each coming to the Buddha with varying degrees of faith and understanding, whom he helped come to freedom and peace through the power of his love and wisdom.

One discourse the Buddha gave that is particularly helpful in understanding the open spirit of investigation and discovery in Dharma practice is known as the *Kalama Sutta*. This sutra is named after the Kalamas, a village people who had asked him how they could know which among the many different religious teachings and teachers to believe. The Buddha said that they should not blindly believe anyone—not their parents or teachers, not the books or traditions, not even the Buddha himself. Rather, they should look carefully into their own experience to see those actions that lead to more greed, more hatred, more delusion, and abandon them; and they should look to see what things lead to greater love, generosity, wisdom, and peace, and then cultivate those. The Buddha's teachings always encourage us to take responsibility for our own development and to directly investigate the nature of our experience.

When he was eighty years old, the Buddha became quite ill. Knowing he was soon going to die, he lay down on a spot beneath two trees. The legends tell us that these trees were flowering out of season, symbolizing the Buddha's final release into the unconditioned. The very last words of the Buddha sum up all his lifetimes of practice and the forty-five years of teaching after his enlightenment. These are the words that he left to us at the very end of his life: "With the light of perfect wisdom, illuminate the darkness of ignorance. Subject to decay are all conditioned things. Strive on with diligence."

As practice deepens and we come to a fuller appreciation and understanding of our own true nature, there develops a wonderful love and respect for the Buddha, both as an historical figure and as the archetype of the Buddha-nature potential within us all. We become filled with a deep gratitude for the opportunity to walk the path discovered by such a being, a path of the greatest distinction and truest nobility. With mindfulness and insight we can reflect the Buddha's journey in our own.

NATURAL FREEDOM
OF THE HEART
The Teachings of Ajahn Chah

Jack Kornfield

S TARTING IN THE 1960S I had the privilege of practicing
in several of the great temples in the Tradition of the Elders of
Thailand and Burma. My home monastery was Wat Ba Pong, a
forest monastery in Thailand near the border of Laos and Cambodia.
Wat Ba Pong monastery covers several hundred acres of forest with
dense foliage, hanging vines, and a wildlife population that includes
deer, snakes, birds, lizards, scorpions, and bugs. The small huts in
which monks live and practice meditation are connected by paths,
separate enough so that you can't see from one to another. It was
there that I began practice as a monk in ocher robes under the guidance of Ajahn Chah. Ajahn Chah was a meditation master in the
lineage of the ancient Thai forest tradition, where a simple and austere life were stressed as a path to awakening. He carried the Dharma
of liberation in all he did, and he demonstrated the great heart of a
Buddha to all who came to join him in the forest.

In this chapter I would like to convey some of the blessings I received in this training, the inspiration and understanding that came from it, handed down through the simple monk's and nun's life since the time of the Buddha. While the stories of Ajahn Chah's monastery may at first sound like tales of a distant culture, they point to the universal principles of Dharma training experienced by all who undertake a genuine path of practice. Those who enter intensive retreat in the West also face periods of surrender and simplicity. They too must come to terms with the suffering of their own body and mind and must endeavor to find compassion and freedom in their midst. In this way modern retreat practice offers an initiation that carries some of the spirit of the ancient monasteries and forests of Asia.

Ajahn Chah described two levels of spiritual practice. On the first level, you use Dharma to become comfortable. You become virtuous and a little kinder. You sit and quiet your mind, and you help make a harmonious community. There are genuine blessings of this comfortable level of Dharma. But the second kind of Dharma, he said, is to discover real freedom of mind, heart, and spirit. This level of practice has nothing whatsoever to do with comfort. Here you take every circumstance of life and work with it to learn to be free. He told us, "That is what we're doing here. If you want to come join us in the forest, that's our purpose."

Ajahn Chah spoke of the second kind of Dharma the day I arrived at his monastery. He smiled and welcomed me by saying, "I hope you're not afraid of suffering." I was shocked. "What do you mean? I came here to practice meditation, to find inner peace and happiness." He explained, "There are two kinds of suffering. The first is the suffering that causes more suffering, that we repeat over and over. The second is the suffering that comes when we stop running. The second kind of suffering can lead you to freedom."

Ajahn Chah's monastery became renowned in Thailand as a center for very strict practice. The style of practice is broader than the sitting meditation we do in the West. It is a mindful and disciplined way of life where the monks must be attentive to everything they do. There are hundreds of monastic rules in Theravada Buddhism that demand care, and in his monastery Ajahn Chah set up an environment that challenged his monks to follow them. A mindful presence and awareness was expected of all who lived there. Ajahn Chah would tell people when they arrived that if they were coming to relax, they'd come to the wrong place. Everything was disciplined, not with an external force, but out of a beautiful sense of respect; when one saw everything done with such care, it was inspiring to do the same.

Within the monastery, Ajahn Chah's teaching had four levels to it, and each level included wisdom, humor, and a great sense of compassion. The first level of his teaching was Surrender: the surrender of using every experience as your practice. The second level was Seeing Clearly: opening up to each experience to see what is happening. The third level was Releasing Difficulties: overcoming each difficulty, and learning to let go of it. The last level of his teaching was Balance: how to rest in wisdom and balance in the face of all things.

His teachings began with surrender. People were invited to work hard and bring an impeccable spirit to their lives as monks. Our lifestyle was intentionally austere. In the meditation hall we sat without cushions on a platform made of stone. When I began many hours of sitting this way it hurt. My knees were high off the floor. When I tried to lower one knee, the other would push up farther. It made for a lot of pain. Then I discovered that if I got to the meditations early, I could get a seat near one of the supporting pillars in the front of the hall. After everyone closed his eyes and started meditating, I could lean against the pillar. I did that for about two weeks until Ajahn Chah gave an evening Dharma talk. Although he was speaking to the group, he smiled at me and noted that learning to practice Dharma was learning how to be independent, how to not have to "lean on things." I moved my seat.

Ajahn Chah expected surrender and care from everybody, but it wasn't the surrender of blind faith. It simply meant accepting that whatever your experience was in that monastery, that was your practice. He would test us often. We would sit in meditation for long hours. Ajahn Chah used to hold what the Western monks later called "endurance sessions." He could easily sit and give a Dharma talk for five hours. We'd be sitting on the stone floor waiting, thinking, "My

God, when is he going to finish?" He'd go on and on, and he'd look around amused to see who was squirming; we were supposed to stay respectful and mindful until he was finished.

Ajahn Chah wanted people to take impeccable care with whatever they did. We'd be sweeping the paths, and he'd come out and say, "No, no, sweep this way." Or if we were making brooms, he'd come out and show us how to make an elegant bamboo broom that would really work. I discovered from watching him what the real teaching was. He didn't care whether the path got swept or not. After all, a day later the forest leaves would cover it up again. What he cared about was people learning to do what they did to awaken. He would show you how to do something so that it was really done well, whether it was tying a broom, sweeping, or building a wall.

The spirit of meditation in the monastery was to do whatever was needed. This is surrender, and it is part of everyone's practice. For a monk it meant taking whatever came to us—the food, the weather, the tasks of the temple—and working with it, whether it was easy or hard. There were people who were difficult to live with in the monastery, and Ajahn Chah valued them as well. This was like Georges Gurdjieff's community in France where an obnoxious Russian character from Paris was actually hired to stay. Everyone else had to pay Gurdjieff a great deal to live there, but this one man, whom no one could stand, was given a salary to stay there. Gurdjieff said he was like the yeast in the bread. If that man had not been there, then the others would not have seen their reactive minds and learned how to deal with them. If there weren't enough difficulties, Ajahn Chah would play this role for his monks.

On full-moon nights we would renew our vows in the ceremonial hall and then be dismissed to return to the main meditation hall and stay up all night sitting and chanting. Late in the evening the villagers would come and offer us a drink of thick sweet coffee. Since we ate only one meal a day in the morning, that one drink was really wonderful. One night Ajahn Chah had a visitor, an older monk, one of his teachers. The two of them were having a lengthy conversation, and it appeared that they had simply overlooked dismissing the monks; they sat and talked from eight o'clock until about midnight.

I was sitting, wanting my coffee, wanting to get up, wanting to move. Every once in a while Ajahn Chah would look around just to see how people were doing. He'd sit quietly for a moment, and then he and his teacher would start talking again. I kept thinking, "When is he going to get done? When will I get my sweet coffee?" It got to be one in the morning, then two in the morning. I got more upset as the night went on, until about three o'clock. I figured that my meditation practice had better happen then and there, because it wasn't going to happen anywhere else that night.

In the morning, as he got up to leave, Ajahn Chah smiled in a kindly manner. He'd seen what we'd gone through in the night. I had realized that meditation practice takes place wherever you are sitting, not just in the meditation hall or upon getting sweet coffee. This was his teaching: the surrender of knowing that wherever you are is your place of practice.

As much as he demanded from his monks, he also did from himself. I remember the coldest morning in a remote mountain cave monastery, when we went out for a long alms round. There was a strong wind, and it was below forty degrees outside. I had my cotton robes on, and I also had a towel that I had managed somehow to wrap under my robes so that it came up and covered my ears a little bit, since they're a big part of my body. It was five miles each way to the village where we went for alms every morning at dawn. By the time we got there, my teeth were chattering from the cold. After the villagers put rice and whatever they could afford in our bowls, we turned to go back to the monastery. Ajahn Chah looked at me and said, "Cold?"

"Freezing!" I replied.

He laughed. "Well, this is as cold as it gets in Thailand!"

His spirit was right there with you. He was there when it was cold, and if you had to sit a long time, he sat there, too. He was there with you in a strong and compassionate way, giving you the sense that whatever the difficulty might be, you could learn to work with it and use it.

Ten years after I left the monastery, I returned and reordained for some months to continue my training. On the full-moon night when the monks gather to recite the rules of the order, I fixed my robes in the formal fashion for this ceremony and went to the hall. Right before the ceremony was to start, Ajahn Chah looked at me and said, "You're not supposed to be here. Go back to your cottage." Usually those who are asked to leave are people who may be impure, visiting monks who may not be keeping their vows, who may not be upholding the standard of conduct of the order. I was upset. It seemed he wasn't aware of my considerable efforts. I was trying to be a good monk, and he didn't believe it. He kicked me out. I heard later that as I was walking down the steps he turned to a couple of the senior monks there, and said, "Oh, he's a meditation teacher, he won't mind."

For over three months he wouldn't let me join the community in that ceremony. At first I was upset, then when I saw it as just another attachment, I let it pass away. The last day before I was leaving to go to Bangkok, I was attending Ajahn Chah under his cottage. He had just taken a bath, and I was helping to dry his feet. He looked down at me and kind of chuckled. Then he nudged me and said, "Well, how did you like being treated just like any other visiting monk?" testing to see if I was still upset.

I said, "Actually, it was appropriate since I am a visiting monk. I'm only here for a short while."

He laughed, and he said, "It's wise of you to see that." He was always trying to see what you were attached to, in order to teach you to surrender and let go.

After one surrendered to the reality of one's circumstance, the second step of Ajahn Chah's teaching was to open up to each experience and see it clearly. It's essential in sitting practice, and in our Dharma life, to see our situation clearly and to see what is true of our mind. Ajahn Chah called this being honest with yourself. He demonstrated this quality quite openly.

I once asked Ajahn Chah how he became a monk, what attracted him to that kind of life. He said that when he was a small boy playing games with the other village children, one of them would want to be the village headman, someone else would want to be the nurse, and someone would be the teacher. "I always wanted to be the monk,"

Ajahn Chah said with a laugh, "so I would seat myself on a higher place than all the other little kids, and I'd get them to bring me food and candy."

He would talk candidly about his own years of practice. Throughout his training, he had lots of problems, doubts, difficulties, and suffering. His body hurt and his mind gave him a hard time. He talked of sitting in the forest in the dry season when unexpected rains came. The water soaked his robes, his bowl, and his few books—everything that he had. He told me, "I was sitting in the forest feeling discouraged. The rain coming down was drenching everything, and tears were streaming down my cheeks. I couldn't tell what was rain and what were my tears, but I just sat there anyway. Sometimes in practice you just weep. I sat and sat and sat, because I had a quality of daring in my practice. No matter what came, I wanted to understand, I was willing to face it." There were times he was very sick. He had malaria like many of the old forest monks, but there was little medicine in those days. He said, "At one point people thought I was seventy years old, when I was about thirty-five. I had just wasted away, and my skin was all dry. But I kept on practicing. I just did it."

Just as Ajahn Chah spoke honestly and directly about himself and his difficulties, he was equally honest about people around him. He would tease people and laugh about their hang-ups. In the 1970s I brought a group of friends to visit him, including Joseph Goldstein and Ram Dass. Ram Dass had just come from surfing and lying on the beach in Bali; although he was fifteen years older than the rest of our group, he was in a mode of looking young and fit, and was obviously taking good care of himself. We sat down at the teacher's cottage, and Ajahn Chah looked around and started in on Ram Dass right away. "Oh," he said, "who's the old man you brought with you?"

At times we would be sitting at his cottage, and laypeople would come. He'd introduce his monks, sometimes in a very formal and respectful way, but other times he would make fun of them. He would say, "Oh, here's the monk who likes to sleep all the time. He's my sleeping monk. Whenever you look for him, he's always sleeping." He'd point to another monk: "And this one's always sick. He's got this thing about getting sick, I don't know why. . . . And this monk is a big eater. This is our eating monk. . . . And this one likes to sit a lot. This monk is really attached to meditation. You can't get him to move or do anything. . . . And this old monk, would you believe it, he had two wives before he ordained—at the same time, poor guy. No wonder he looks so old!" He would go through the monks around him, teasing them, and being very accurate about what that particular person's roles and attachments were. He'd say, "Me, I like to play teacher. That's my role here." Then he'd laugh.

Once a Western monk who had been in a Chinese temple for ten years came to visit. He requested to stay at the monastery. Ajahn Chah said he could, and then he started questioning him, because he was quite stout. "Why are you so fat? Do you really eat that much?" Finally he said, "All right, you can stay, but only under one condition. We have a cottage that's really tiny. You'll just barely fit into it now, so if you eat too much, you'll squeeze into your cottage one morning and you won't be able to get out. Then we'll just lock the door, and you'll have to stay there." The irony of this, of course, is that Ajahn Chah himself was kind of fat, which he readily admitted. So it was wonderful to see that for him, there was nothing sacred. Whatever happened to be true was the place to look. "Pay attention to that."

When I translated for him he would tease me. "I know that you translate what I say in a general way, but I'm sure you leave out some of the biting and difficult parts. Even though I don't speak English, I can tell that you're a little too soft on them, you don't really tell them all that I'm saying, do you?" The method of his teaching was not to be coy, but to be straightforward and very honest, to look directly at our difficulties so that we too could see ourselves freshly.

I asked him once what was the biggest problem with his students. He said, "Opinions. Views and ideas about all kinds of things, about themselves, about practice, about the teachings of the Buddha. Many who come to practice have had worldly success—they're wealthy merchants, university graduates, teachers, government officials—

and their minds are filled with opinions about the world. They're too clever to listen. It's like water in a cup. If the cup is filled with dirty, stale water, it's useless. Only when the old water is thrown out can the cup become useful. You must empty your minds of opinions, and then you will begin to learn." To see clearly, you must learn to be simple, to see things as they are.

Ajahn Chah also taught about seeing one's own limits clearly. Ram Dass asked him how people should teach if they hadn't finished their own practice yet. If we are still suffering, how can we teach others to be free? He replied, "First of all, be very honest. Don't pretend that you are wise in ways you are not. Tell people how you are yourself. And then take the measure of things. In weight lifting, if you're strong, you know that through practice you can lift a really big weight. Maybe you've seen someone lift a weight bigger than you can. You can tell your students, 'If you practice, you can lift that big weight, but don't try it yet. I can't even do it, but I've seen people do it.' Be willing to express what is possible without trying to fool someone that you've done it. Be scrupulously honest with yourself and in your teaching, and all will be well."

In seeing clearly, Ajahn Chah stressed where it was important to look—at ourselves. I remember feeling very frustrated in my first few months at the monastery, wanting to leave because my practice wasn't going well. I wanted a quieter place where I could sit eight, ten, fifteen hours a day. Instead, I had to go on alms rounds and chant and work with other monks and was only able to sit five or six hours a day. He said our practice was to live wisely, and sitting would help with that. But sitting was simply the support for wisdom, not our main task. I was angry at what I saw as interruptions in my meditation. I told him that I didn't like it there and that I was going to go to a Burmese monastery. Because I was frustrated I said to Ajahn Chah, "And another thing, you don't seem so enlightened to me. You often contradict yourself. One time you say one thing, one time you say another. And sometimes you don't look truly mindful to me. I see you eating, and how do I know you're mindful? You drop things on the ground like anybody else. You don't look perfect." He thought this was very funny.

He said, "It's a good thing that I don't look like a Buddha to you."
I said, "Well, how come?"

He said, "Because if I did, you would still be caught in looking for the Buddha outside yourself. You cannot look outside and find enlightenment. Each person is different. Freedom does not come by imitating others. If you want to know about freedom, it only comes in your heart, when you're not attached to things."

He went on, "Wisdom is for you yourself to understand and develop. Take from the teacher what's useful and be aware of your own practice. If I am resting while you all have to sit up, does this make you angry? Or if I say that the sky is red or that a man is a woman, don't follow me blindly. Look at what is true and beneficial for yourself. One of my own teachers ate very fast. He made a lot of noises as he ate, yet he told us all to eat slowly and mindfully. I used to watch him and get very upset. I suffered, but he didn't. I was only watching the outside. Later I learned how some people can drive fast but carefully, and others drive slowly and still have many accidents. So don't cling to rules, to outer form. If you observe others ten percent of the time and attend to yourself ninety percent, this is proper practice. Looking outside yourself is comparing, discriminating; it will bring you more suffering. You won't find happiness or peace looking for the perfect man or the perfect teacher. The Buddha taught us to look at the Dharma, the truth, not to look at other people."

This was his second level of practice: to be honest. To see clearly is to look at your own ego, fears, and patterns with compassion. "Really look at yourself," he said. Keep the attention inside, rather than comparing with others outside.

The third level of Ajahn Chah's teaching was how to work with difficulties as they arose. To do this he most frequently offered two skillful means. The first was overcoming the difficulties and the second was letting go. He expected people to face their difficulties as a place to discover freedom. When people were having a hard time, he'd ask them, with a smile on his face, "Are you suffering today?" If they said no, he'd laugh and say, "Very well." When they said yes, he'd say, "Well, you must be very attached today." It was so simple to see. If you're suffering, you're attached. And right there is the place to learn to be free.

If people were afraid, he'd direct them right into their fears. If they were afraid to be in the forest alone because of ghosts or wild animals, then he would send them into the forest. His teacher told him that at night, when the mind is attacked by fear, the forest monk forces himself to do walking meditation in the open. "This becomes the battle between fear and Dharma," his teacher said. "If fear is defeated, the mind will be overwhelmed by courage and enjoy profound inner peace. If fear is the victor, it will multiply rapidly and prodigiously. The whole body will be enveloped by perspiring heat and chilling cold, by the desire to pass urine and defecate. The monk will be suffocated by fear and will look more like a dying than a living man. The threatening roar of a tiger from a nearby place or far away at the foot of the mountains only serves to increase his already desperate fear. Direction or distance mean nothing to such a monk, his only thought being that the tiger is coming right now to make a meal of him. No matter how vast the area might be, he will be hypnotized by his own fear into believing that the tiger knows of no other place to go but to the very spot where he is walking. The passages for recitation on lovingkindness to prevent fear disappear and ironically what remains is that passage, which serves only to increase it. He will thus recite to himself, 'The tiger is coming. The tiger is coming.'"

But simpler fears were to be overcome as well. Ajahn Chah once had his seniormost Western monk, Ajahn Sumedho, give a Dharma talk for an hour. For a new monk it was hard to give Dharma talks and not be afraid of appearing foolish, boring, or insecure. So when Sumedho was finished, Ajahn Chah said, "Go on," so he talked for another forty-five minutes. Ajahn Chah said, "Go on. More." And he made him do this over and over again until he had talked for four hours. He had nothing to say, and he went on and on. It was so boring! When he'd stop, he'd hear, "More." By the end he learned not to care whether he was boring or foolish or not, not to be afraid of what anybody thought, just to do it.

The first big Dharma talk I ever had to give was done without preparation, in the middle of the night. On big Buddhist holidays we would sit up all night. The hall would be filled with up to a thousand villagers, and we'd alternate one hour of Dharma talk and an hour of sitting. At around two in the morning Ajahn Chah said, "We will now hear a Dharma talk from the Western monk." I'd never given a Dharma talk before, much less in Lao to hundreds of people. I just got up there, and he said, "Tell them what you know of the Dharma, go to it." He knew I was nervous. He said, "That's an even better reason to do it!"

It is a tradition in forest monasteries to push monks into what they dislike, and over the years Ajahn Chah would find out what your soft spot was. If you were afraid to be alone, off to a remote forest with you; if you have trouble dealing with people, you might be sent to a big, busy city. He could really seem like a rascal. He'd find out just what you didn't like and make you do it. If you were bored or restless, then he'd put you in a position where you would have more boredom or restlessness to deal with, and make you feel it. He'd say, "You simply feel it until you die." That was the spirit of his practice. Whatever resists is the sense of "I" or ego or self, and you have to work with that until it dies. That's overcoming the difficulty.

I was extremely sleepy in my meditation practice at first. Ajahn Chah instructed me, "Sit up straight; open your eyes if you're sleepy. Walk a lot, walk backwards." I'd walk backwards; I'd still be sleepy. "Okay, walk backwards in the forest." Then I'd really have to wake up, to avoid trees and vines. Walking backwards in the forest kept me awake. But as soon as I sat down, I'd get sleepy again. Finally he said, "We have a cure for people like you. There's a well near your cottage. Go and sit right on the edge of the well." So I sat down on the edge of the well, closed my eyes, and began to meditate. I soon felt a little sleepy and started to nod. As I did, I looked down and saw fifty feet of space below me. The rush of adrenaline from the fear kept me wide awake. I learned that sleepiness was workable, like any other state.

If you were angry or restless, Ajahn Chah would say, "If you want to be angry, go back into your hot cottage, wrap yourself in your warmest robes, and spend the day being angry and feel it, experience it. Just keep sitting with it." He would speak about "putting the tiger of anger in a cage of mindfulness." He said, "You don't have to take it out and butcher it. You just make mindfulness around whatever it is, and then let it exhaust itself. Let it be your teacher."

For those of us who were young monks, celibacy was especially difficult. A Westerner who had been made abbot of one of Ajahn Chah's small monasteries told him he had a lot of lust and fantasy coming up in his practice. At this particular monastery, the villagers would come every afternoon for Dharma talks. So Ajahn Chah said, "Well, did you tell the villagers about yourself? Tell all the old women. Tell them." He made him get up there and admit what was in his mind. He made him look at it.

At the same time, he wouldn't push too much. He had creative ways of helping people overcome the things that they got caught in, and he did it with a lot of balance. He wouldn't allow long periods of fasting or long solitary retreats unless he thought you were ready for it. He said, "You have to know the strength of your oxcart. You can't load it up with too much or it'll break down." He made space for each person to grow at his or her appropriate pace.

The first way he taught us to work with difficulties was by being willing to face them, going directly into them, to overcome them. The second way was by letting go. This is the heart of the teachings of the Buddha.

Being around Ajahn Chah challenged any territory you were clinging to. I remember a rich man coming to the temple saying that he had made a lot of money. He was starting to give his money to charity. He said quite proudly, "I don't know whether to give it to the hospital, or to orphans, or perhaps I should give some to your monastery to provide for nuns and monks."

Ajahn Chah looked at him and said, "I know what you should do with it."

The man said, "What?"

Ajahn Chah said, "Throw it off the bridge over the river on the way to the monastery." The man's jaw dropped open. It was just the right thing for him to hear, because he was really saying: "See how great I am, see what I've done with my money." Ajahn Chah's teaching was to look at whatever you're attached to and learn how to let go of it.

For some students, doubts would arise. Someone asked, "What can I do about my doubts? Some days I'm plagued with doubts about the practice, or my progress, or the teacher."

He answered, "Doubting is natural. Everyone starts out with doubts. You can learn a lot from them. What's important is that you don't identify with your doubts, you don't get caught up in them. That will spin your mind in endless circles. Instead, watch the whole process of doubting, of wondering. Ask who it is that doubts. See how doubts come and go. Then you'll no longer be victimized by your doubts. You'll step outside of them, and your mind will become quiet. You'll see how all things come and go. Just let go of what you're attached to. Let go of your doubts. Let them be there and simply watch. This is how to put an end to the trouble of doubting." Learn to see the movements of the mind and not get caught in all of its lures, its traps, and its intricacies.

No matter where he went, Ajahn Chah taught directly about freedom. When he was in England to teach, a staid, upper-class English lady who had been part of a British Buddhist Society came to visit. She asked him a series of complicated philosophical questions about Buddhist Abhidhamma psychology. Ajahn Chah asked her if she had ever done much meditation practice, and she said no, she hadn't had time, she'd been too busy studying the texts. He told her, "Madam, you are like a woman who keeps chickens in her yard and goes around picking up the chicken shit instead of the eggs."

He later explained to me that his way of teaching is very simple: "It is as though I see people walking down a road I know well. To them the way may be unclear. I look up and see someone about to fall in a ditch on the right-hand side of the road, so I call out, 'Go left, go left.' Similarly, if I see another person about to fall in a ditch on the left, I call out, 'Go right, go right!' That is the extent of my teaching. Whatever extreme you get caught in, whatever you get attached to, I say, 'Let go of that too.' Let go on the left, let go on the right. Come back here to the center, and you will arrive at the true Dharma."

Ajahn Chah taught how to let go, to put down our struggle and make the heart peaceful. "Learn to let go of doubts, let go of the obsession with thinking. Let go of desires and fears," he said. "Make your mindfulness patient, like a parent with a child. Your mind is a child and mindfulness is the parent."

You have a little child who says, "Daddy, can we have an elephant?"

"Sure, kid."

"Daddy, I want an ice-cream cone."

"Later, kid."

"Daddy, can we buy a new car?"

"All right, kid." You attend to the child with kindness and wisdom. You don't have to react to everything. Just say, "That's fine," and watch.

You observe how the child of your mind can come up with a thousand desires. You see them arise, and you let them go.

The same is true for special states in meditation. Ajahn Chah used to say that one of the great difficulties in practice for people comes when they start to develop some concentration and they think, "Oh boy, I'm going to get enlightened now!" or "I must be right on the edge of one of those great experiences." When you think like that, the quiet of concentration disappears and slides away. To practice wisely, you must let go of expectations. Let things be just as they are for you. Don't try to make something happen. Simply be open to each experience as it occurs.

If judgment arises, that's fine, let judgment be there. If you have a lot of judgments, make them the subject of your meditation. There's nothing wrong with that. Being aware of the rise and fall of judgment is just like being aware of the in and out of the breath. The practice of meditation is not to change anything, but to see how things arise and how they pass away, to experience things fully and yet not be caught with them. Anger, fear, doubt, sleepiness—let them come, let them go, and rest in the pure knowing of them. Just be here and be mindful. This does not mean withdrawal, and it doesn't mean suppression. It means to be open to all experience. That's how you learn to be free.

Ajahn Chah said, "Sitting for hours on end is not necessary. Some people think that the longer you can sit, the wiser you must be. I've seen chickens sit on their nests for days on end. Wisdom comes from being mindful in all postures. Your practice should begin as you awaken in the morning, and it should continue until you fall asleep. What's important is only that you keep attentive, whether you are working or sitting or going to the bathroom. Each person has their own natural pace. Some of you will die at age fifty, some at age sixty-five, and some at age ninety—so, too, your practice will be different. Don't think or worry about this. Try to be mindful, and let things take their natural course. Then your mind will become quieter and quieter in any surroundings; it will become still like a clear forest pool. Then all kinds of wonderful and rare animals will come to drink at the pool. You'll see clearly the nature of all things in the world, see many wonderful things and strange things come and go. But you will be still. This is the happiness of the Buddha."

So the practices that Ajahn Chah taught were surrender and opening to experience. Then he taught how to work with difficulties by overcoming them and letting go. This led to the fourth level of his teaching: living in balance, the simplicity of the Middle Path. Ajahn Chah rarely taught about levels of enlightenment. He didn't think the system of stages of enlightenment and levels of insight was helpful, because it took people out of the reality of the present. He said, "When you teach that, people get attached to it. They want to get there. They have a gaining ideal. But freedom comes directly from letting go." He emphasized this again and again. "If you let go a little, you will have a little freedom. If you let go a lot, you will have a lot of freedom. And if you let go completely, your heart will be completely free."

I remember coming back to him after doing intensive practice in another monastery. I described a wide range of extraordinary and wonderful experiences. For him these were just something else to let go of. When I finished my account he looked at me and said, "Do you still have any fear?"

I said, "Yes."

"Do you still have any greed and desires?"

"Yes."

"Does anger still come?"

"Yes, it still comes."

He smiled. "Fine, continue." And that was it.

He wouldn't let people get stuck in practice. Just be here, where you are, he would teach. He asked me if I had learned anything in my travels and studies with other masters. He said, "What have you learned by traveling that wasn't present at the monastery?"

I thought about it and I said, "There really wasn't anything new. It was the same Dharma. I could have as well stayed here."

He laughed. "I knew that before you left, but it would have done no good to tell you. You had to go on that journey to discover it. But from where I sit, no one comes and no one goes."

Learning the Middle Path, the life of balance, allows the heart's natural awareness and compassion to grow. We become free and gracious. I heard a story from the first Western monastery that Ajahn Chah set up in a forest two villages away from his main monastery. One December the Western monks there decided to have a Christmas tree. The villagers who built the monastery got upset and came to Ajahn Chah to complain. They said, "We have made a Buddhist monastery for the Western monks that we're supporting, and they're having a Christmas celebration. It doesn't seem right to us."

Ajahn Chah said, "Well, in the simple way I have been told, Christmas is a holiday that celebrates the renewal of generosity and kindness. As far as I'm concerned that is beneficial. It is very much the spirit of the teaching of Buddhism. But since you are concerned, the monks won't celebrate Christmas anymore. Instead, we will call it ChrisBuddhamas." With that, the villagers were content and they went back home. He taught us to be kind and flexible. "The point is to learn how to let go and be free, how to be happy," he said.

Ajahn Chah encouraged us to continue to use our Dharma practice to come to what he called the natural freedom of the heart, beyond all forms and conditions. He said, "The original heart/mind shines like pure, clear water with the sweetest taste. But if the heart is pure, is our practice over? No, we must not cling even to this purity. We must go beyond all duality, all concepts, all bad, all good, all pure, all impure. We must go beyond self and nonself, beyond birth and death. When we see with the eye of wisdom, we know that the true Buddha is timeless, unborn, unrelated to any body, any history, any image. Buddha is the ground of all being, the realization of the truth of the unmoving mind."

Ajahn Chah's way of teaching combines the ultimate level of Dharma with the practical level. The ultimate level invites us to see the timeless dance of existence, all arising and passing, days, experiences, eons, and galaxies alike. The practical level teaches us to take care of the moments we are given, to live with impeccability and compassion, to sweep the paths with mindfulness, delight, and fullness, to be honest with oneself and caring with others. He wouldn't let people get caught in either level.

To help us find freedom, Ajahn Chah taught about selflessness, the essential realization of the Buddha's liberation, in simple and remarkable ways. "If our body really belonged to us, it would obey our commands. If we say, 'Don't get old,' or 'I forbid you to get sick,' does it obey us? No, it takes no notice. We only rent this house, not own it. In reality there is no such thing as a permanent self, nothing solid or unchanging that we can hold on to. The idea of self is merely a concept. Ultimately no one exists, only elements that have combined temporarily. There is no me, there is only *anatta*, nonself. To understand nonself, you will have to meditate. If you only intellectualize, your head will explode. When you see beyond self, you no longer cling to happiness, and when you no longer cling to happiness, you can begin to be truly happy." One day I had a further conversation with Ajahn Chah about this Buddhist teaching of nonself and he said, "Nonself, anatta, is not true." This was an amazing thing for a Buddhist teacher to say. "It's not correct," he said, "because self is one extreme and nonself is the other extreme. What is true is neither of those, because both are concepts. Things are as they are."

In the midst of the strict discipline and impeccable training of the monastery, Ajahn Chah had a great laugh and a playful spirit. He reminded us that the sole task of Buddhism is to help people be happy and free, develop their heart's resources, and open to what's true. From surrender, seeing clearly, and learning how to deal with the mind in a balanced way, "you yourself can become a Buddha." To know Ajahn Chah over many years brought great joy into my life. His spirit of freedom and simplicity was contagious. His maturity and delight in the Dharma brought all he touched closer to liberation.

When Ram Dass, Joseph Goldstein, I, and others left Ajahn Chah in 1977, he said, "When Thai people come to me and only ask for amulets, clay buddhas, or blessing rituals, they insult themselves. Now you have come to ask me questions. You want somebody outside to teach you the Dharma. You insult yourself, too, because the truths discovered by the Buddha are already in your heart. There is a One Who Knows within you who already understands and is free. If you can turn toward this natural awareness and rest in it, then everything will become simple." He went on, "Over the years you can deepen your freedom in many ways. Use your natural awareness to see how all things come and go. Let go and live with love and wisdom. Don't be lazy. If you find yourself lazy, fearful, or timid, then work to strengthen the qualities that overcome it. With natural wisdom and compassion, the Dharma will unfold by itself. If you truly dedicate yourself, you will come to the end of all doubts, you will be liberated. You will live in that place of silence, of oneness with the Buddha, with the Dharma, with all things. Only you can do that."

Awakening Confidence
in Our Own Capacity
The Blessing of Dipa Ma

Sharon Salzberg

I N T H E T R A N S I T I O N of the Buddhist teachings from Asia to the West, there is an understanding that doesn't come easily into our culture—the importance of confidence in oneself. Traditional Asian teachings emphasize Right Effort, one of the elements of the Eightfold Path as reflected in the very last thing the Buddha said to his disciples: "Strive on with diligence." Meant to be empowering and personally liberating, that message is somehow not understood in the same way in the West. Effort seems burdensome, or even terrifying. We might disdain or dismiss the whole idea that the path demands effort. At the heart of many of these reactions is, I believe, a feeling of helplessness. We might subtly think, "I can't do it. I don't have what it takes to 'strive with diligence' or to bring about a change in my actions." The Dharma has worked for twenty-five hundred years, but we assume, "I am the one who will defeat the entire methodology preserved for all of these centuries"!

Because we tend to think in this way, it is so important to understand what having confidence in ourselves means. For me the person who exemplified the power of transforming self-deprecation into self-confidence—perhaps more than anyone else I have studied with—was my teacher Dipa Ma. Her teaching of Right Effort was coupled with her ability to mirror to each of her students a powerful sense of his or her own ability.

Dipa Ma was born in Bengal, and, as was customary in the India of her time, her family arranged a marriage for her when she was twelve years old. At fourteen she left her home to join her husband, who was working in the civil service in Burma. She was lonely and homesick, but her husband was gentle, and they actually fell in love and grew quite close. However, when it appeared over time that she was unable to bear a child, their happiness was tested. Her husband's family even urged him to put her aside and take another wife, but he refused. Year after year her inability to have children continued to be a source of great shame and sorrow to her. After twenty years a child was finally born, a daughter who died at the age of three months.

Some years later another daughter, Dipa, was born and lived. So significant was this occurrence that Dipa Ma acquired the name by which we know her: Dipa Ma—Dipa's mother. The following year Dipa Ma became pregnant again, only to bear a son who died at birth. As she mourned the death of this baby, Dipa Ma's health began to deteriorate severely. Just at the point when she was beginning to overcome her great sorrow and make some peace with all of the losses she had sustained, it was discovered that, at forty-one years of age, she was suffering from a severe heart condition. Her doctors feared that she might die at any moment.

Struggling with her own frailty and the possibility of her imminent death, Dipa Ma had to face yet another trial. Her husband, who had been in fine health, came home one day from the office feeling ill. Later that same day, he died. Dipa Ma was devastated. She couldn't sleep, yet on the other hand she couldn't get out of bed because she was so distraught. But she had Dipa, who was only five years old, to raise.

One day a doctor said to her, "You know, you're actually going to die of a broken heart unless you do something about the state of your mind." Because she was living in Burma, a Buddhist country, he suggested that she learn how to meditate. Dipa Ma very carefully considered his advice. She said she asked herself, "What can I take with me when I die?" And she considered the "treasures" of her life: "I looked at my dowry, my silk saris and gold jewelry, and I knew I couldn't take them with me. I looked at my daughter and knew I couldn't take her. So what could I take?" Dipa Ma's answer was: "Let me go to the meditation center. Maybe I can find something there I can take with me when I die."

Clearly everybody suffers to some degree or another in life, but it is a great mystery why some people emerge from their suffering with greater faith and determination to understand, to love, to care, to go deeper, while others do not. The Buddha said that the "proximate cause," the condition that most readily gives rise to faith, is suffering. Dipa Ma endured tremendous suffering and loss and pain, and she transformed it into motivation to find a deeper truth. Somehow, despite all she had undergone, she seemed to have a belief in her own capacity to awaken, to make something out of all her pain and suffering. She was empowered by her suffering rather than defeated.

Dipa Ma went to a monastery, so weak from her physical and emotional suffering that she actually had to crawl up the temple stairs in order to get to the meditation hall. Her motivation was so strong that nothing was going to stop her. I often think about the intensity of Dipa Ma's motivation to practice. I find it deeply inspiring to imagine her—a tiny, exhausted, worn-out, grief-stricken woman—crawling up the temple stairs to learn how to meditate, to find something that wouldn't die. The strength of our motivation is the foundation of our practice. When we nurture our motivation to be free, we simultaneously nurture the confidence that our efforts can, in fact, lead to freedom.

When Dipa Ma first started meditating, Right Effort meant simply not giving up. As she tells the story: "When I started doing the meditation, I was crying all the time because I wanted to follow the instructions with full regard, but I couldn't do so because I only fell asleep. Even standing and walking, I fell asleep all the time. I just needed to sleep. So I cried and cried, because for five years I was trying to sleep and couldn't—and then, when I was trying to do meditation, all I could do was sleep. I was trying so hard not to sleep, but still I couldn't do it."

When she went to her teacher to report her difficulty, he said, "This is a very good sign that you're falling asleep, because for five years you've been suffering so badly that you couldn't sleep, but now you're getting sleepy. That's wonderful. Sleep mindfully. Just do the meditation as instructed." With her powerful perseverance, Dipa Ma continued, and, as she relates, "One day all of a sudden my sleep disappeared, and I could sit."

Movement, or progress in the practice, is not so much a matter of learning a skill, although there are skills involved, as it is a reflection of our motivation, of our depth of commitment and care. Because of this, it isn't necessarily a sign of failure if you find yourself falling asleep all the time. What's actually happening is not as important as the willingness to open, to look, to persevere, to carry on. Unfortunately, our extremely judgmental minds find that kind of progress hard to measure. It's much easier to reflect on a meditation period and say, "Wow, this spectacular vision happened." But to look back and say, "I kept going, even though it was hard," is a true measure of progress.

When Dipa Ma began to experience the fruits of her practice, she began to say to people, "Come to the meditation center. You've seen how I was disheartened by the loss of my husband and my children and because of my disease. But now you are finding that I have changed and I am quite happy. There's no magic to it. It simply comes from following the instructions of the teachers. I followed them and I got peace of mind. You come too, and you'll also get peace of mind."

Having come through that tremendous suffering to some level of peace, Dipa Ma was left with the gift of an extraordinary ability to love and care and have compassion. Her presence itself was a blessing. Students would go up to her, and she'd put her arms around them and stroke them; she'd do that with everyone. I never saw her interacting with people in a way that excluded them or created a feeling of separation. I think that came from her own experience of pain and her recognition that we are all vulnerable to suffering. Even if the current circumstances of our lives are happy, we all share this vulnerability. Our pleasure rests on a fulcrum in a very fragile balance, and the next breath might bring something very different, something undesired. Her own sense of this fragility translated into tremendous love and care.

Dipa Ma exhibited no pretense, no fabrication. She was quite simple and direct, and there never was a sense that she was assuming the persona of a great spiritual being. Her lovingkindness poured out of that very simplicity and graciousness. She could be as interested in feeding you dinner as in hearing about your meditation practice. The expression of her lovingkindness could center on an ordinary event, but she was so completely present with everybody that it became extraordinary.

She had raised her daughter by herself in great poverty, all the time doing her meditation practice. When Dipa got married and had a son, Dipa Ma became a grandmother. She then had a great many chores and responsibilities. When someone asked her if she found her worldly concerns a hindrance, she said, "They're not a hindrance, because whatever I do, the meditation is there. It never really leaves me. Even when I'm talking, I'm meditating. When I'm eating or thinking about my daughter, that doesn't hinder the meditation."

When she was visiting the Insight Meditation Society in Barre in the late 1970s and early 1980s, I would watch her as she played games with her young grandson, both of them laughing with pleasure; then she would get up and give somebody meditation instruction, then do her laundry by hand and hang it outside on the line, then do some walking meditation, then go back in the house and sit for a while. Her grandson would be running around the room, and her daughter would be cooking and watching television, and she would meditate in the midst of all that activity. Someone would arrive and sit down in front of her; she would open her eyes and bless them, caress and hug them, and then go back to meditating. It was all quite seamless.

Later in her life, someone asked her what went on in her mind, what were her prevalent mind-states. She said, "There are only three: concentration, lovingkindness, and peace." Her consistent response to life events reminded me of the Buddha, who rested upon the same qualities no matter what situation he was in—unlike many of us, who react one way in one circumstance and another way in others. We might be filled with lovingkindness when we're all alone but have much fear and difficulty when we're with people. Or we may feel connected and happy when we're with people but uneasy at being alone. Our lives can be fragmented without this strength of integration. Dipa Ma seemed to be simply who she was, at all times and in all circumstances. I will always remember Dipa Ma for those three qualities of simplicity, love, and integrity.

The power of her tremendous motivation could be felt behind her warmth and lovingkindness. It was obvious how meditation practice had given her back her life. She did not take the practice casually in any way and was a very demanding teacher. She was resolute about everybody's capacity to be free, and she insisted that we all do our absolute best to realize and actualize that capacity through Right Effort. She had powerful faith and confidence in each one of her students, and in the Buddhist techniques of awakening.

Once in Calcutta she was asked about a teaching that is recorded, not in the actual scriptures based on the Buddha's words, but in the later commentaries, which says only a man can be a fully enlightened Buddha. If you were a woman, you would have to be reborn as a man in a future life in order to attain the state of complete Buddhahood. Hearing this, Dipa Ma drew herself up to her full height of four feet and said, "I can do anything a man can do." In a traditional context this was a radical statement. It symbolized her conviction that the power of endeavor and motivation to bear fruit is not limited in any way. That was the gift she gave to those who came to her. She knew, and she let each of us know, that we could be free. The practice was meant not only for somebody in a long-ago time and faraway place, not only for the Buddha sitting under a tree or for people who had the luxury of leaving their responsibilities behind. We can do it ourselves. We can be free. And our effort to be free, which we are fully capable of, is a valuable measure of our success.

In 1974 I went to Calcutta to say goodbye to Dipa Ma when I was leaving India for what I thought would be a rather quick trip home before I returned. I was convinced that I was going to spend the rest of my life in India. "I'm going back for just a short time to get my health together," I told her, "to renew my visa and get some money, and then I'll be right back." She looked at me and said, "When you go to America, you'll start teaching meditation with Joseph [Gold-stein]." I said, "No, I won't," and she said, "Yes, you will." I said, "No, I won't. I 'm coming right back," and she said, "Yes, you will." "No, I won't," I insisted. The amazing accomplishments I had seen in my own teachers had convinced me that I would need to be a student for the rest of my life. I told Dipa Ma that and continued, "I'm not capable of that. I can't teach meditation." She looked at me and said, "You can do anything you want to do. It's only your think-ing you can't do it that can stop you." Of course she was right.

So she sent me off to America with that blessing, which was a great empowerment. I knew the encouragement was not only about me; it was about everyone's capacity for goodness, for wholeness, for understanding, for love. We are much more capable than we can imagine. Having confidence in ourselves is not to be confused with conceit, which focuses on the individual self. Instead we can have confidence in the potential for the innate human goodness within all of us.

We are all vulnerable to pain, and, like Dipa Ma, we are capable of using painful circumstances to understand more clearly, to con-nect more deeply. The tremendous urgency in someone like her can spark an urgency within us to find the truth, to live in a better way, to give up counting on superficialities for happiness, to not be depen-dent on that which crumbles, changes, and dies. Such a deep passion for freedom, for the Dharma, can evoke passion in us, and Dipa Ma's willingness to practice through any circumstance can inspire us to do the same. With such inspiration, those times when we are uncer-tain and afraid can become doorways into the unknown that are as wonderful as they are terrible.

We really can do it. We can be perfect embodiments of the coherency of being that Dipa Ma revealed. We can know who we are and be who we are through all of our changing circumstances. We can transform suffering into compassion. We can do so much with this precious life, with the innate capacity of our minds to awaken and to love. Right Effort arises from the joyful confidence that we too can be free.

JUST WASHING DISHES

Kamala Masters

IN 1976 when I was twenty-nine years old, I used to listen, starry-eyed with fascination, to the exotic stories of my friends, and friends of friends, who had gone off to India, Thailand, and Nepal to practice with their guru or teacher. It was a time of aspiring for "enlightenment," of understanding one's "true nature," and becoming "at one with the divine." I had so much admiration for my friends' courage to go beyond the familiar structures of family and Western society in order to seek out what might nourish their hearts more profoundly. Silently, I was also searching for a deeper meaning to life. But I knew that going to some far-off place like India or Tibet was not in the cards for me.

At the time, I was a single mom raising three small children. Caring for rambunctious kids, and sometimes needing to work at two jobs in order to make ends meet, kept my day-to-day focus right around home—cooking, cleaning, wiping runny noses, working, paying bills, and on and on. Through all the rewarding and hard times of family life, I was clearly aware of my own strong aspiration to know firsthand what the experience of true peace or "liberation" was all about. Reading books and hearing about spiritual awakening from others was no longer satisfying. There were some great teachers who could guide me in Burma, I had heard. But the only realistic chance for me was to find this peace, to know this truth, in my own heart, amid the joys and struggles of my ordinary life.

I had lots of questions: How could I fulfill my aspirations with so much to do—with a home, children, and a job? To have a spiritual practice, do I need to be near a teacher? Should I actively look for a teacher, or do I wait until the teacher "appears because the student is ready"? How will I recognize the right teacher for me? What qualities do I need to have or develop in order to fulfill my heart's desire? What commitments do I have to make to be able to work with a teacher, and be worthy of his or her care?

Even though I was nowhere near having any answers, just knowing my questions clarified what was important to me and what my intentions were. That gave me enough confidence to point myself in the right direction.

Maybe it was because I was surrounded by three playfully active and clamorous children that I had an indescribable thirst for stillness and deep silence. I happened to go to one of those "spiritual fairs" that were popular in the seventies. This one was held at the University of California at Santa Cruz. The campus grounds were teeming with activity and a festive atmosphere. In the air was the sweet aroma of Indian incense, a group of "flower children" were playing drums and flutes, and people of different colors and walks of life were just wandering around contentedly. But my kids were tugging at me, hungry for some lunch and wanting to go home, so I knew there was only time for a quick scan. The cavernous gym was buzzing with many different spiritual groups, sects, and ashrams that had set up booths displaying their teachers, practices, and reading materials. As I stood at the entryway and looked around, I felt dazzled and, at the same time, barraged with information and opportunities. But my attention was immediately captured by a simple sign: SILENT RETREAT.

That sign was an invitation to a weekend *vipassana* retreat, and I signed up to participate. This retreat was to mark the beginning of an enduring relationship as a student of the teachings of the Buddha and the practices of insight and lovingkindness meditation. During all these years, and especially since I've been teaching, I have noticed that the most frequently asked questions are very similar to the ones I was asking when I took my first steps on the path of fulfilling my spiritual aspirations.

I love to tell stories about my own trials and tribulations along the path of spiritual practice, because when I hear others tell their stories, it feels as though all my senses are open, and I can sympathetically participate in the experience of the storyteller. The humanness and relevance of someone's true experience often answers questions I didn't even know I had, dispels doubts, and infuses me with more confidence so that I don't give up on myself in times of struggle.

Here are a few stories about what led me to practice meditation, the qualities of heart and mind that inspired me, how I continued to practice without a teacher nearby (which was most of the time), and the balance of determination and surrender I needed in order to keep steady through the ups and downs of practice.

My first teacher was Anagarika Munindra, and over the years he has continually guided, influenced, and inspired my spiritual practice. He lives and teaches in Calcutta and in Bodhgaya, India, and has been a meditation teacher for more than forty years. He was also an early teacher of Joseph Goldstein and Sharon Salzberg, who were instrumental in establishing the teachings of the Buddha in the West after their own practice in Asia. So it can be said that Munindra is one of the grandfathers of vipassana and lovingkindness meditation in the West.

It was during that weekend retreat in San Jose, California, that I first heard about Munindra (or, as he was often called, Munindraji, the ending *-ji* conveying affectionate respect). He was described as a highly esteemed and well-loved meditation teacher with a great deal of textual knowledge, and a wealth of experiential wisdom from his meditative practice as well. In a few months he would arrive in America for the very first time to visit his students and to teach intensive retreats. The planning was underway for Munindra to teach a one-month retreat right in San Jose, near the town of Aptos where I lived.

Unexpectedly, I found myself filled with joy and anticipation at the thought of being able to devote myself to a month of practice, which was quite a big jump after having just done a weekend retreat. And I didn't even have to go to India—a part of India was coming to San Jose! Out of sheer intuition, and a bit of impetuousness, I signed up for the one-month retreat, not really knowing if this was the teacher for me or how I would work out the details of being away from home and job for that long. As I took the steps to fulfill that decision, a mysterious flood of confidence filled my heart.

There were many arrangements to make so far in advance in order to be away for that long: getting responsible care for my children, working overtime to save enough money to cover expenses for the time off without pay as well as the cost of the retreat, stocking up on food and supplies, cooking and freezing some dishes ahead of time, and the usual endless clothes washing and housecleaning. The hardest part was preparing the children for my being away for so long. As it turns out, I was only able to participate in half the retreat because I just couldn't stay away from the kids the entire time.

By the time I arrived at the retreat venue, I felt worn to the bone with exhaustion from working so hard to get there. The retreat was at a large estate with a two-story home and beautiful garden in a suburban area. It was called the Stillpoint Institute and was founded by the late Sujata, a former monk and student of Munindra's. They would be teaching that retreat together. Because I arrived late and all the regular beds were taken, I was assigned a sleeping space on the floor in the upstairs hallway next to the large bathroom to be used by the teachers.

As I was nervously laying down my narrow folding mat and bedding in that hallway, Munindra came walking toward the bathroom and me. I had never met him before, but I knew from his shiny dark Indian skin, shaven head, and long white robes that it must be him. As he approached, I remember feeling totally at ease with his presence, which was unpretentious and light. His grounded composure helped me to relax more. Being a newcomer to this ancient spiritual tradition, I somehow thought he would say something mystically profound. But he just stood there for a moment and looked curiously at the mat I was putting down on the floor, then at my haggard-looking face, then at the mat again. He surprised me when he asked in a matter-of-fact way, "Is that where you will sleep?" After a short conversation, during which he found out I was so tired mainly because I was a mom, he paused, pensively figuring out what to do next. What I remember most about our encounter was the look of concern and compassion in his eyes when he said (as I recall his words), "You cannot sleep well here. You must take good rest in order to practice. I will take your mat, and you take my bed."

Munindraji's kindness came forth with a practical directness. His giving came from a place of a very natural compassion for another human being and obviously not from a place of needing to impress. I was struck by the observation, *though he is a meditation teacher, he truly doesn't consider himself to be more important than me.* In fact, it was as though he was treating me as respectfully as his own mother.

In an intensive one-month retreat, most of the day is spent in silent moment-to-moment mindfulness practice while sitting in the meditation hall or walking on the pathways in the garden. Even the activities of eating, bathing, dressing, and doing chores during the morning work hour are all done silently with intentional mindfulness. Then, each evening in the meditation hall, the teacher offers an hour-long talk regarding some aspect of the teachings of the Buddha.

Listening to those first Dharma talks, I took it all in as if the words and the meaning were long-overdue nourishment to my heart. In many ways the teaching felt very familiar to me. Munindra would speak of the importance of cultivating generosity, lovingkindness, compassion, and respect for others, and how these qualities help us to live harmoniously with our family and community. He spoke of how a harmonious life would naturally create inner harmony, a restful composure, and happiness, and that this would support the training of calming and concentrating the mind. He spoke further on how when the mind and heart are calm and concentrated, it's easier to experience more clearly what's going on beneath the veneer of our busy lives and to see into deeper understandings and truths. And finally, the Dharma talks pointed the way to how those behaviors and trainings lead to an ever-deepening, unconditioned peace.

Though Munindra can expound on profound aspects of the Dharma, he has a way of making it sound like it's just common sense and applicable to everyday life. Hearing the Dharma in this way filled the deep wells of my heart with more confidence—confidence that I would need to draw on during challenging times of meditative practice, and life in general.

It didn't take long for me to see that this teacher's words were not just from a book, but that he really and truly exemplified what he was teaching. Respect, kindness, generosity, compassion, inner quiet, and profound wisdom were clearly evident in him. As far as I could tell, he was "walking his talk."

When we see the teachings embodied in someone, that living reality infuses us with faith that we have the same potential. And that faith holds us together through our practice. It's not just "good theory" holding it together. In this way, Munindra's example awoke in me the confidence and determination to realize my own spiritual aspirations. This is how I recognized Munindra as a true spiritual teacher for me.

A few years later, I began to organize retreats out of enthusiasm to share with my community the teachings I so revered, and also because I wanted to continue to hear the Dharma and practice with my teacher. We had moved to Maui, and it made me very happy to invite Munindraji to teach in a climate that he was familiar with and could be comfortable in, one similar to his own motherland. One time when he spent a few days at our home after a ten-day retreat, he tried to get me to do sitting meditation every morning. It was pretty hopeless with the three kids —I just knew I couldn't do it all the time. Not giving up easily, he asked me where I spent most of my time in the house, to which I quickly replied, "In the kitchen, washing dishes." So we went to the kitchen, and he gave a Dharma talk right there about how much freedom and happiness there can be in the simplicity of being present with whatever is happening, and how the power of that presence of mind would uncover deeper and deeper truths. He stood right next to me at the sink, and with his lilting East Indian accent, he gave on-the-spot mindfulness instructions for washing the dishes.

He said, "Have a general awareness of just washing the dishes, the movement of your hands, the warmth or coolness of the water, picking a dish up, soaping it, rinsing it, putting it down. Nothing else is happening now—just washing the dishes." Then he told me to experience my posture, or just notice that the process of seeing was happening. He said that I didn't need to go slow, or to observe everything moment-by-moment, but that I should have a general mindfulness of whatever was happening as I washed the dishes. "Just washing the dishes."

So I continued, just washing the dishes. Once in a while Munindraji would ask me, "What's happening now?" When I replied, "Now I'm worried about paying the mortgage," he would further instruct, "Just notice 'worried,' and bring your attention back to washing the dishes." When I told him, "I'm planning what to cook for dinner." He repeated, "Just notice 'planning,' because that's what is in the present moment, and then return to just washing the dishes."

Even though we were standing in my kitchen, Munindra offered those instructions with as much seriousness as though he were teaching in a formal retreat. Learning something from his sincerity, I practiced earnestly as I washed the dishes many times during the day. Doing this ordinary task with intentional mindfulness has helped me to notice and experience many things more clearly: the changing physical sensations, the flow of thoughts and emotions, and my surrounding environment are all much more alive. This has been a steadfast training in bringing awareness back to my original intention, the simplicity of what I am doing at the time. This helped collect or focus my mind so that it was not so scattered. To do this has required me to develop more perseverance, patience, humility, clear intention, honesty with myself, and much more. These are no small things. Just from washing the dishes! So day by day, dish by dish, a lot of the training of the mind and heart can be accomplished.

The resulting enjoyment of being more fully present with life is a rare treasure in this world.

But that training wasn't enough for Munindra. He also noticed that I walked through the hallway from my bedroom to the living room many times each day. The hallway was only about ten steps long, and he suggested it could be a perfect place to do walking meditation. As we stood at the threshold of my bedroom door, he gave me some simple instructions.

"Every time you step into this hallway, see if you can use the time as an opportunity to be present with the simple fact of walking. 'Just walking.' Not thinking about your mother, or about the children . . . just experiencing the body walking. It might help you to make a silent mental notation of every step. With each step, very quietly in your mind you can note, 'stepping, stepping, stepping.' This will help you keep your attention connected to your intention of 'just walking.' If the mind wanders to something else, as soon as you notice that it has wandered, make the silent mental note, 'wandering mind.' Do this without judging, condemning, or criticizing. In a simple and easy way, bring your attention back to just the walking, noting, 'stepping, stepping, stepping.' Your practice in this hallway will be a wonderful training for you. It will also benefit those around you because you will feel more refreshed."

It didn't seem like much of a spiritual practice, but every day as I walked back and forth through that hallway on my way to do something, I would have a few moments of clear presence of mind—unhurried, unworried, at ease with life for a precious ten steps.

As I look back now, in my heart I regard that hallway and kitchen sink as very sacred places. I extended that mindfulness practice to all the everyday chores in our household—washing clothes, ironing, wiping counters—essentially to all my activities during the day.

This was my main practice for a few years because I couldn't sit every morning. I didn't make it to many retreats, and most of the time there was no teacher nearby to guide me. What helped me the most when one of my teachers wasn't accessible was mindfulness itself. It is said that mindfulness is like an inner mentor. It's just common sense that if we can experience what's truly going on within us and around us with more honesty and clarity, we already have a great teacher in our midst. The constancy and accessibility of simply being present with whatever was happening helped me tremendously in terms of training the mind.

There is a saying, "Not to look to the teacher, but to the teaching. And not to look to just the words of the teaching, but to the meaning. And not to look to the meaning of the interpreter, but to the meaning for oneself." Understanding this deeply, we begin to have more reliable faith in ourselves. This transfers easily to confidence in our practice, and trust in the teachings because we begin to verify them for ourselves.

Sometimes we may have misgivings about our teachers because we discover they are not as perfect as we imagined them to be, or maybe their behavior is inappropriate according to our standards or even harmful. But that need not derail us from staying in alignment with our own highest potential, if we can maintain faith in ourselves. One time I asked Munindra about a popular teacher whose controversial lifestyle was making news headlines. I was perplexed because the literature coming from this person was quite beautiful, and his students (some of them were my friends) seemed to be benefiting greatly from their practice with him. Munindra replied with one of his wisdom-filled one-liners, "A perfect rose can come from an imperfect giver."

Later, when I was able to attend retreats of a month or more, the strengths that came from practicing at home all those years clearly paid off. Being accustomed to bringing mindfulness to every activity, whether it was tying shoelaces, opening a door, eating, or sitting on a meditation cushion, made meditation practice comfortable and seamless during those long retreats. The unbroken continuity of mindfulness practice during a day generates strong concentration, which is vitally important for the opening of the mind and heart. My gratitude for Munindraji's simple yet deep-reaching guidance runs deep.

After some years passed I remarried, and my family grew to four children. At the time, Munindraji needed some medical procedures done in the United States, so a few of his students got together to help him out. I volunteered to make arrangements with a surgeon on Maui so that I could take care of him after his surgery for about three months. It was a challenging time keeping up with all the kids and Munindraji too! Sometimes it was like I had five children. In fact, the children would kiddingly call me the "dhamma mama," and Munindra would call me Mom. We all had fun with that.

Being a gracious guest, Munindra shared the Dharma with me each day he spent in our home because he felt that was the most valuable offering he could make. Every morning I went to his room to receive some guidance and instruction. His enthusiasm for sharing the Buddha's teaching is quite remarkable. Sometimes in the morning I would ask him a simple question, and he would take several situations that arose during the day to illustrate the Buddha's teaching in response. In this way he exposed me to some of the most esoteric of the teachings of the Buddha, such as the truth of impermanence, the empty nature of self, dependent origination, and karma.

A phrase he would use many times is "This is the law." I came to understand that when he used this word, it meant "the Dharma." One of the meanings of *Dharma* is the natural unfolding of the law of cause and effect. Another is the truth of this moment, or the way things are. He often said that phrase, "This is the law," when inviting me to simply open to and accept the reality of the situation.

For example, one time I asked him (probably with a complaining and blaming tone) why my life had been full of hardship. And he replied, "This is the law. What is happening now is the result of actions in the past. But in this moment, depending on how you respond, you can create a different future—one of happiness. That future will eventually become this present moment. And this present moment will become the past. In this way, it is possible for your life to be surrounded by more happiness . . . in the past, the present, and the future. Everything depends on this moment. If you are mindful, you can choose with wisdom how to respond. If you are not mindful, your life is run by reactivity. It's up to you."

I learned from the meaning of that phrase that accepting or surrendering to the truth of the way things are didn't mean that I had to resign myself to some predetermined destiny, or that I just had to give up on life. It is a potent reminder that if we are clearly mindful, it is possible to take part in creating our destiny. Otherwise we live over and over again in the realms of delusion and unhappiness because our lives are dictated by the reactive habits of our mind. The realization that this present moment carries with it such incredible potential changed the course of my life. By compelling me to make mindfulness practice a priority in my life, it redirected my destiny.

After Munindra's surgery, I tried my best to keep the atmosphere in our home peaceful and healing for his recovery. In retrospect, I probably also wanted to impress him with how well I had raised the children and what a "meditative" life I had. At the time, the eldest three children were well into their teenage years, and the youngest, my ten-year-old, was beginning to test her strength. One day Munindraji and I were quietly sitting at the dining table having a meal. All of a sudden in the adjacent family room, my youngest daughter and her father got into an argument over something fairly petty that quickly escalated into a shouting match. Then she tore through the dining room, around us at the table, down the hall to her bedroom, and with all her might slammed and locked her door. Her father came right behind her, all steamed up and trying to open her door.

Munindraji calmly continued to eat, but I could tell by his darting eyes that he was apprehensive. I felt embarrassed, angry, protective, helpless, confused. It wasn't the peaceful home I wanted it to be. The shouting continued, "Open this door right now!" "No!" my daughter shouted back at the top of her lungs. The whole neighborhood must have heard them. Ugh. I cringed.

We were a pretty average family, so hot tempers and arguments happened sometimes, but this wasn't a family scene we were used to on a regular basis. By this time, I didn't know whether to run away from embarrassment, cry, or start screaming at them too. In the midst of all this chaos, Munindraji reached over, placed his steady hand on my forearm, looked at me very compassionately, and said, "Surrender to the law."

Those few words, and the teaching they offer, have served me well many times since then. The lessons are clear. In surrendering or accepting how it is, there is a clear experience of the moment. In this way, we are cultivating nondelusion, or wisdom. From that wisdom, we can let go of our attachment to how we think it should be or how we want it to be. Letting go helps us to cultivate nonattachment, or acceptance and understanding in this case. When both wisdom and nonattachment are present, there can be no resistance to how it is. We are simply able to see clearly what is going on so that we can take compassionate action from that place of clarity. This engenders love.

As soon as I did "surrender to the law," to the reality of what was happening in the moment, my reactive and chaotic mind settled. I was able to draw from the deep well of equanimity, and from that place I did what I could to help make peace between father and daughter.

But I also saw with deeper understanding that they had their own stuff to work out, so to speak. It wasn't something I could control. Certainly, my desire for it to be perfect, or my aversion to how it was so imperfect, only brought more suffering and confusion to everyone involved. From that experience, I saw again that it was only from acceptance, clarity, and understanding that the most compassionate action could come. And with compassion, there is a better chance to *beneficially* influence what is happening around us, even though we can't control it.

Munindra did not comment much on that event afterward. I imagined that he might judge or criticize us, but he didn't. His behavior showed us that he didn't expect our home to be a heaven or a monastery. And in fact, our home was as valid a place as any for spiritual practice. He just proceeded as usual to offer the same teachings. It didn't matter what transpired; his invitation to be more aware, to be kind and compassionate, and to point oneself toward wisdom and peace were always the same.

Doing a major part of my spiritual practice using everyday life situations has given me the opportunity to experience an organic, homegrown opening of the heart. I have found that it is possible to fulfill one's deepest aspirations even within a busy and sometimes chaotic life. I have also learned that at times we also need to go deep within and drink from the wellspring of stillness, silence, and clarity. For this, being guided by a teacher who inspires faith and confidence in our practice, and who shows us how to verify the teachings for ourselves, is of immeasurable value. If we are sincere about our practice and have faith in ourselves, that deep wellspring of peace is closer than we can imagine.

SONGS OF
THE SISTERS
The First Buddhist Women

Carol Wilson

O NE OF THE TREASURE CHESTS of Buddhist literature is the *Therigatha*, "Songs of the Sisters," a classic collection of poems by some of the women who went forth into homelessness under the protection of the Buddha. When I read the poems in the *Therigatha*, I experience the living presence of these women. Their lives were as varied as ours are today. Some came from wealth and privilege, or possessed great beauty and used it to rise to high position. Many more were poor; some were servants or even slaves. Some came to the Dharma as a result of enormous suffering and grief, while others experienced suffering after they joined the order of nuns (*bhikkuni*), brought to the point of despair by their frustration at not achieving their goal as quickly as they might have wished. One hears desperation in some of the poems, as well as the peace and joy that radiate when the fetters of suffering have been seen through. In these stories I hear and feel myself and all those I've had the privilege to share time with during meditation retreats. The yearnings, fears, and struggles we go through today are not so different from those of twenty-five hundred years ago.

The inner lives of the first Buddhist women are our inner lives. The steadfast devotion to awakening that they discovered in themselves, with which they inspired and supported one another, is also available to us, here and now. An enlivening of confidence and strengthening of intention can occur for us when we read the *Therigatha* because these women are so obviously real. They share not only the joys of their deep inspiration but their self-doubts and fears as well. Sometimes the strongest resistance in spiritual life is the fear of having to give up one's attachments. Yet they did so. If it was possible for them, then it is possible for me, and for each one of us who is willing to trust in that potential and to commit our devoted and sincere energy to the task.

I would like to share the stories of a few of these women, beginning with Mahapajapati (or Pajapati) Gotami, the stepmother of Siddhartha Gotama, the man who became the Buddha. Pajapati's devotion, courage, and persistence are largely responsible for creating the first community of nuns. I think her story deserves to be told in some detail.

Pajapati Gotami and her older sister Maya, the mother of Siddhartha Gotama, were both married to King Suddodhana. When Maya died seven days after the birth of her son, Pajapati raised him and loved him as her own child. She later had a son and daughter of her own as well.

After his enlightenment the Buddha visited his family to share what he had discovered. Many of his relatives became lay disciples, Mahapajapati among them. On hearing her stepson preach, she awoke to the first stage of enlightenment, called *sotapanna*, when the belief in the separate sense of self is eradicated. Pajapati became a devoted disciple of the Buddha while continuing in her daily life as wife and mother. Some years later, both her son, Nanda, and her great-nephew, the Buddha's son Rahula, left home to become monks with the Buddha. Then King Suddodhana died. This left Pajapati on her own. Although she lived with a large community of women attached to the court of her late husband, her status and security in society as an Indian woman derived largely from her male relations. So Pajapati was effectively left alone. Many other women in the society at that time were sharing her experience. A great number of men were inspired by the Buddha to enter the homeless life, and quite a few others were killed in ongoing disputes between clans.

Mahapajapati was apparently a natural leader. As many women were left without fathers, husbands, or sons to protect them or tell them how to live their lives, they naturally turned to her in their confusion. These women had been just as inspired by the Truth they had heard from the Buddha as their men had, yet there existed no women's Sangha that they could join. Together, under the leadership of Mahapajapati, they resolved to request that the Buddha ordain them, thus establishing an order of nuns similar to the *bhikku* (monk) community in which the men lived and practiced. They asked the Buddha three times, the traditional number after which the Buddha would usually agree to any request. Surprisingly, he refused, saying: "Enough. Do not be eager, Gotami, to obtain the going forth of women from home into homelessness in the Dharma and Discipline proclaimed by the Tathagata."

At this point, Pajapati's true courage came into play. Being partially awakened, she had great devotion, both to the Buddha and to the Truth he manifested as well. She would have had no doubt about her ability to understand and live it. Her faith gave her confidence and strength. She and the other women shaved off their hair, donned yellow robes, and walked barefoot for some hundred and fifty miles, following the Buddha to his next resting place, in Vesali.

Barefoot, exhausted, with bleeding feet, Pajapati stood outside the Buddha hall. Ananda, the Buddha's attendant known as the Guardian of the Dharma, saw her and was deeply moved with compassion. He himself then went to the Buddha and requested that the women be permitted to form an order of nuns. Again the Buddha three times refused. But Ananda was persistent when moved by compassion in the service of Dharma, and he tried another angle. He asked the Buddha whether women would be able to realize all four stages of awakening, if they entered into homelessness, and the Buddha said yes. Ananda then reminded the Buddha of all that Mahapajapati had given him, raising him, teaching him, even nourishing him with her own milk after his mother died. "Therefore it would be good if the Blessed One would allow women to leave home for the homeless life. . . ." And at this point the Buddha agreed.

It is difficult, if not impossible, to understand the basis for the Buddha's reluctance when viewed from our contemporary context. Because he went on to establish eight extra rules for the bhikkuni order, beyond what was required of the bhikku order, my belief is that he was attempting not to shock the societal structures of the time too much. However, that is speculation. What we can know for sure is that the courage and commitment of Mahapajapati Gotami were largely responsible for establishing the order of nuns. Within this order grew up many teachers, very powerful teachers, strong and inspirational women, who by sharing their insight with other women in the community brought many nuns to awakening. We can hear the voices of these women across the centuries in their poems, as recorded in the *Therigatha*.

Here is the voice of Mahapajapati herself. The immediacy of her presence, devotion, confidence, and joy sings across the years:

Buddha! Hero! Praise be to you!
You foremost among all beings!
You who have released me from pain,
And so many other folk too.

All suffering has been understood.
The source of craving has withered.
Cessation has been touched by me
On the Noble Eightfold Path.

See the gathering of followers:
Putting forth effort, self-controlled,
Always with strong resolution—
This is how to honor the Buddhas!*

*Translated by Andrew Olendzki.

Thanks to Mahapajapati, the Sangha of nuns under the Buddha's dispensation became a source of refuge and awakening for many, many women. When I reflect on how easily, at times, I can be diverted from my deepest intentions simply by conflicting interests, not to mention how discouraged I can feel when some seeming obstruction appears on my path, I respect Pajapati and her followers all the more. Each woman came to the Sangha from her own unique situation, from her personal motivations, just as each of us today comes to the Dhamma for different reasons, from varying backgrounds. According to our personalities and inclinations, each of us will express our understanding in a way that is unique, and the same was true during the time of the Buddha. Some of these first Buddhist women became great leaders and teachers, inspiring others with their words or insights, while others quietly expressed their awakening by living in harmony with the community. The lives of all of them were instrumental in keeping the Buddhadharma alive for us who follow in their footsteps today.

Another nun whose songs are preserved in the *Therigatha* is Khema. Khema was named by the Buddha as one of his two foremost disciples in the bhikkuni Sangha, the disciple who was greatest in insight. The story of how she came to be a nun reflects the resistance that many of us, in our modern lives, may have to hearing the truth, especially when we fear it will mean changing the way we live.

Khema was very beautiful, and on reaching adulthood she became one of the main consorts of King Bimbisara. Far from being a shameful connection, serving as the chief consort to a king brought great wealth and privilege to a woman. Khema thoroughly appreciated her beauty and enjoyed the pleasures and comforts of her position. Although King Bimbisara was a devoted follower of the Buddha, whom he often invited to his palace to teach, Khema refused to go to meet the Buddha. She had heard that he spoke of the dangers of attachment to beauty and sense pleasures, and being quite happily attached to these very things, Khema had no interest in hearing otherwise. Perhaps she feared to hear otherwise.

We may discover ourselves in a similar predicament today. There are many stories of people who come to the Dharma through the vehicle of enormous suffering, times when our usual responses to life no longer seem to work, and in desperation we open our minds and hearts to meet ourselves and our lives in a new way. Many of the people I know have begun their spiritual quest in this way, as did many of our early sisters. It is a rarer thing for one to be inspired to question one's life and worldview when it all seems to be going well. More likely, we do not want our happiness threatened.

Khema found herself in this situation. She finally went to hear the Buddha only because King Bimbisara, out of concern for her, tricked her into going. He had donated his Bamboo Grove to the Sangha as a monastery. Knowing that Khema loved the beauty of nature, he hired poets to compose songs about the tranquillity and beauty of this spot. Khema could not resist. Once there, she was drawn to the hall where the Buddha was preaching. He could read her thoughts, and he psychically created an image of a celestial woman far more beautiful than she. As Khema watched, transfixed, the lovely image gradually aged and decayed to old age, with broken teeth, gray hair, and wrinkled skin, finally falling down lifeless. Khema was deeply impressed with the truth of impermanence. The Buddha then spoke to her, describing how people who are enslaved by attachment to beauty and pleasure are bound to this world, while those who can renounce this are free. Right on the spot, Khema became completely enlightened.

Khema then asked and received permission from her king to become a nun. She had penetrated into the truth so deeply that she was praised by the Buddha as the nun foremost in wisdom. What she had feared did indeed come to pass. As she states in her poem, her attachment to pleasure was destroyed. Far from destroying her happiness, however, this understanding ended her suffering instead.

Everywhere the love of pleasure
Is destroyed,
The great dark
Is torn apart,
And Death, you too are destroyed.
(Fools,

Who don't know things
As they really are,
Revere the mansions of the moon
And tend the fire in the wood
Thinking this is purity.)

But for myself,
I honor the Enlightened One
the best of all
and, practicing his teaching,
am completely freed from suffering.*

A story from the *Samyutta Nikaya* illustrates the depth of Khema's wisdom. Once King Pasenadi, a devout follower of the Buddha, was traveling through the country of Kosala, and on arriving in a town, he wished to have a discussion with whichever wise ascetic might be staying there. After much searching, his servant found no male ascetic, but he did find the bhikkuni Khema. King Pasenadi went to Khema and, after greeting her respectfully, asked her many questions concerning the Dharma. She answered him so profoundly and skillfully that when, sometime later, King Pasenadi asked the Buddha the same questions, he answered exactly as Khema had done, even using the same words.

This story illustrates the power and the purity of awakening. In the society at that time, it must have been somewhat unorthodox, if not radical, for a king to sit at the feet of a woman and ask for teachings. Yet Pasenadi did so without prejudice or hesitation. Perhaps he recognized the presence of awakened truth, where distinctions of class and gender are irrelevant. The Buddha reinforced this fact by his deliberate use of the very same words that Khema had used. I find this tremendously liberating. It helps me to recognize how easily my mind can become caught in the habit of evaluating a person's wisdom and compassion through the filters of personal background,

*Translated by Susan Murcott, *The First Buddhist Women: Translations and Commentaries on the* Therigatha (Berkeley: Parallax Press, 1991), p. 66.

gender, or spiritual affiliation, all of which may or may not have any bearing on his or her understanding. Khema's story helps me to drop this limiting view and listen with an open heart and mind. In the process I have discovered that truth and real spiritual inspiration often shine where I might not have looked.

Not all women entered the Sangha from such a position of ease and privilege as did Khema. Many came to the Dharma to find a way out of the enormous suffering in their lives. Patacara is a perfect example. She became one of the most trusted and influential teachers in the Sangha, yet when she first met the Buddha, she was literally insane with grief.

Patacara was the daughter of a wealthy banker in the city of Savatthi. She fell in love with a servant in her father's household and eloped with him to a distant village. After some time, Patacara became pregnant, and following the custom of the day, she wanted to return to her family to have her child. Her husband was less than enthusiastic, and they waited so long to travel that Patacara gave birth on the journey. They then returned to their small village.

When Patacara became pregnant again, the same scenario occurred. She wanted to give birth in Savatthi, her husband resisted, and she finally took her young son and started out by herself. This time, as her husband caught up with them, a terrific storm began, and so did Patacara's labor. Her husband went into the nearby brush to construct a shelter, where he was bitten by a poisonous snake and died. So she had her baby alone in the midst of the storm. The next morning, filled with grief and self-blame, she could only continue the journey to Savatthi.

Before long, she came to a river that was immensely swollen from the rain, flowing with a strong current. Still weak from the birth, Patacara could not carry both children at once, so she took the newborn across first and laid him on the far bank while she went back for her firstborn. When she was in the middle of the river, a hawk swooped down and scooped up her baby. The older boy heard her cries and plunged into the river toward her, only to be swept away and drowned in the current.

Patacara must have been half crazed with grief as she continued toward Savatthi. As she neared the town, a passing man told her about her family. During the violent storm of the previous night, their house had collapsed, killing both her parents and her brother. He pointed out the smoke of their funeral pyre in the distance. At the sight of the smoke, Patacara went completely mad. She tore off all her clothes and ran about in circles, wailing and mourning the deaths of all she loved. People began to call her names and pelt her with rubbish.

Eventually she came to the Jeta Grove, where the Buddha was staying. He saw her and called her to him, saying, "Sister, regain your mindfulness." Instantly, she came back to her normal state of mind. A compassionate man threw her a cloak to cover her naked-ness, and she prostrated herself before the Buddha, told him her tragic story, and asked for his help.

The Buddha listened and responded to Patacara's great grief with such deep compassion and wisdom that on the spot she asked for the going forth, the ordination into the Sangha of nuns.

What did the Buddha say that had such a profound transforma-tive and healing effect? This is a point of inspiration to me. My idea of a compassionate response might be to "make it better," to help distract someone from focusing on her pain. The Buddha, knowing that only the truth will free our hearts, with great compassion told Patacara, "This is how it is. Not only today have you mourned the deaths of those you love, but throughout countless lives you have wept over the loss of those dear to you. The four oceans contain but a little water compared to all the tears we have shed throughout our many lives."

He went on to say that no one, however dear, can provide us shelter when it is our own turn to die, and he taught her the path of virtue and restraint, the path of the Dharma. So deeply did Patacara listen, so fully did she comprehend that all things are impermanent, that we all share in the universal nature of suffering, that she opened to the truth on the spot. She entered the community of nuns, and after a period of struggle and diligent practice, she saw through the cause of suffering and her heart was freed. She describes this mo-ment vividly in her poem:

. . . But I've done everything right
and followed the rule of my teacher.
I'm not lazy or proud.
Why haven't I found peace?

Bathing my feet
I watched the bathwater
Spill down the slope.
I concentrated my mind
The way you train a good horse.

Then I took a lamp
And went to my cell,
Checked the bed,
And sat down on it.
I took a needle
And pushed the wick down.

When the lamp went out,
My mind was freed.*

How vividly this moment is described—it could be happening
today. The frustration expressed in the beginning of the poem is certainly familiar enough, the frustration of impatience. (What? All this
sincere practice and I'm not enlightened yet?) She transcends it simply, by returning her attention to the present moment, using the
world around her to remind herself to pay attention. The recommitment to diligence brings about a moment of such total and relaxed
presence that her heart fully awakens. Yet it is a moment like any
other, an ordinary moment. "When the lamp went out, my mind
was freed." That line breathes life into mindfulness practice. That
simplicity of total presence is available to each of us, the potential to
be so immediate, so free from clinging, that something as natural as
a lamp going out can awaken us to our true nature.

*Translated by Susan Murcott, *The First Buddhist Women*, p. 34.

Patacara became a great teacher in the women's Sangha. She was a natural magnet, attracting women who were in states of loss and despair. Many came to her for help in understanding and overcoming their grief, and her wisdom and compassion guided them to freedom. It is deeply affirming to hear women of such wisdom and commitment sharing the Truth with one another, helping their sisters to realize the happiness of peace. The vibrancy of their commitment to freedom touches and awakens the same stream of energy and joyful confidence in me.

When I think of Maechee Roongduen, a present-day Buddhist nun whom I had the pleasure to know, the timeless aspect of the Sangha of nuns is striking. I spent several months as a nun in a small forest monastery in northern Thailand in 1982; Maechee Roongduen was the head nun of the meditation section. She was a young woman who had grown up in the countryside; her family still lived in a nearby village. From my first glimpse of her, I could see that she took her life as a nun very seriously.

The women's Sangha still exists in the Theravada Buddhism of Southeast Asia today. Yet it has survived in a form that outwardly appears less rigorous than the original bhikkuni order founded by the Buddha. Nuns in Thailand formally commit to following eight rules instead of more than three hundred. In addition to the eight formal precepts, a nun must live by many implicit rules, most of which I learned only by failing to follow them! Roongduen added two more: not handling money and never wearing shoes. Going barefoot is one of various ascetic practices any ordained person can choose to follow. Her decision not to handle money, however, reflected a commitment to the renunciate life that called for great courage and fortitude in a *maechee* (nun). While monks must refrain from handling money as one of their required precepts, they routinely are served by attendants who deal with any financial arrangements that must be made. An example might be purchasing train or airline tickets. Maechees, however, have no such attendants. So the commitment not to handle money was a serious one. It imposed complications and restrictions on Roongduen's life that must have required her to live very simply.

While it is true that as an institution the nuns' Sangha does not receive the same cultural support that the monks' Sangha receives, my personal experience showed me that as individuals, the Thai people have great respect and love for nuns when they meet them personally. During the entire period of time that I spent as a nun, I was overwhelmed by the joyful generosity that met me everywhere I went. I never lacked for food, and my robes were provided from the day of my ordination by lay supporters who were filled with gratitude at having the opportunity to support me. Being a foreigner, I was treated as an honored guest when I arrived at a monastery, often being given the best accommodation that was available for women.

My experience at Thum Thong, the monastery where I met Roongduen, was no different. The women's meditation section consisted of six small huts along the bank of a river that ran through the forest. Across the river were about twenty huts for the monks. When I first arrived, Roongduen gave me a hut to myself. My experience in the West led me to assume that as head nun she would have her choice of hut and that she would be the last one to move if a crowd should arrive. One of the beautiful aspects of Buddhist temples is that any monk or nun, and usually layperson as well, who turns up, even unexpectedly, is completely welcome. It often happened that several nuns would arrive for an indeterminate amount of time, and space would always be found, willingly and happily. I lived in fear of having to share or even give up my small hut to visitors, since I was the most junior of the nuns. To my surprise, Roongduen was always the first one to give up her hut, at times staying in a cave high above the forest floor. Along with a small cot, this cave was home to hundreds of bats! Even when the *wat* (temple) was at its most crowded, I was given a hut to myself. I was very grateful for this.

Roongduen was a young woman of strong resolution and tremendous energy. Her duties as head nun included overseeing many of the practical details of running the temple day to day as well as ensuring that we nuns maintained an appropriately contemplative atmosphere in the meditation area where we lived. She carried out her obligations with fervor and attention to detail. In contrast to the slower pace of life I was becoming accustomed to in Thailand, I found her energetic enthusiasm refreshing.

At first, I interpreted Roongduen's obvious commitment to the outer form of ordained life as pride in her ascetic lifestyle, and I thought perhaps she was a trifle carried away by acting as the "good nun." I had come to Thum Thong with the intention of spending months living in nature as an integral aspect of intensive meditation practice. While I hoped that the nun's lifestyle would be a support for this practice, I had never given serious consideration to the possibility that the ascetic lifestyle could itself become the primary form of practice. How limited my perspective was! I felt Roongduen was missing out on deeper aspects of the spiritual life by giving her energy to preserving the outer form so meticulously.

Over the weeks, I slowly came to see that although she carried out her responsibilities with great generosity and impeccability, her heart was called to deep inner silence as truly as mine was. Whenever she had the opportunity, she would retreat into her hut or cave, emerging only when her next duty called. She would meet whoever needed her assistance with presence and grace, yet it was clear that she had had to pull herself back from a state of deep *samadhi*, or strong concentration. This is a very delicate balance to hold, to be able to move from deep inner stillness to relational activity at a moment's notice, yet Roongduen did so with a natural generosity of heart that impressed me strongly.

I began to realize that the outer form of the ordained, ascetic life was much more than a convenient way to find a time and place to meditate. I also discovered that what I had mistaken for naive rigidity in adhering to the rules was not so at all. Watching Roongduen, I learned that a commitment to impeccability in life can actually become the crucible that allows the fire of urgency that feeds our awakening to burn strongly in our heart. The rigorous way of life and the steady but unforeseeable nature of the demands placed on her did not get in the way of her inner stillness. For Roongduen, the serious nature of her commitment to the nun's vows and her responsibilities was the structure that permitted a truly wholehearted commitment to a life of awakening. Had she met the outer form with less rigor, perhaps her inner discipline would have been equally lax. In fact, the differentiation between inner and outer form becomes meaningless. Roongduen's life was an expression of dedication to generosity, virtue, and awakening that equals any of the stories I have read about the nuns or monks at the time of the Buddha.

It is not easy to live a nun's life now, and I cannot suppose it to have been any easier twenty-five hundred years ago. The austerity and discipline required are immense. Were it not in the service of freedom of heart and mind, the simplicity and restrictive nature of the lifestyle would be almost impossible to live with for long. Even when one is sincerely inspired by the potential of awakening and enters the Sangha with heartfelt commitment and urgency, the road can be long and rough. I often wonder whether Roongduen is still a nun, or whether the logistics became exhausting or overwhelming and she found it necessary to return to her family.

Once again, the present is reflected in the past. Contrary to what we might believe, not every nun in the first Sangha came swiftly and easily to complete enlightenment as soon as she ordained. Some of the poems in the *Therigatha* convey heart-rending despair: the despair of someone who has practiced sincerely for years yet still feels far from her goal. Oddly enough, these poems inspire me the most of all. As anyone knows who has committed her life to the path of awakening, it is quite possible, if not probable, to dedicate months and years to serious meditation practice, and the whole of one's life to the intention to be aware, and at times to feel that one is getting nowhere.

Listen to Vaddhesi, who was Mahapajapati's nurse. She was one of the five hundred women who joined the Sangha with Pajapati, but she was not one of the lucky ones who was immediately enlightened. Her poem speaks for itself:

It was twenty-five years
Since I left home,
And I hadn't had a moment's peace.

Uneasy at heart,
Steeped in longing for pleasure,

I held out my arms and cried out
As I entered the monastery.

I went up to a nun I thought I could trust.
She taught me the Dharma,
    The elements of body and mind.

. . . .

I heard her words
And sat down beside her.

. . . .

I have great magic powers
And I have annihilated
All the obsessions of the mind.
The Buddha's teaching has been done.*

It eases my frustration to know that even when people could hear the Buddha teach in person, these fallow periods still occurred. The poems these women have shared with us can help us to ease up on our unrealistic expectations of ourselves and of awareness practice. We remember that truth is not a product of time; there is no equation guaranteeing a certain experience if we practice a certain number of hours or years. Far from increasing discouragement, these poems strengthen my faith in the power of the sincere mind and heart to awaken. They instill trust in the mysterious methods of the Dharma. So I thank these women for their greatness of spirit and persistence in their discouragement, and for giving voice to their experience.

For other women, the life of a nun brought ease and joy right away, which they express with a lightness and humor that is delightful. This is from a woman known as Sumangala's mother:

I'm free
Free from kitchen drudgery
No longer a slave among my dirty cooking pots

*Translated by Susan Murcott, *The First Buddhist Women*, pp. 28–29.

(My pot smelled like an old water snake)
And I'm through with my brutal husband
And his tiresome sunshades
I purge lust with a sizzling sound—*pop*
"O happiness," meditate upon
this as happiness.*

"This is happiness." These voices of our ancient sisters, singing to us today, remind us that liberation is indeed possible. Listening to their voices, we find the courage and trust so that we may live a life of compassion and wisdom also.

The Buddha taught
Seven Factors of Enlightenment.
There are ways to find peace
And I have developed them all.

I have found what is vast and empty,
The unborn.
It is what I've longed for.
I am a true daughter of the Buddha,
Always finding joy
In peace.

—UTTAMA†

*Translated by Andrew Schelling and Anne Waldman, *Songs of the Sons and Daughters of Buddha* (Boston: Shambhala Publications, 1996), p. 51.
†Translated by Susan Murcott, *The First Buddhist Women*, p. 53.

SACRED
FRIENDSHIP
Bridge to Freedom

Steven Smith

I N B U D D H I S T L I T E R A T U R E the word *kalyanamitta* is usually translated as a good, honest, or spiritual friend. But *kalyanamitta* means more than just that. The words "sacred friendship" come closest to describing the depth of connection and commitment, the pure and unconditional relationship, that can exist between a student and a spiritual teacher, as well as between friends.

Kalyanamitta, sacred friendship, has two aspects: empathy and wisdom. Empathy is the capacity to resonate and connect on a level deeper than the persona, to feel what another is feeling in one's own heart. Free from judgment or interpretation, empathy means being right there with another on a pure, energetic level. The other half of sacred friendship, wisdom, attunes to the other person's inherent goodness, a sacred place within. A spiritual friend might see this goodness long before we know it is there. Overtly or subtly, he or she then skillfully brings that goodness out and inspires us to live up to our true potential. As a student on retreat once joked, "I want to become the person my dog thinks I am!"

It feels good to be unconditionally loved by someone who is faithfully attuned to our goodness, ever forgiving our faults. Sacred friendship is unconditionally inclusive. Undesirable aspects of the friend are not excluded from the depth of one's heart. Being unconditionally loved by someone radically affirms our core being.

While being attuned to our goodness, a spiritual friend also accepts our less desirable traits and forgives our imperfections. To offer this rare kind of love to a friend requires both commitment and courage. Sacred friendship may be easiest to see in archetypal relationships between great leaders and their fold or between teachers and students. Sometimes even an "ordinary" friendship develops this uncommon sacred character. These relationships suggest the possibility of what complete sacred friendship can be.

Kalyanamitta is beautifully evoked in one of the *Jatakas* ("birth stories"), which are tales of the previous lives of the Buddha, or the "Bodhisattva," a Buddha-to-be.

This legend tells us that once upon a time, the Bodhisattva was born as a Monkey King. He grew up stout and strong, and became a vigorous leader of eighty thousand monkeys who all lived together in one mammoth mango tree. Imagine the size of such a magnificent tree! It grew on the bank of the great river Ganges, spreading its branches partly over water and partly over land. This mango tree was an elaborate mansion of thickly layered leaves, like a forested mountain with richly landscaped regions down its flanks. The mangoes were as large as water pots and had a sweet fragrance, brilliant sunset colors, and the taste of ambrosia. The monkeys loved their mango tree. For timeless generations their ancestors had lived in the region. Now, bodhisattvas have intuitive knowledge about unforeseeable events and other mysterious things, so throughout their residence in this mango tree, the Monkey King laid down one rule: they must never allow even one of the mangoes to fall into the river.

But the palatial mango tree was home to many other beings as well, including a giant colony of forest ants, and their huge nest stretched out along a large limb growing over the great river. The monkeys didn't see that the ant's nest was hiding a cluster of mangoes. One day a large ripened mango fell into the flowing river and floated away.

After a long journey downstream the shiny orange orb became caught in a fisherman's net set to catch river flotsam upstream from where a great Human King of the province happened to be bathing. Seeing this brightly colored object, the king climbed out onto the riverbank and ordered the fisherman to fetch it. "What is that?" the King wondered aloud. The fisherman didn't know. They stared at the strange-looking forest jewel. Then the King's forester came and identified it as the "mango" fruit. The forester ran a sharp knife across the thick skin until the succulent yellow interior was exposed. Instantly an otherworldly aroma arose. The King reached for the fruit and bit into it. Flavor pervaded his entire being. Never had he tasted anything so divine. He said, "We must have more."

The Human King and his retinue sailed upstream for what seemed like a long time, seeking the source of the mango. At last they came to the huge mango tree along the banks of the river in the early evening. No one was around. Mango clusters hung like lamps from the deep green tree and lay like large jewels on the ground. The travelers feasted on mango, enjoying the sublime flavors. Then they built fires around the boundaries, and the King camped at the base of the tree with his archers on guard.

Around midnight the Monkey King returned with his retinue of eighty thousand. The monkeys happily swung into their home tree after their evening forage in the forest. Immediately the archers alerted the sleeping King. Spying the plump monkeys, the King ordered, "Shoot some of them before they flee. We'll have monkey meat with our mango in the morning."

Quickly the archers readied deadly arrows in their bows. Commotion in the mango tree erupted as the Monkey King soothed his tribe: "Do not fear, I will give you life"—and in a flash he led a retreat to the higher reaches of the great tree, where they were momentarily safe from harm's way. But the archers jockeyed for a better shooting position with their deadly poison-tipped arrows. The great Monkey King then leaped from the tallest branch, across the wide

Ganges, and onto the far bank. When the Human King saw this, he said to his archers, "Don't shoot them yet," and all the humans watched what was to unfold.

Expertly, the Monkey King broke several long lengths of bamboo, strung them together, and attached one end to the trunk of a tree, the other end to his waist. With the speed of a thundercloud torn by wind, he jumped back across the river, aiming for a mango branch in order to form a bridge of bamboo that would stretch from bank to bank. But the width of the Ganges was a hundred bow lengths, and the Bodhisattva had forgotten the part he wrapped around his waist. Just as he was about to reach the mango tree, he realized he would fall one bow length short. His mighty body became the last link. He then implored his monkeys, "Go quickly across my back and slide down the bamboo to safety." They began their escape to the other side.

Among the monkey tribe was an envious and resentful monkey named Devadatta. When Devadatta saw the outstretched body of the Monkey King, he thought, "Here is my chance to see the last of my enemy." With the other 79,999 monkeys safely across the bamboo bridge, Devadatta leaped from the highest branch and jumped hard on the Bodhisattva's back, breaking his heart. The Monkey King looked up and said, "Oh, Devadatta, you fool. Now just save your life from the deadly arrows." Devadatta shamefully slid across the Bodhisattva's broken body and joined his tribe, now safe on the other side. The Bodhisattva was alone, and mortally wounded.

The Human King, who had witnessed the unfolding of the entire drama, was overwhelmed with emotion. He said, "This is a great being indeed. He offered his life for the safety of all of those in his care. Now I will care for him. He is a pure friend and a great teacher." The King had the dying Bodhisattva brought carefully down from the tree. He gently washed him in the Ganges and wrapped his own kingly robes around him. He made a comfortable bed and offered fresh fruit and water. Then the Human King asked the Bodhisattva, "Great King, why did you do that? You have sacrificed your own precious life for them. Who are they to you?"

The Bodhisattva answered, "I am their sacred friend, their refuge.

I do not fear death. My monkeys are safe now. Freedom was won for those in my care. My dear friend, if you wish to live by the Dharma, the Truth, then the happiness of all in your realm should be most dear to you. This is the way of a true friend, a true King."

As the Bodhisattva made his transition into his next life, the Human King's heart awakened as if from a long sleep. He remained a long time at the site of his transformation. Then he made a shrine at the foot of the mango tree depicting his great friend's fantastic leap across the wide Ganges for the sake of his tribe. And for the rest of his days he honored the Great Being's memory. Established in the Bodhisattva's teachings of generosity, compassion, and wisdom, he found his true calling as a leader in the joy of serving others. He left a legacy for generations of leaders who followed. The Human King, like his teacher, became a friend to all, a protector of life, justice, and peace.

The Monkey King is the complete kalyanamitta: no being is excluded from his care. He is the savior of his tribe and the protector even of his enemies. He has both the compassion and the wisdom that understands the supreme value of giving everything, even his own life, for the benefit of others. Such sacrifice is a movement of the heart motivated from a place of loyalty that is beyond time. Just as the Buddha spent countless lives as a bodhisattva developing the qualities that would eventually enable him to awaken, so the kalyanamitta is also a bodhisattva cultivating these qualities. When seen from this perspective, the entire world, including our internal and external "Devadattas," can be our benefactor, offering ceaseless teachings of compassion and understanding. Envy, conceit, lust for power, anger, and fear, whether seen within or experienced in others, can teach us patience and forgiveness. It is because Devadatta is not excluded from the tribe that the Bodhisattva is charged to protect, that the Bodhisattva both grieves and feels grateful when Devadatta strikes him a mortal blow. He is grieved by the harm Devadatta causes himself, and glad that as a bodhisattva he is able to offer his life to save all beings. The Human King understood the entire scope of the Monkey King's sacred friendship—and seeing this in action is what transmitted to the Human King the most essential teachings of kalyanamitta.

We need not turn only to legends and literature for inspiring examples of sacred friendship; in our contemporary world there are also great leaders who exemplify this ideal. Aung San Suu Kyi, the Nobel Peace laureate from Burma, is one such hero. Suu Kyi is a good friend with whom I have enjoyed numerous meaningful conversations, great Burmese curry, and afternoon tea at her home in Rangoon. We discovered we had a mutual regard for the Jataka of the Monkey King. We discussed the great power of the Jatakas to encourage the development of qualities of awakening, called *paramis*, in the midst of life's vicissitudes. I noted the parallels of the Monkey King tale to the difficult situation in Burma.

As a leader in the struggle for democracy, Suu Kyi is virtually confined to her home by the opposing military authorities. Yet, like the Monkey King, she and her colleagues strive to create a bridge to freedom for millions of followers. She has said that she does not like to be regarded as a hero, someone separate from the many people who are struggling for freedom. We discussed the quality, or parami, of "courageous energy and strength of heart" (*viriya*) as a deep motivation of the heroic actions of a bodhisattva. She feels that a leader with courageous energy is not a grandstanding "hero," but rather one who tries to work selflessly and courageously with others for the benefit of all.

Although Suu Kyi has a strong intellect, her passion is simple: basic needs such as health, education, and liberty to express oneself. Using the nonviolent forces of love and compassion to bring about change, she inspires courage through her renunciation of self-interest and her loyal friendship. I think the reason millions of people in Burma and throughout the world respect and love her is that she genuinely offers herself as a friend to all. Her spirit of generosity, sacrifice, and friendship nurtures the light of hope in an era of darkness. In the intimacy of friendship, the sense of kinship with all beings creates a "sacred canopy" under which we all live in a natural morality and integrity of intention.

When we were talking about the Monkey King, I observed that

Suu Kyi herself seemed to be a living aspect of this Jataka tale. There are many people who rely on her as a symbol of hope. And she said, "You know, if there was only one person, one friend, left in all of Burma, I would not leave." I thought of the Monkey King's assertion: "I am their refuge."

The Burmese have an expression that describes sacred friendship: *yezed sounde*, which literally means "water-drop connection." It describes the experience of meeting someone and feeling an immediate bond. The image evokes what happens when water drops come close to one another: they combine and become one, the confluence of two streams. In Buddhist cosmology, our lives are viewed as streams of interrelated cause-and-effect energy, a movement of mental and physical forces in ceaseless flow from moment to moment, and life to life. Burmese people would think, "In some past life I did something good for you, you did something good for me, or we performed skillful actions together for the benefit of others. The power of these past actions set in motion a current of complex forces that result in the reunion in the present life of these separate streams of existence." Much more simply said: yezed sounde, water-drop connection. The two meet once again. Pure friendship of this intensity kindles a feeling of recognition and the sense of being "seen."

Meeting my teacher Sayadaw U Pandita was yezed sounde, an immediate recognition, a reunion, and a radical love at first sight. I had traveled to Burma with a dear friend to ordain as a monk at the monastery of the great Mahasi Sayadaw. My mission was principally Dharma practice and study, and the rich discipline of wearing the robes of a monk. I was not looking for a teacher in Burma, rather a profound lineage of teachings. I found such teachings, I found an abounding spiritual home, and unexpectedly, I found a teacher. Sayadaw U Pandita was the senior meditation master at the time I took robes. The moment our eyes met in his modest monastic cottage, I realized that I had found a teacher. It was not exactly like finding him. There was just this powerful connection: yezed sounde.

His initial gaze was at once profoundly reassuring and deeply unsettling. The Sayadaw seemed to see into the very core of my being. Light and shadow, vulnerability and shame, were all laid bare—and accepted. The power of his spiritual friendship was immediate. I felt seen, exposed, yet unconditionally accepted.

The gift of a teacher's unconditional acceptance is a significant condition in creating an inner rest and freedom. From this ease and clarity the truth of things as they are is naturally revealed, and our life flows out of wisdom and compassion.

The power of sacred friendship is not only a catalyst for awakening to truth. It also creates a cohesive and protective surround in one's psyche that heals, empowers, and liberates. We see with eyes of compassion and understanding. When we see in this way, we can begin the long and rewarding journey of accepting all the disparate and fragmented regions of our psyche, and we discover the goodness enfolded within.

Years after I left the monastery and resumed life as a layperson, I asked for U Pandita's blessing for my marriage to Michele McDonald. His response was just as concerned with the heart of the matter as if I were still in robes asking about one of the rules of conduct. He questioned my motivations. He wanted to know if it was *kama* or *kamma*—desire or deep karmic (water-drop) connection. It was a good question, and an important one. Was my wish to marry based on sensual desire and clinging to comfort and convenience—possibly undermining commitment to practice and awakening? Or was it the kind of affiliation between two people that is rooted in an underlying ground of deep spiritual friendship? The ultimate motivation of a *yezed sounde* connection would be the mutual wish for and support of one another's liberation, not simply the satisfaction of worldly desires. As a true spiritual friend, U Pandita pointed me back to the most important aspect of my decision to marry.

The staggering range of joys and sorrows all beings experience is the way of the world. It is natural law, the truth of things as they are. Just as the nature of the physical world is turbulent systems with the ever-changing conditions of wind, water, heat, and earth, so too our inner environment is a turbulent system. We are ever challenged with changing fortunes of gain and loss, pleasure and pain, praise and blame, fame and disrepute. Spiritual friendships show the way of the wise; with wisdom and lovingkindness one can skillfully navigate through these systems with equanimity. It is acceptance of one-self, and life as it is, that is the secret of navigational success.

The Dalai Lama says that we can survive without religion but not without affection. Unconditional love is a nutriment as essential to our being as food. Because it is rare to receive unconditional love, we yearn for it; we long for the experience of being seen, of being recognized to the core in a genuine and authentic way. The trust experienced with a spiritual friend nurtures the places in the psyche that have always longed to love and be loved unconditionally. The power of association with a wise friend helps us to live from our depth, wherein all of life is experienced intimately and as very real.

As an adolescent I had a friend whom I loved and trusted more than anyone else in the world. It was an archetypal friendship, a water-drop connection. I met Peter in the ocean one Saturday while body-surfing at Sandy Beach, a popular yet treacherous shore break. Waves the size and force of Mack trucks were rising up out of deep water, cresting, and pounding down several yards shoreward in a few feet of water. Peter was gracefully riding these dragons, and I saw him as a beautiful youth at skillful play in the foaming intensity of Hawaiian surf.

Confidence—which is essential in riding these massive volumes of water and escaping them before being crunched against the sandy, shallow bottom—was still a developing quality in me. Those waves instilled fear in me. Peter looked at me in a way I still clearly recall four decades later. It was a look of affection and acceptance that at once transmitted confidence, truth, and trust. Under Peter's caring tutelage, I entered a higher level of big-wave body surfing that day at Sandy Beach.

As a lowly freshman, I was an unlikely partner for Peter, a senior "god," yet we formed a deep bond. It was a magical and adventurous friendship: journeys to rural island valleys, caves, and hidden beaches. Yet all these beautiful outer forms mirrored an inner nature more profound than I realized back then. It was an innocent, original spiritual friendship. The beauty of Peter's being was in loving others in such an unconditional, good-hearted way that each of his friends felt their goodness in his presence. He was a "friend to all."

Tragically, Peter died nine years after our meeting at Sandy Beach. When I learned at my family's seashore home about his untimely death, I swam into the surf in a desperate attempt to wash away the pain of unbearable loss. A short time later, on the island of Molokai, I stood on a high, lush valley ridge between two tropical waterfalls looking out over the ocean. A strong feeling of Peter came to mind. I sought him in the beauty of the land we had so often played in throughout our youth. Now he was gone and the pain of it was too unbearable to let in. So I just pushed it away.

Twenty years later, about a month into an intensive *metta* (loving-kindness) retreat, a strong feeling and image of Peter arose in the depths of very concentrated practice. The force of concentration and metta was strong. Yet so potent was the feeling of Peter that I felt impelled to come out of the deep meditation and go with the feelings. My body then began to surge with energetic contractions, releasing emotions of sadness, grief, and loss. I wept.

And something shifted. All those years I had been looking for Peter in each of my relationships, but nothing could compare with the idealized memory of its perfection, and so I rarely felt fully met. Who can compete with perfection? In the wake of this deep and mindful mourning, my view of Peter altered, and I could appreciate the gift he had left in my heart. Only when I let go of Peter as an ideal, and fully mourned his loss, could I accept and appreciate the depth of true-hearted friendship.

Our wisdom tradition of love and understanding teaches us the practice of letting go. When we let go of striving for the perfect, archetypal friendship and just practice being a friend, we discover it is not about *finding* friendship; it is about *being* a friend.

Whenever we are unconditionally present, the friend before us feels affirmed, safe, and seen on the deepest level so that the goodness and authenticity of his or her being shines forth. In this moment the friendship is a sacred connection. And it flows both ways: when we are living from our own depth, everything and everyone is experienced as real, not as an interpretation or idealized image. We also become more forgiving as we accept our failings. We experience in lifelong friendships a compassionate acceptance of each other's longtime flaws.

A movement into intimacy reveals imperfections as well as strengths. Though we may seek supportive and nurturing relations, the closer we become with someone, the more our disturbing, difficult, and dissatisfying traits are revealed. But here is where we meet depth and emotional closeness. Sacred friendship is a way of being, an intimacy with oneself and the world that invites the presence of another into that space.

In this process, friendships can be a crucible of healing. A history of fear of abandonment and longing for connection might be deposited in this crucible. The journey into intimacy may trigger old emotional wounds that have nothing to do with the friend in question. Or maybe an old karmic "knot" simultaneously attracts and repels two individuals in a tension arc of contradiction. The shadowy side of friendship, the competition and jealousy, needs to be recognized and acknowledged.

How do we hold a friendship when the cord of connection has been frayed or broken, when the water drops have separated and cannot seem to find their way back to cohesion? Some betrayals may feel too hurtful to forgive. Yet by allowing ourselves to feel the pain, to forgive our own failure to forgive, eventually we may be able to still feel the sacred in broken friendships.

Within the wide embrace of sacred friendship, acceptance and forgiveness are what make real intimacy possible. Intimacy rests in the simplicity of being fully present, responsive to what is there in the moment, with no agenda or anticipation. By fully being in the moment we are there in just the right way. We rediscover the mystery of who we are through this interchange of opening and surrender. Such friendships create heaven on earth.

> There are such connections, which must be a very great, an almost unbearable happiness, but they can occur only between very rich beings, between those who have become, each for their own sake,

rich, calm, and concentrated; only if two worlds are wide and deep and individual can they be combined.

For the more we are, the richer everything we experience is. And those who want to have a deep love in their lives must collect and save for it, and gather honey.

—RAINER MARIA RILKE

SEEING THE
TEACHINGS AS
THE TEACHER

Sylvia Boorstein

SOME BUDDHIST GROUPS have the tradition of honoring
their teachers by chanting their names, beginning with their
immediate teacher and naming back in time, tracing their lineage to the Buddha as their original teacher: "My teacher So-and-So,
disciple of So-and-So, disciple of So-and-So . . . ," and so on. Those
traditional lineages are vertical; my sense of my own lineage is horizontal. My teachers are primarily contemporaries of mine, and of
each other. Some of them were students of more than one teacher. I
learned Dharma through many voices, often in different styles and
with differing emphases. And, since I began my meditation practice
when I was forty years old, my understanding had also been shaped
by my psychology and biology teachers and by Western modern culture as well as by my Buddhist teachers. With each of these teachers,
there have been moments in which I have felt radically re-informed.
I sometimes think of my learning life as having moved, not from

one teacher to another, but from one insight-inspiring comment to another—a lineage of teac*hings*.

Here are some of the teachings from my Buddhist practice life that I have found transformative. I hesitated before presenting them in this abbreviated form since a list, all by itself, cannot transform, and I was concerned that however graciously I might present these teachings, reducing a great deal of careful instructions into one or two "sound bites" might seem glib or trivializing. I also am convinced that the power of each teaching depended on my being especially attentive when I heard it. I decided I could write this when I remembered a remark made by my friend Sharon Salzberg: "You never know when seeds will be ready to sprout, so you broadcast them widely, and when the time is right, they will grow."

''I'M NOT INTO HASSLING.''

An insight into the possibility of peace was part of my first retreat experience. It occurred in response to an overheard casual remark that I might have missed, had it happened five seconds earlier or five seconds later. It was an insight into *dukkha* (the extra struggle we create around the inevitable challenges of life). It had all the hallmarks of "insight." It was startling; it was surprising; it offered a new perspective.

Somewhere in the middle of the retreat the bell rang marking the end of a period of sitting meditation. I had been struggling to keep my body and mind comfortable. The schedule was rigorous. I was confused about the instructions. The teachers spoke about "clarity of intention," and I knew I didn't have it. I stood up, massaged my aching knees, and began to walk toward the door to begin a period of walking meditation. I passed the teacher just as the manager of the retreat center was whispering a message to him about a problem.

"Bzzz, bzzz, bzzz." Worried face. Furrowed brow.

The teacher thought for a moment, and then, in a very kind voice, said, "Look, I'm not into hassling. . . ."

"Not hassling?" I was surprised. I realized, "That's an alternative! Another possible way to respond." I understood that the teacher was not being dismissive, that the problem would be addressed without *extra* upset. The Buddha taught that a noncombative response, a mind unclouded by the tension of struggle, assures that pain does not become suffering. My first important experience of insight, and I don't know whether it had to do with undelivered groceries or malfunctioning plumbing.

''NOTHING IS WORTH THINKING ABOUT.''

My first five years of meditation practice were pleasant, albeit unre-markable. I liked going away on retreat. I liked sitting quietly. I liked the food. I enjoyed hearing stories about the Buddha. I *loved* the idea that it was possible to live peacefully, regardless of the particular circumstances of one's life.

Although I certainly passed the time at retreats following the schedule—sitting, walking, sitting, walking—my attention was all over the place. I believe, in retrospect, that I probably thought about *more* stories and *more* fantasies on retreat than off. At home, I had lots of tasks, busywork for the attention. On retreat, my mind was free to spin endless stories. And it did.

One day I was walking along a path, most likely telling myself yet another story. My teacher Joseph Goldstein was coming toward me, engaged in conversation with another person. I didn't hear the whole conversation or even the sentence that preceded Joseph's re-mark. But just as they passed by me, I heard Joseph say, "Listen, nothing is worth thinking about."

"Nothing is worth *thinking* about?" I was stunned. I had spent my whole life thinking about everything. I come from a long line of heavy thinkers. I pride myself on my thinking. I also knew that Jo-seph was a pretty good thinker himself. How could he *say* that?

Somehow, by grace perhaps, or just because the necessary condi-tions had been met for me to "get" it, I "got" it. If the point of prac-tice is to experience in *this* moment, as in every moment, the truth of arising and passing away, the truth of eternal change, I need to be here, *now*, to realize it. Stories are always mind-elaborations on the mythic past or the hypothetical future.

I took a vow not to tell myself stories. Not forever, but for the period of time I was on retreat, practicing. It wasn't a vow against all thinking, because cognitions—"moving, stepping, hungry, tired"—are thoughts, too. It was a vow about *discursive* thinking, which is what stories are.

As soon as I took the vow, my meditative experience changed dramatically. I determined that my attention, when I sat, would not move from the breath. The initial minutes of resolve, perhaps the initial hours of resolve, were difficult. Very soon, however, I found I *could* relax. It wasn't that I humbled the attention into submission. What happened was that the breath became interesting. In fact, fascinating. Even (can you believe it?) thrilling! That's when my serious practice began.

Years later, I told Joseph the story of his overheard remark and how it had transformed my practice. He said, "Maybe I didn't mean, 'Nothing is worth *thinking* about.' Maybe I meant, '*Nothing* is worth thinking about!' "

"EVERY MOMENT OF MINDFULNESS ERASES A MOMENT OF CONDITIONING."

I learned about how to use the energy of mindfulness to condition ongoing clarity from U Sivili, a Sri Lankan monk who was teaching at a retreat at which I was a student many years ago. I had described to him my dismay over a particular practice hurdle I was experiencing at retreats. It was my habit, in those days, to go to bed quite early. I would awaken refreshed in the middle of the night, dress, and go to the meditation hall to practice sitting and walking. Although I would arrive filled with enthusiasm, five minutes later I would find myself drowsy. The rest of the night was sitting-dozing-walking-dozing-sitting-dozing. "Perhaps," I said to U Sivili, "this doesn't count for anything. Maybe I should stay in bed."

"No," he replied. "Don't stay in bed. First of all, the intention counts. More than that, it doesn't matter how many times you doze off. What matters is that from time to time you wake up. Every moment of mindfulness erases a moment of conditioning!"

That last line, the idea that every moment of mindfulness *erases*, was an enormous boost to my capacity for patience. I imagined that my mind was erasing scribbles. I thought to myself, "We never *know* how near we might be to erasing the last scribble. I might be one scribble away from enlightenment!"

"*BE* THE EXPERIENCE."

For the first years of my meditation practice, I studied with teachers who emphasized the technique of "mental noting."

"I'm breathing in, I'm breathing out. I'm lifting my foot, I'm moving it, I'm putting it down. I'm lifting, I'm moving, I'm putting down." Mental noting is a Burmese practice instruction associated with the teacher Mahasi Sayadaw. I found it a valuable instruction. I learned to carefully rest the attention with current experience, and I named it meticulously and (possibly) somewhat obsessively. I then studied with Christopher Titmuss, who said to me in an interview, "Don't do that anymore. It gets in the way. Stop naming. Just *be* the experience."

"*Be* the experience?" I remember going into the chapel to do my walking practice, and discovering that it was hard for me to unlearn my habit of talking to myself. Then I remembered that I had taught myself to ride my bike without holding the handlebars by getting going, reaching a certain speed, and then letting go. I did walking meditation the same way. I walked, and noted, and brought all my attention to the experience of touching and lifting and moving. When I felt present, I let go of the noting, just as I had of the handlebars. I discovered that staying present required unwavering attention, an attention that enhanced the intimacy of the experience.

"DO WHATEVER YOU NEED TO DO TO STAY BALANCED."

Some years later, I was practicing in Barre, feeling clear and confident about my progress and organizing my days in a way I believed supported my practice. I began my day at two or three in the morning. I rationed my cups of coffee strategically, and I chose food carefully to assure that I was neither hungry nor sleepy. One day a notice appeared on the bulletin board that said, "Tomorrow is Oxfam day. If you elect to fast, we will contribute $9.00 on your behalf to Oxfam. Check below if you plan to fast, so we will cook that much less food."

Suddenly a storm arose in my mind. Fasting is not a problem for me under normal circumstances, and I certainly wanted to support Oxfam. But I had my whole practice day organized: now a cup of coffee, now the bowl of rice, now this, now that. When I had my interview with Joseph, my teacher, I said, "Listen, I've gotten everything so carefully arranged. I really want to fast tomorrow, but if I fast maybe I won't feel well or perhaps I'll lose my concentration. What should I do?"

Retrospectively, this all seems silly. I can't imagine what I was worried about. We concentrate. We become distracted. We concentrate again. Not a big deal. But Joseph's answer was important to me. It was the perfect generic answer to every practice question: "Should I eat more?" "Should I eat less?" "Should I stay up later?" "Should I go to sleep earlier?" "Should I walk more?" "Should I sit more?" He said: "Do whatever you need to do to stay balanced."

Mindfulness balances composure in the mind with relaxed vigilance so that the mind stays clear, so that we understand fully, so that we respond compassionately. "Do whatever you need to do to stay balanced" is a fine instruction for practice and a fine instruction for life.

"MAYBE THIS ISN'T YOUR RETREAT TO HAVE ZEAL."

I was practicing for several weeks at a spring retreat that I had anticipated with joy and great expectations. My experience, to my great dismay, was one of seemingly impermeable torpor. I sat and walked and sat and walked and rigorously followed the schedule, but my mind felt flat. Uninterested. Bored. Attention just wasn't there. I struggled with it because I am usually a very zealous student. I had a reliable pharmacopeia of antidotes for all of the hindrances. I was always tinkering, trying to fix things. This time nothing I tried inspired more enthusiasm.

I went to see my teacher Jack Kornfield for an interview. I said, "I am concerned. I am sitting and walking and sitting and walking and *trying* to be attentive, but I don't have any energy. My normal zeal isn't here."

Jack said, "Maybe this just isn't your retreat to have zeal." What a relief! I didn't have to be the perfect retreatant all the time. More than that, though, I understood his intervention quite directly as an insight into impermanence—in this case, the impermanence of mind-states. Sometimes there is energy in the mind; sometimes there isn't. When there's energy, we have zeal; when there isn't energy, we don't have zeal. It became something to pay attention to, not something that required struggle.

I had been complicating my experience with demoralizing stories—"I'm a terrible meditator. I'm not trying hard enough. All these other people have zeal. I'll never get enlightened if I don't have zeal."—and depressing myself, probably further depleting my energy. As soon as I could think, "I guess this is not my retreat to have zeal," I relaxed. I thought, "Maybe in the *next* retreat I'll have zeal. Or maybe *tomorrow* I'll have zeal." I felt so reasssured by Jack's remark that five minutes later I had zeal. Such a remarkable insight into impermanence, just from admitting I was sleepy!

"ASSUME THE NATURAL PEACE AND EASE OF THE MIND AND BODY."

In the early years of my practice, my understanding was conditioned by exotic ideas about enlightenment. I had heard stories of magical psychic powers, incredible feats of body and mind control, exalted states attainable by a very select few. I had heard about "fully realized beings" who seemed tranquil in the face of every conceivable grief or challenge. Comparing my own experience with theirs, I felt sure that there was some experience *outside* myself that I had yet to discover, some permanent state that I was meant to attain. What I've come to trust most deeply is that the capacity for peaceful response is natural to all of us, as a birthright, and that the presence or absence of peace at any moment is the result of habits of our mind and of circumstances in our lives. My confidence in life and in myself depends on knowing that life *is* difficult, challenge *is* inevitable, distress is *not* failure, and returning to peacefulness—at least some of the time—is a possibility.

These days I give meditation instructions using a phrase I heard Ajahn Amaro use that presents practice quite simply as a form of remembering. He said, "As you sit, allow your mind and body to assume the natural peace and ease that *is* the natural peace and ease of the mind and body. Then just stay that way. Be attentive to anything that comes up that disturbs that sense of peace. If nothing comes up, just sit peacefully."

"Where is it written that you are supposed to be happy all the time?"

Although this list has been my lineage of Dharma teachers, I am including my grandmother's instruction, since she was my principal caretaker when I was a child, and I think of her as my first Buddhist teacher. Although her life, first in Europe and then in the United States, had been difficult, she was even-tempered, resolute, sensible, and kind.

My grandmother was entirely solicitous of my physical needs. She cooked the things I liked to eat. We took walks together. She bathed and dressed me and braided my hair. She sat by my bedside and sang to me until I fell asleep. And she was philosophical about my moods. Sadness didn't worry her. On those occasions when I said, "But I'm not happy!" she would say, "Where is it written that you are supposed to be happy all the time?"

I don't remember this comment as a rebuke. I think of it now as my introduction to the first of the Four Noble Truths of the Buddha. Life is difficult by its very nature because things change. Change means loss and disappointment. Bodies and relationships are, from time to time, painful. I was reassured by my grandmother's re-

97

sponse. I didn't feel I was making a mistake by feeling sad, and she didn't feel obliged to fix me.

As I think about these teachings and how helpful they were to me, I realize more than ever that it was the degree of attention with which they were met that made them valuable. This inspires me to say what has been important to me over and over again in the hope that they will be heard by an attentive listener.

Tricia, the secretary at the Angela Center in Santa Rosa, California, reminded me, at the end of a retreat that I was teaching there, of the first time we met. "It was sixteen years ago," she said, "before you were a mindfulness teacher. I think you were teaching hatha yoga. Anyway, I only remember one particular thing you said."

"What was that?" I asked.

"You said, 'When, at the end of time, the curtain comes down on history and everyone comes out to take a bow, everyone will get applause because everyone will have played their role as well as they could.' You said, 'Everyone gets handed a part to play, certain talents, and individual circumstances.' That's been very helpful to me to think about all these years. It's a very good teaching."

"Thank you," I said, remembering that it was Rabbi Zalman Schachter-Shalomi I heard use the phrase "everyone will applaud" in 1973 in a class in Berkeley. I also thought of Gwen, in the Wednesday morning Spirit Rock meditation class, who taught the same truth when she said, "I always answer the question 'How are you?' by saying, 'I couldn't be better.' "

The place to end is where I began, with Sharon's teaching, "You never know when seeds will be ready to sprout, so you broadcast them widely, and when the time is right, they will grow."

When I hear that I have been helpful, and when I remember the particular ways in which my teachers have been helpful to me, I am inspired by both the potency of mindful speech and the importance of paying attention.

The Dharma and Understanding Practice

INTRODUCTION
TO PART TWO

T HE TEACHINGS OF THE BUDDHA are not traditionally known as "Buddhism"—that is a relatively recent Western term and concept. The body of teachings and practices was classically known as Buddhadharma, or the Way of the Buddha. The crucial point of this Way is to recognize that there is a realistic path to freedom, and to know that it is not something that worked only for the Buddha long ago. The practice of freedom can work for each of us, immediately and directly, whoever we are and whatever our lives look like.

It is said that even without a Buddha, the Dharma is; even without a Buddha, the truth of things still exists. A Buddha doesn't create the Dharma or the truth; a Buddha uncovers it and reveals it. Our own task in spiritual life is the same. Thankfully, we do not need to create, fabricate, or contrive the truth. Our task is, instead, to see the truth of our moment-to-moment experience clearly. Seeing the truth of our experience is so powerful that it frees us from suffering, from a sense of meaninglessness, from apathy and disconnection.

The Dharma has many aspects, like the many different facets of a jewel. Each is compelling, and ultimately each is not separate from the other. There are facets of acceptance, silence, commitment, strength, and love. The chapters in this section describe various different elements of this jewel of Dharma—present, pragmatic, applicable ways to seeing the truth of our lives. All are authentic ways to freedom.

In following the Way of the Buddha, we face a radical challenge to our conditioned assumptions about aloneness, our need to turn away fearfully from suffering, and our ideas about whether or not we deserve happiness. We come to realize that we can live with respect for ourselves and for all beings. We can be open to others rather than habitually anxious, and we can live our lives rooted in loving-kindness and mindfulness rather than in our ordinary limiting habits of thought and behavior. We can begin to live in a way that is commensurate with our own extraordinary potential for happiness. That is the ultimate invitation of the Dharma.

THE FOUR
NOBLE TRUTHS
Path of Transformation

Christina Feldman

ORE THAN TWENTY-FIVE HUNDRED years ago a
young man sat down beneath the branches of the Bodhi
Tree and vowed to be still until he understood what it
meant to awaken, to be free. Prior to that evening Prince Siddhartha
had lived a life that embraced both the heights of gratification and
the depths of deprivation. In his life as a child and young man in the
palace of his father, he had been surrounded by every conceivable
sensual pleasure and protected from pain in every way possible. It
was a life of delight and enchantment but not a life of enduring
happiness and peace. Guided by both discontent and a vision of
more profound freedom, he left the palace to begin a quest for awakening that was shaped by the leading spiritual teachers of his time.
For six years he explored the pathways of endurance, self-mortification, hardship, and self-denial, until he saw that these, too, did not
lead to the peace and awakening he sought. Forsaking all extremes,

he resolved to sit in stillness and discover for himself the wisdom that would liberate.

The teaching that emerged from that night of stillness is the heart of all Buddhist teachings, the Four Noble Truths. The First Noble Truth is the simple statement that there is suffering, or unsatisfactoriness, in life. The Second Noble Truth asserts that this suffering has a cause, a beginning. The Third Noble Truth is that there is an end to suffering. The path to the end of suffering is the Fourth Noble Truth. This simple yet extraordinarily profound teaching is the core of a body of teaching that embraces goodness of heart, liberating wisdom, and transforming compassion. It is a teaching that is universally accessible; it invites us to look within our own life and to explore its truth. The Four Noble Truths are radical invitations that challenge many of our cultural and personal assumptions about suffering and freedom. They invite us to discover for ourselves the same liberation the Buddha found.

The First Noble Truth

The First Noble Truth asserts that there is *dukkha*, or unsatisfactoriness in life, and this is usually quite apparent for us. Usually *dukkha* is translated as "suffering," but suffering is only one aspect of this word. We face suffering in life in countless moments and circumstances. The media provide endless images of starvation, poverty, and violence. In a single day we may encounter those who are homeless, confused, angry, or despairing—people who are clearly far removed from happiness, safety, or peace. When we honestly explore our own lives, we meet the frailty of our bodies—from the extremes of grave illness or pain to the unpredictable aches and imbalances that catch our attention. Every breath is one step nearer to our death. Our hearts and minds endure countless moments of confusion, restlessness, discontent, fear, and anger. From depression to elation, we carry within us the whole spectrum of experiences and feelings that appear to hold the power to make us suffer.

We are deeply related to people around us, and to our world of sights, sounds, and touch. This relatedness is intrinsic to life. It is a dimension of our lives that can give birth to moments of intimacy, joy, and depth—equally it can give birth to frustration, disappointment, and disillusionment. There is the pain of not being able to get what we want, whether it is the promotion at work or the approval of a friend. And getting what we don't want is equally a source of pain: disapproval, rejection, the company of people we dislike, even the wrong brand of shampoo. The world, it seems, holds an inexhaustible capacity to provide us with opportunities to look at aversion. Even when we do get what we want, rarely does that attainment provide enduring interest and delight. We usually become bored and uninterested quite quickly. Then the mind sets forth again on its search for a happiness and peace that are separate and apart from the world we inhabit.

How do we respond to this maze of suffering we inevitably encounter in our lives? We live in a culture that promotes a mythology that has little room for the acknowledgment of pain or unsatisfactoriness. It is a mythology that seeks endless happy endings, and supports the pursuit of satisfaction and pleasure that is mistakenly equated with happiness. Freedom is often misnamed permission—the license to pursue our own desires regardless of consequences. In the atmosphere of this mythology, we usually respond to suffering by suppressing it, denying it, avoiding or distracting ourselves from it, or numbing ourselves to its presence. One of our most immediate responses to pain is to shout, "This shouldn't be happening." There are times when our strategies of avoidance are effective in postponing our encounter with pain or in increasing our capacity to distance ourselves from it—yet rarely do they lead to profound happiness or freedom.

The simple statement that there is suffering in life is not life-denying, negative, or depressing. It is avoidance that is life-denying. The First Noble Truth is not an encouragement to pursue pain or sorrow, but to cultivate a radical change of heart that allows us to turn toward our own encounters with pain and explore whether there is a way of relating to this maze of suffering with wisdom, balance, and compassion.

There is pain that is intrinsic to being human—aging, sickness, and death. On the other hand, there are whole realms of sorrow that are not intrinsic to life but are born of misunderstanding and confusion. The failure of our car to start in the morning isn't intrinsically accompanied by feelings of rage. Even the death of someone dear to us is not necessarily a sentence of interminable grief or depression. We can learn the skills of balance and wisdom that allow us to embrace pain with grace and understanding.

Most important, the Buddha spoke of dukkha as being not only the variety of sorrowful experiences we encounter, but also the unsatisfactoriness of identifying with anything that is impermanent, anything that cannot offer a true sanctuary of peace and freedom. He spoke of the unsatisfactoriness of identifying our sense of self with any changing phenomenon, whether it is the body, the mind, or the changing world of opinions and feeling. He spoke of the unsatisfactoriness of believing blindly in a world perceived as being formed by many separate selves.

THE SECOND NOBLE TRUTH

All types and levels of dukkha have the same root. The Second Noble Truth is that suffering has a cause: *tanha*, or craving. *Tanha* can also be translated as "unquenchable thirst." Although the teaching that suffering has a cause may seem self-evident, it actually challenges many of our cultural assumptions. We are at times tempted to believe that suffering is random; we just happen to be in the wrong place at the wrong time, and as a result of outside forces, misfortune happens to us. We may feel we suffer because we are unlucky or we simply didn't try hard enough to avoid it. Even when we explore the sorrow in our lives, we may believe it is too simplistic to say that craving is the only cause of suffering. Perhaps we can create a list of people and circumstances that are the source of pain in our lives. We struggle with colleagues at work, our in-laws, traffic jams, our past, the endless intrusion of the world upon our desires, our minds, our personalities—it seems there is no end to the events and people in our world who cause us to suffer. The Buddha says these may be factors that we relate to with distress, resistance, or unease, but to understand what truly causes suffering, we need to dive beneath our superficial reactions and seek their source.

Tanha, or craving, wears many different disguises. There is the restlessness that accompanies a sense that something is missing or incomplete within ourselves. We may call this sense of emptiness a lack of happiness, authenticity, freedom, or security. We want what seems to be missing, and so we search the world looking for an end to dissatisfaction through experience, roles, accomplishments, and achievements. There are whole realms of experience we want to get rid of, from our perceived personal imperfections, to people and encounters that disturb us. There are times when the very hint of an unpleasant sensation in our bodies or minds sets off cycles of resistance and aversion. There are also realms of experiences, sensations, possessions, and achievements that we believe we must possess in order to be happy. This may be the new car, the improved personality, the more profound spiritual experience, the better relationship, or the promotion that really matters. The object of desire is extraneous; the wanting mind is a powerful force, compelled by the endless shopping list built upon discontent. The power of wanting intrudes into our relationship with others and ourselves in the form of expectations, demands, and lofty ideals, which promote nonacceptance, resentment, and anger. In the grip of craving, our mind and heart are gripped by restlessness and discontent; rarely is there either stillness or happiness. The wanting mind perpetuates its own mythology that happiness rests upon fulfilling desires. This is despite the evidence from our whole life that getting what we want, while producing a momentary relief from the tension intrinsic to craving, never produces enduring peace or happiness.

In the Tibetan tradition there is a realm of existence inhabited by beings called hungry ghosts. These beings have enormous bellies, yet their mouths are the size of a pin, and their throats are tiny. Driven by hunger, they roam the world seeking satisfaction and ease, but the very nature of their dilemma is that they can never be full. This is the essence of craving. It leads us to war with ourselves, to battle with the present moment, and to struggle with others. It is the root of dissatisfaction, and its offspring are judgment, greed, rejection, and disappointment.

There are some desires that are valid in our lives and on our spiritual path. The desire for safety, for intimacy, for understanding, for depth and freedom, are yearnings of our heart we need to honor. These desires do not cast us out of ourselves to wander restlessly in search for ease. They encourage us to turn toward the present moment, to understand the forces that move us, to seek understanding, and to ask important questions such as "What is peace?" "Where is freedom found?"

It is not easy for us to accept that the many forms of craving are the primary source of suffering. To do so would mean questioning many of the values that move in our lives, and a willingness to embrace pain with patience, compassion, and understanding. When we explore the Second Noble Truth, we are invited to look at the restlessness and hunger of our own hearts and minds, to learn to be still and to discover the peace and freedom that are born of our capacity to let go. It is not avoiding the necessary changes in our inner and outer worlds. It is not an invitation to passivity or resignation. It is an understanding that discovers the peace and freedom of acceptance, forgiveness, tolerance, patience, and wisdom.

THE THIRD NOBLE TRUTH

The Third Noble Truth of the Buddha is a statement of vision and freedom. It reveals the end of suffering, discontent, alienation, and sorrow. This truth is discovered through a profound understanding of reality that frees us from the confusion and misunderstanding that causes sorrow. When we understand that everything changes, that when we cling to that which changes we suffer, and that there is no abiding solidity or self in anything at all, we are freed to live in harmony with the way things actually are. Our bodies will still age and die, we will continue to encounter the losses and changes that are intrinsic to living. Understanding liberates us and our world to unfold according to the natural rhythms that we can then learn to embrace with wisdom and compassion. Our capacities for letting go, calmness, clarity, and balance mean that we are not imprisoned anywhere or by anything.

The Buddha describes the Third Noble Truth as awakening to the truth that shatters suffering and its cause—an awakening that holds within it profound depths of happiness, peace, and well-being. If craving with all of its restlessness is the cause of suffering, then it is the end of craving that brings freedom. Bringing about the end of craving is sometimes called "extinguishing the fire"—the fire of struggle, resistance, anger, aversion, and the attempts to fulfill our endless desires. Ending craving does not come through suppression, willpower, or a rejection of the world. It is born of wisdom. Deeply understanding the nature of change, we are not invited to dismiss or reject the world with its delights and its sorrows, but to live in harmony with its essential rhythms. Shunryu Suzuki Roshi once said, "We are not asked to get rid of the things of this world but to accept that they pass away." Through our own meditation practice we discover depths of well-being, happiness, and richness that radically alter our relationship to the world of sense impressions. Our happiness is no longer dependent upon them—the world is appreciated with a fullness of sensitivity. We no longer approach it with the mistaken belief that our happiness relies upon what we do or do not receive in this life. It is the happiness of nonclinging and nonbecoming that allows the radiance of all that is true to shine. In awakening to what is true, we discover a profound stillness of being amid the storms of existence.

The Third Noble Truth describes an end to suffering that goes against the current of society. Our culture frequently presumes that the end of sorrow relies upon our capacity to "fix it." Sorrow is linked in our culture to there being something "wrong," "imperfect" in ourselves or in our world, and so the end of suffering is seen to lie in the pursuit of "rightness" or "perfection." The pursuit of perfection has become a driving force in our culture as we are faced with countless prescriptions of how to achieve the "perfect" body, personality, mind, relationship, spiritual experience, and lifestyle. The underlying message is that if we are "good" enough, strive enough, manipulate enough, we will find the perfection that is believed to be the prerequisite to the end of pain. Lost in the pursuit, we may find it difficult to be still long enough to question whether this ideal of perfection is anything more than an image, an illusion created through our resistance to turning toward the actuality of sorrow and its cause. There is a need in our world for boundless compassion, skillful action, and wise effort to bring about the end of pain that is rooted in greed, hatred, and delusion. This is not in the service of creating a perfect world—it is in the service of peace and freedom.

THE FOURTH NOBLE TRUTH

The Fourth Noble Truth describes the path to the end of suffering. It is a path that embraces every area of our lives and prompts us to touch every moment with wisdom and compassion. It is called the Noble Eightfold Path because it invites us to live in a sacred and wise way. Rather than following the pathways of avoidance or denial in response to pain, the Noble Eightfold Path shows us the way that our consciousness can be transformed through wisdom and compassion, through being present in every moment. The Noble Eightfold Path portrays a discipline and practice that are cultivated, fostered, and developed. It also illustrates the way that the fulfillment of understanding is manifested and embodied.

The Noble Eightfold Path should not be seen as eight separate areas of training or exploration; rather it represents a tapestry of our being that is endlessly interwoven. The eight links or threads are Wise Understanding, Wise Intention, Wise Speech, Wise Action, Wise Livelihood, Wise Effort, Wise Mindfulness, and Wise Concentration. Clearly, these do not only describe the path we undertake when seated in meditation, but fully embrace the choices and avenues we follow in our lives and relationships. The Buddha spoke of this path as a path to happiness that purifies our mind and heart, that brings peace and freedom to every dimension of our lives. It is not a passive path but one that invites boundless creativity, exploration, questioning, and vitality. Its aim is transformation and the end of suffering.

As with all of the Four Noble Truths, the Noble Eightfold Path invites us to question our assumptions about how suffering and pain are brought to an end. This is not an easy invitation to respond to. Our habits of denial and avoidance may be deeply entrenched. We are accustomed to the attempts to overcome pain, to close our hearts to its presence, or simply to seek solace in distraction. When none of these strategies work, we may try to track the source of pain in our personal histories, or find relief from personal pain by dumping it upon others. Another attempt to distance ourselves from pain is to become numb, to drown it in sensory pleasure. The refrigerator, TV, drugs and alcohol, all become habitual pathways in a search for refuge from distress. Their solace is temporary, and too often avoidance can become a habit of a lifetime. These methods call not for judgment but for honest questioning. Do they help us to live in a sacred way? Do they heal us or contribute to healing in our world? Do they lead to a clear mind and an open heart? Do they end suffering? If the answer to these questions is no, the understanding ripens in us that it is time to follow new pathways in our lives, to learn the art of freedom.

The Noble Eightfold Path

The Noble Eightfold Path begins with Wise Understanding, also called Wise View. Wise Understanding is the foundation of the whole path of meditation and a meditative life. When we begin on the path, our understanding of the true nature of reality may only be embryonic, yet our awakening is sufficient to bring about a radical change of heart and mind that leads us to question the nature of both suffering and freedom. Our understanding of the nature of reality is the source of our values, our choices and actions, and the quality of our relationship to every moment. Wise View holds within it the seeds of vision, the possibility of transformation and liberation, and from these seeds come the commitment and effort to turn our ideals into reality.

Wise View embraces many aspects of the path of meditation—it includes some understanding of the value of an ethical life based upon an experiential understanding of karma: that all our actions, speech, and thoughts have ripples of consequence that lead either to suffering or well-being. It is an awakening that encourages us to be a conscious, discerning, and compassionate participant in all of life, rather than being governed by the habits of greed, anger, and delusion. Wise Understanding is beginning to see existence as it actually is; it is no longer mistaking the unsatisfactory for the satisfactory, and ceasing to misname pleasure as happiness. It is a deep acknowledgment of the reality of impermanence. It is a movement away from the struggle and distress of grasping, away from the sorrow of being out of step with reality when we endeavor to maintain what is already passing. Wise Understanding means we are beginning to question all of our views about "self," solidity, and separateness.

The second link in the Eightfold Path is the cultivation of Wise Intention. Wise Intention addresses the quality of our thoughts, from which arise our actions and responses. The Buddha pointed to three intentions that are the forerunner of compassionate and wise relationship and inner clarity of heart and mind. These are the intentions toward renunciation, lovingkindness, and compassion. When these are cultivated and developed, they lead to calmness, inner simplicity, wisdom, and harmlessness. Their opposites lie in the habitual or reactive intentions of craving and grasping, ill will, and harmfulness that lead to division and sorrow. In the *Dhammapada* the Buddha says:

We are what we think.
All that we are arises with our thoughts.
With our thoughts we make the world.
Speak or act with an impure mind
And sorrow will follow you
As the wheel follows the ox that draws the cart.
. . . .
Speak or act with a pure mind
And happiness will follow you
As your shadow, unshakeable.

. . . .

Your worst enemy cannot harm you
As much as your own thoughts, unguarded.

But once mastered,
No one can help you as much. . . .*

Wise Intention is not a doctrine to be accepted with blind faith but a teaching that can be explored on a moment-to-moment level in our own lives. What qualities of speech and action are triggered for us when we are in the grip of craving or grasping, ill will or aversion, harshness or cruelty? Do they lead to happiness, well-being, closeness, and freedom? Or do they have the opposite effect? When we are moved by a willingness to let go, by lovingkindness and compassion, with our minds calm and peaceful, we feel closer and more forgiving and tolerant toward others. We feel more profoundly free within ourselves. The significance of Wise Intention is a life lesson we are invited to learn for ourselves. Mindfulness practice gifts us with the capacity to pause and see clearly in those moments before we speak or act, to sense the source of our responses. Wise Intention is not a magical benediction but a path of cultivation and letting go.

Wise Speech is the third link in the Eightfold Path. A wonderful line of Zen graffiti says: "I open my mouth and *samsara* jumps out." Our words make a powerful impact upon this world. They can be harbingers of deep pain or profound healing. Speech that flows from habitual reactions, our own unresolved pain, or aversion has the power to wound others deeply and to leave residues of regret and unease within ourselves. The cultivation of Wise Speech is an ongoing exploration that involves both restraint and mindfulness.

Unwise speech essentially means speech that harms, is unmindful and is rooted in patterns of greed, anger, and confusion. Wise Speech involves restraint from speaking words that are untrue, deceiving, manipulative, or exaggerating. Unwise speech is speech that is slanderous, that condemns others for one's own gain, or that creates

*From *Dhammapada: The Sayings of the Buddha,* translated by Thomas Byrom (New York, Alfred A. Knopf, 1976).

alienation. Words that are spoken in anger, that are intended to cause pain in another, that are abusive or insulting, are a level of unwise speech that calls for remarkable restraint. The Buddha equally speaks of the pitfalls of idle chatter and gossip, or speech that simply provides food for the restless mind.

The antidote to unwise speech is not only restraint and mindfulness but also the conscious cultivation of Wise Speech. Wise Speech involves a commitment to honesty and truthfulness that heals relationships and brings understanding. Cultivating speech and forms of communication that are rooted in lovingkindness and a genuine concern for the person on the receiving end of our words produces harmony and friendliness and promotes trust and openness. Just as aversion is the root of wounding speech, so patience, forgiveness, and tolerance are the roots of speech that are respectful and filled with love. Wise Speech equally includes finding time in our lives for communication that is meaningful, inspirational, and inquiring. Following the pathways of Wise Speech brings into our lives a flowering of relationships that are rooted in openness, trust, and honesty. Wise Speech leaves little residue of regret in our hearts, and our minds can settle in calmness.

Wise Action, the fourth link, means cultivating pathways of responsiveness in our lives that are free from harm, greed, and cruelty. We are active participants in life. Giving attention to our actions is a direct means of dissolving the frustration that arises when there is a gap between our values and the way in which we live our lives. The quality of our presence in this world endlessly impacts upon the quality of our world. Our actions on every level can be embodiments of compassion and sensitivity that directly contribute to a culture of compassion and sensitivity. Wise Action is born of Wise Intention and a clear sense of connectedness with each moment. Through giving attention to the way we act and move and the choices we make, we learn to undo the habitual patterns of insensitivity and live with integrity and honesty, with sensitivity and compassion.

Wise Livelihood, the fifth link, is one specific dimension of Wise Action. We spend a major proportion of our lives engaged in earning a livelihood and cannot divorce it from our spiritual path. Few people are blessed with the opportunity to do work that has a deep spiritual core or emphasis, yet to engage in a livelihood that requires deceitfulness or has harmful consequences is to face endless disharmony inwardly. The work we do may not have universal significance in its impact, yet approaching our work with a commitment to integrity and compassion has the power to deeply touch our immediate world. The quality of relationships we have with our colleagues also deserves reflection; they can be a source of inspiration and creativity, providing the opportunities to cultivate honesty and compassion. When ignored, however, they can become a source of struggle and resentment. The attitude with which we approach our working lives is what makes the difference between working with reluctance and aversion and working with a deep willingness to learn.

The final three links in the Eightfold Path are Wise Effort, Wise Mindfulness, and Wise Concentration. These address specifically the dynamics of our meditative path and also have real implications in the way in which we live our lives. The encouragement throughout this teaching is not to regard our meditation cushion as the only place where transformation happens, but to look upon the whole of our lives as our meditation room.

Wise Effort reflects upon our attitude and approach to the cultivation of wisdom. Wise Effort teaches us to find the middle path between passivity, where we feel fortunate if we happen to be struck by a passing insight, and striving, where we become preoccupied with distant goals whose achievement relies upon our willpower. Wise Effort cultivates the wholesome and skillful factors of mind and heart that provide an inner environment conducive to the flowering of wisdom and compassion. We learn in our meditation, and in our lives, to cultivate calmness, equanimity, patience, acceptance, and attentiveness. When they are present, we explore and investigate them, and as we become intimate with them, they become a natural resting place of our mind. We cultivate the commitment to let go of unskillful or unwholesome factors of mind and heart that obscure clarity and depth. Aversion, restlessness, doubt, wanting, and dullness may all be familiar places to us. Rarely are they places of happiness and well-being, yet through fear, habit, and inattention they become frequent visitors. We explore these places within ourselves and begin to understand the ways in which they disconnect us, obscure our capacity to be present, and lead to confusion. In the service of happiness and freedom, we learn the art of letting go.

Wise Mindfulness is a practice of cultivating sensitivity and clear seeing in every moment. Mindfulness has the effect of bringing us closer to ourselves, to others, and to the simple actuality in each moment. Mindfulness is a path of simplicity—we learn to be present without the endless stories and constructions we tend to weave around the sights, sounds, sensations, thoughts, and feelings that compose our world. Our stories usually become the springboard for our associated reactions of resistance, wanting, anxiety, and aversion. Wise Mindfulness is the cultivation of bare attention that strips away the coloring of our stories, freeing us to be present in each moment as it actually is, with confidence and balance. The Buddha said, "In the seeing there is just the seeing. In the feeling, just the feeling. In the hearing, just the hearing." With mindfulness we explore the dimensions of our bodies, feelings, minds, and every impression that comes to us from our world. With simplicity, sensitivity, and understanding we learn to be at peace with all things.

Mindfulness is a radical shift in how we approach our lives. Mindfulness is a way in which everything is greeted as being worthy of our wholehearted attention. Nothing is irrelevant, nothing is dismissed—dualities between worldly and spiritual, sacred and mundane, are dissolved. Mindfulness is a clear expression of sensitivity and reverence—seeking what is true, authentic in each moment, in our speech, actions, thoughts, and choices. Habit and mindfulness cannot coexist. Through mindfulness each moment is illuminated in the light of wise attention, and understanding is brought to life. We see in our lives where we need to let go, and where we need to foster generosity, compassion, lovingkindness, and understanding. We see where we are making our home in suffering and where we choose freedom.

Wise Concentration is the path of learning to collect and focus our attention. It is the aspect of meditation that leads directly to calmness of being. We learn to attend, to care for one moment at a time. Concentration is the factor that allows insight to penetrate deeply, transforming us on a cellular level. In the absence of concentration we may have many insights, yet they become lost in the swirl of our thoughts, ideas, plans, and preoccupations. Learning to focus our attention helps to bring the storms of the mind to stillness and enables us to see clearly and deeply. Through the direct experience of profound calmness, the mind loses its addiction to busyness; we discover depths of happiness and well-being that no sensory pleasure can compare with.

Concentration does not liberate us but provides an inner environment that is deeply receptive to transforming wisdom. There are different dimensions of concentration, from the moment-to-moment attentiveness that is brought to each instant of our changing experience to the great depths of *samadhi* (a refined, clear, one-pointed attention that rests with ease in its object) and absorptions that are born of sustained concentration practice. Throughout those different depths, the intention remains the same—wise and simple attention is brought to the primary focus of the moment, whether it is the breath, a sound, a thought, or a feeling. Attention frees the focus from all of the complex stories we can surround it with. The simplicity of seeing directly and deeply provides the richest environment for understanding.

The Four Noble Truths are a path of transformation accessible to all of us. They are not an instant answer to difficulty, but rather a process that asks of us a deep commitment to ongoing exploration. They are not a philosophy to be held only intellectually; insight is liberating only if it is lived and applied. All of our explorations, all the ups and downs, then ripen into a path that is in the service of happiness, compassion, and freedom. Along the way our inner explorations and meditations provide a wealth of understanding about the processes of our minds and bodies. We begin to see more and more clearly where suffering exists and how it is caused. The application of the Four Noble Truths then reveals how to end the path, to bring about the end of suffering, to discover freedom.

THE SCIENCE
AND ART OF MEDITATION

Joseph Goldstein

M EDITATION PRACTICE is an investigation of who we are. It is the investigation of our bodies, our breath, of the sensations of subtle energies, of movement. It is the investigation of our minds: thought, emotion, the nature of awareness, of consciousness itself. It is the investigation of silence. In meditation practice we explore all these aspects of ourselves. Although we each have different backgrounds and conditioning, the nature of pain, the nature of happiness, sadness, anger, love, and joy, is the same in all of us; and the nature of the mind is the same here and now as it was in India in the time of the Buddha. This is one reason why the Dharma is called timeless. Because it is timeless, the understanding of ourselves automatically and naturally brings understanding of one another.

There are two approaches to meditation practice that support and complement each other. The first perspective is the understanding of meditation as a science of the mind. The great power of the Buddha's enlightenment was that he saw clearly and exactly how the mind works. He saw that our lives are not unfolding by chance, that nothing is accidental or haphazard. There are certain laws at work. One law that is at the heart of our unfolding experience is karma, or the law of cause and effect. Cause and effect are relatively easy to see and understand in the physical world. For example, it is painfully obvious that if we continue to pollute the environment, the results of those actions will be holes in the ozone layer and global warming and toxic waste; people will be less healthy. Over thirty years ago, after two years in the Peace Corps in Thailand, I went to the Kathmandu Valley in Nepal. At that time, it was a clean and beautiful place. In the last five years I have gone back several times, and with each successive visit the pollution in Kathmandu Valley had increased significantly. Some people actually walk around with masks on to avoid breathing the polluted air. This is just one example of something that is occurring in many places around the world. It is not happening accidentally. It is happening because of causes and conditions. It is the result of actions. On the other hand, when we take care of the environment, there are other results: polluted rivers being restored, toxic dumps being cleaned up, people leading healthier lives. So this law of cause and effect is not difficult to see operating in the world.

Just as there are physical laws of nature, there are also laws of the mind. The Buddha understood that the underlying causes of suffering and of happiness lie in the motivation behind our actions. Through meditation practice, our deepening wisdom begins to reveal the relationship of actions to their consequences. But it is not always obvious. Sometimes we can have a great deal of pleasure or gratification in the moment—feeling ease, joy, and happiness—but the actions may actually lead to more suffering. We see this, for example, in the great power of addiction, where something we do may make us feel good in the moment, yet lead to disastrous consequences later. And sometimes discomfort or pain or unease in the moment can actually have very beneficial consequences. For example, sitting for long periods in a meditation retreat can be difficult, yet we may eventually realize great happiness from it. Or suppose that being generous is very difficult for you: you have not yet developed that quality, and although you struggle with being generous, you do it anyway. You are doing an act that is difficult, that causes some discomfort, and yet it has good consequences.

The Buddha spoke about two types of happiness: one kind to be avoided and the other kind to be pursued. Usually we don't make this discrimination. Consider the following from the *Digha Nikaya* (Long Discourses of the Buddha): "When I observed that in pursuit of such happiness, unwholesome factors increased and wholesome factors decreased, then that happiness is to be avoided. When I observed unwholesome factors decreasing and wholesome ones increasing, then that happiness is to be pursued." The criterion is not whether something makes us feel good or not, but what factors in the mind are being cultivated. If they are the wholesome, skillful factors, they lead to genuine happiness and peace. If they are unwholesome, even if we feel good in the moment, they will be the cause of future suffering. So we need the wisdom and understanding that our actions *are* going to have consequences. We want to be making the right choices.

One of the implications of seeing that our lives are a lawful unfolding of nature—a meaning of the word *Dharma* is "law" or "truth"—is that the path of awakening is available and accessible to us all. We can each undertake this journey of investigation for ourselves. It is not limited to a special few people who have some magical gift. Our path of practice explores the nature of our own lives, of our bodies and minds. This is why the Buddha's teachings are frequently introduced in the Pali texts with the word *ehipasiko*, which means "Come and see." The Buddha invites us to come and see for ourselves whether the teachings are true for us.

Meditation as a science of the mind understands this lawfulness and encourages us to sharpen or hone the mind's power of observation. We hone this power so that we can see more deeply and clearly what is actually happening from moment to moment. All the forms, techniques, and methods are just tools in the service of this investigation.

The first tool of this investigation is the form of sitting and walking meditation. We use the simplicity of alternating periods of sitting and walking to help settle the mind and collect the attention. This practice helps protect us from the myriad distractions of our worldly life. If an outside observer were to look at the schedule of a meditation retreat, it might seem as if not much is happening—sit, walk, sit, walk, eat, sit, walk, sit, walk. And yet settling into the simplicity of the form reveals exactly how much *is* happening. In one sitting or one walking period, there is so much going on—a cascade of sensations, thoughts, feelings, and sense impressions.

We also use a primary object—the breath is a common one—as a focus or anchor for training the mind in concentration and insight. The seventeenth-century bishop Saint Francis de Sales wrote something about Christian prayer that applies very well to this Buddhist practice: "If the heart wanders or is distracted, bring it back to the point quite gently. And even if you did nothing during the whole of the hour but bring your heart back, though it went away every time you brought it back, your hour would be very well employed." We give the mind an object of attention, a basic primary object, and we bring our attention back to that point over and over again, even if that is all we are doing for an entire meditation period.

From this simplifying of the form, giving the mind a primary object, and bringing the mind back again and again, we begin to enter into the first insight of insight meditation. This is the very clear and immediate experience of how often the mind is lost, how often it is distracted. Do not underestimate the value of seeing this. This is knowledge about our own minds that most people do not have. If you went out and asked someone on the street, "Does your mind wander?" you would probably hear, "Oh, no, I know what I'm doing." But we have little idea of what our minds are doing, until we actually sit and observe it. We give the mind a very simple object—just the breath—and yet, after one or two or three breaths, the mind is off and running. We jump on a train of association, with one thought leading into the next. We do not know when we hopped on the train, we have no idea where it is going, and then thirty seconds or a minute or five minutes or half an hour later, we are deposited somewhere, at some station down the track, often leaving us in a completely different inner environment. As another example of the distracted mind, imagine going to a movie theater where they change the movie every ninety seconds. Would you pay to go to that theater? But that is what is happening in the wandering mind: one movie after another, endlessly.

It is also quite amazing that we get caught up and lost in thoughts, memories, or fantasies that are often not even pleasant. We frequently get lost in reliving old hurts, vendettas, judgments, and arguments. Not only may these be unpleasant; sometimes they are not even true. Mark Twain commented that "some of the worst things in my life never happened." Keep that in mind during your meditation practice, especially when you come out of these trains of association. How much is just a proliferation of imagination and fantasy? This first insight into what our minds are actually doing in the moment, and its consequences for how we live our lives, leads us to understand the great value and importance of stabilizing the attention. Much of the world that we create in ourselves and around us has its origin in our own minds.

In the simplicity of the form of sitting and walking, we give the mind a primary object to come back to, and slowly the mind is trained. It starts to stabilize. It starts to steady a bit. Then, even though the thoughts or images are still there, they begin to get a little quieter. They are no longer so predominant or compelling. There is a growing sense of relief, of letting go, and we have the experience of some inner relaxation and stillness.

As the attention stabilizes, we begin to investigate and understand a very critical meaning of the Pali word *sati*, which is usually translated as "mindfulness." Sati is at the heart of our practice. One aspect of its meaning that I find very helpful is its quality of being *undistracted*. When we are undistracted, we begin to notice how effortlessly and spontaneously mindful awareness arises. When we see this for ourselves, we then stop struggling to create awareness, struggling to make it happen. Being mindful is not difficult. It is difficult to *remember* to be mindful. For example, when you are sitting, settled into the body, undistracted, and a sound appears, is there any problem in being mindful or aware of that sound? No. There is nothing special we have to do or create. So every time we become distracted, lost in thought, lost in some fantasy where we do not know what is going on, it is simply a matter of coming back to this place of awareness, which is the basic nature of the mind itself.

Notice carefully the difference between being lost in thought and being aware that we are thinking. There are countless opportunities to do this, because thoughts are arising most of the time. What is it like when the mind is lost? What is it like when we are aware that a thought is present? The difference is quite amazing. Becoming aware of one's thoughts is like waking up from a dream. Each such awareness is a moment of awakening. And instead of judging the fact that you got lost, can you delight in the awakening? This greatly changes the tone of the practice. Every time you notice that you're thinking, there can be that moment of delight.

Often people have the idea that meditation means *not thinking*. I have heard this misunderstanding repeated many times. If this idea is present, then every time a thought arises, there is a struggle or a judgment. This is incorrect. Meditation is the practice—and it is *practice*—of not getting lost in thought. It is not about stopping thinking; it is about being aware when thoughts arise and, to use an expression from the Tibetan tradition, watching them "self-liberate." In the moment of being aware that we are thinking, we see the impermanent, insubstantial nature of thoughts. Often in that moment of awareness, thoughts simply vanish. We practice remaining undistracted as thoughts arise. Can we be with a thought in the same way that we are with a sound? We are sitting, feeling the body, feeling the breath. A sound appears, and we are simply aware of hearing. If a thought appears, can we simply be aware of thinking? If so, there is no problem.

A great Korean Zen master of the eleventh century named Chinul said: "Don't be afraid of your thoughts. Only take care lest your awareness of them is tardy."* This is what we are practicing: alertness and undistractedness. In this way, we allow everything to come, whatever it may be, without getting lost in any of it.

*Robert E. Buswell, *Tracing Back the Radiance: Chinul's Korean Way of Zen* (Honolulu: University of Hawaii Press, 1991).

Why is this so important? Why give so much emphasis to understanding this difference between being aware of thought and being lost in thought? The distinction is tremendously significant, because very often we not only are lost in our thoughts, but are also acting them out. When we look at the many places of suffering in the world—places of war, of violence, of injustice, of exploitation—and really examine what is happening in those situations, we see people acting out various mind states of fear, of hatred, of greed. All of these thoughts and feelings have tremendous consequences.

We can observe this pattern even in an ordinary activity. One spring I was doing a self-retreat in my house, and every day I would walk over to IMS for lunch. One time, as I was taking my food, I saw a sign in front of one of the dishes: MODERATION, PLEASE. For some reason, these signs always seem to appear in front of one's favorite food; in this case, it was sesame spinach. Going through the line as mindfully as I could, I saw the MODERATION, PLEASE sign, and the first thing that my mind did was wonder, "How much can I take and still be moderate?" And that is how much I proceeded to take—as much as I thought I could get away with. But about thirty seconds later I was seized by guilt: "I took too much. There won't be any left for the people behind me." So for the whole lunch period I was looking over my shoulder . . . did they get their spinach? Although it was not a very peaceful lunch, the experience, in retrospect, was very instructive. It pointed out once again the importance of being mindful in even the simplest of activities. Now, every time I go through that line and see the MODERATION, PLEASE sign, it is like a mindfulness bell: watch what the mind does with this.

The second tool of investigation is slowing down so that we can open to experience fully, without rushing through things. An example of one important level shift that happens when we slow down is the difference in experience between simply knowing we're moving as we walk and actually feeling the sensations of the movement. As we settle into the level of changing sensations, it becomes possible to go beyond the concepts of "foot," "leg," and "body" to experience for ourselves the impermanent and insubstantial nature of phenomena.

Also notice times of rushing, and the feeling of getting ahead of ourselves, which often happens when we think there's some task to do or place to go. Notice if you rush through work or through taking a shower. Even at times when I've been on retreat and moving quite slowly, I can often notice the difference between the formal walking meditation and walking to the dining room—that slight energetic leaning forward in anticipation of the meal. Don't skip over things or think that some experiences are less important than others. Everything is revealing the nature of our minds and bodies; everything becomes a vehicle for awakening.

The time of a meditation retreat is a good opportunity to practice this continuity of awareness, of not overlooking the small things. A story told about the famous naturalist Louis Agassiz and his student Samuel Scudder illustrates the importance of paying attention.

> [Agassiz] intended, he said, to teach the student to see—to observe and compare—and he intended to put the burden of study on them. Probably he never said what he is best known for: "Study nature, not books," or not in those exact words. But such certainly was the essence of his creed, and for his students the idea was firmly implanted by what they would refer to as "the incident of the fish."
>
> His initial interview at an end, Agassiz would ask the student when he would like to begin. If the answer was now, the student was immediately presented with a dead fish—usually a very long-dead, pickled, evil-smelling specimen, personally selected by "the master" from one of the wide-mouthed jars that lined his shelves. The fish was placed before the student in a tin pan. He was to look at the fish, the student was told, whereupon Agassiz would leave, not to return until later in the day, if at all.
>
> Samuel Scudder, one of the many from the school who would go on to do important work of their own (his in entomology), described the experience as one of life's memorable turning points.
>
> In ten minutes, I had seen all that could be seen in that fish . . . Half an hour passed—an hour—another hour. The fish began to look loathsome. I turned it over and around:

looked it in the face—ghastly; from behind, beneath, above, sideways, at three-quarters view—just as ghastly. I was in despair.

I might not use a magnifying glass; instruments of all kinds were interdicted. My two hands, my two eyes, and the fish; it seemed a most limited field. I pushed my finger down its throat to feel how sharp the teeth were. I began to count the scales in different rows until I was convinced that that was nonsense. At last, a happy thought struck me—I would draw the fish, and now with surprise, I began to discover new features in the creature.

When Agassiz returned later and listened to Scudder recount what he had observed, his only comment was that the young man must look again.

I was piqued; I was mortified. Still more of that wretched fish! But now I set myself to my task with a will, and discovered one new thing after another. . . . The afternoon passed quickly and toward its close, the professor inquired: "Do you see it yet?"

"No," I replied. "I am certain I do not. But I see how little I saw before."

The day following, having thought of the fish most of the night, Scudder had a brainstorm. The fish, he announced to Agassiz, had symmetrical sides with paired organs.

"Of course, of course," Agassiz said, obviously pleased. Scudder asked what he might do next, and Agassiz replied, "Oh, look at your fish!"

In Scudder's case, the lesson lasted a full three days. "Look, look, look," was the repeated injunction, and the best lesson he ever had, Scudder recalled, "a legacy the professor has left to me, as he has left it to many others, of inestimable value, which we could not buy, with which we cannot part.*

*David McCullough, "The American Adventure of Louis Agassiz," *Audubon* (January 1977), p. 9.

Can we have that intention, that power of observation, directed at our own minds? This is our life; can we look at it with that degree of care?

Sharon Salzberg tells a wonderful story about our first course with Sayadaw U Pandita in 1984. Sharon came in for an interview, with a prepared report of her meditative experience, which was getting more silent and still. She bowed and began reporting. U Pandita interrupted her, "What did you notice when you brushed your teeth?" She hadn't noticed; she had nothing to say. He didn't want to hear anything else, so he rang the bell and she left. The next day she came in, prepared to report what she had experienced when brushing her teeth. Sayadaw then asked her, "What did you experience when you put your shoes on?" She hadn't noticed. He didn't want to hear anything else, so she left. That was the end of the interview. This went on for weeks. Every day she would come in, and he would ask her about something else, until she was paying attention to everything she was doing. One thing was not more important than another. Can we practice in that way? Not with a sense of straining, not with a sense of struggle, but being very receptive, very still, receiving each moment with attentiveness, without rushing through things. When we practice in this way, our perception of the world is quite transformed. Gary Snyder expressed it just in a few lines: "There is a world behind the world we see that is the same world but more open, more transparent."

A third tool of meditation as a science of the mind is mental noting, that is, making a soft, whisperlike note to help us connect with our experience. Mental noting is the simple recognition of what is present. For example, with each breath we might note "in, out" or "rise, fall." When we are aware of thoughts, we could note "thinking" or "planning" or "judging," depending on the kind of thought that it is. Sometimes people note just at the beginning, sometimes they might note many times. You can experiment. When the mind is settled and quite concentrated, you may not need to use mental noting at all. See what happens. Even if you let go of noting as a tool, you might return to it, beginning to note some of the more subtle mental states. You may feel quite connected with your physical experience, but are you noticing the feeling of calm, of peace, of steadiness? Every once in a while, check in with your mood. Label it. This helps cut through levels of identification that you might not have even known were there. Play with the noting; it is a tool in the service of awareness.

We want to investigate and see the truth of our experience, so we can begin to make choices in our lives with discriminating wisdom rather than simply acting out old habit patterns of conditioning. Thoreau wrote about his time at Walden Pond: "I went to the woods because I wished to live deliberately and face only the essential facts of life, and see if I could learn what it had to teach, and not when I came to die, discover that I had not lived." Meditative practice is our own Walden Pond. We come to our practice because we wish to live deliberately, to face the essential facts of life, and see if we can learn what it has to teach.

In meditation practice, using a simple form, coming back to a primary object, consciously slowing down, and practicing mental noting are all tools within the first perspective on practice, meditation as a science of the mind. The second perspective of this exploration is meditation as an art. From this viewpoint, we begin not only to see what is happening, what is arising in the moment, but also to feel and understand how we are relating to our experience. In this sense, meditation is discovering the art of true relationship. And as we discover more about the nature of relationship in meditation practice, we begin to apply these insights to our lives as well.

There are many ways of relating to experience. We can be aware of what is happening and be very reactive, filled with like and dislike, judgment or aversion or grasping. Or we can be aware of what is happening and relate to it from a place of openness, of tranquillity, of compassion. Each moment's experience can reveal our state of mind. Take a very simple situation: how do you relate to the breath? When you are sitting with the breath, the first step is noticing, feeling the breath, and precisely observing the specific sensations of it. But then the art of the practice is to understand how the mind is holding the breath, how we are relating to it. What is the quality of effort that we have? If there is no intentionality or effort to be with the breath at all, then the mind easily slips off. On the other hand, if we are efforting too much, trying to hold on, trying to grasp at it, then we become tight and tense. Or we can be slightly impatient with the breath, being with the in-breath in order to get to the out-breath. Or with the out-breath in order to have the next in-breath. This way of relating keeps us toppling forward instead of simply resting in awareness and letting each breath appear as it does. Can you be with the sensations of each breath in the same receptive way that you are with sound? Can the sensations be like different sounds appearing in the mind? When we are simply resting, undistracted, awareness is spontaneous.

We can also see clearly our relationship to experience when we are having pain or unpleasant feelings. What is our relationship to painful feelings? There is a lot to learn about this, and much opportunity to learn it. We relate in so many different ways to things that are unpleasant. Sometimes we relate by feeling sorry for ourselves. Or perhaps the mind starts complaining about difficult situations. Sometimes fear arises.

Many times in my practice I have been in situations that were tremendously noisy. This happened at certain times in India, with Hindi film music playing on loudspeakers from early morning until late into the night. Years later, it happened in Burma, where there was a lot of construction noise every day, all day long—hammering on metal right outside my window. At that time, I watched my mind fill with aversion. Finally, I went to my teacher, Sayadaw U Pandita, to tell him about this great disturbance, and all he said was, "Did you note it?"

I went through an important process there: after my initial frustration at his response, I saw that when he said, "Did you note it?" he was teaching me that from the perspective of awareness, it really does not matter what the object is. Sometimes it is pleasant, sometimes it is unpleasant. That is all. Can we note it? Not "note it" in terms of making the best of a bad situation or dismissing it. "Did you note it?" means: can you simply rest in awareness, whatever the object? This is sound. Unpleasant sound. Unpleasant, loud sound. Unpleasant, loud, *unremitting* sound. It does not matter. Meditation is not about having one experience rather than another. It is about settling back into the awareness of whatever is arising, realizing that sometimes it is pleasant, sometimes it is unpleasant, and that is fine. It is simply to be aware. With this one insight, our whole practice will be transformed. The great power of vipassana, of mindfulness practice, lies in the understanding that when we discover the art of true relationship, nothing is outside the domain of awareness. It is tremendously liberating when we can simply be present for whatever arises.

The art of meditation is the art of true relationship. What is the relationship that we have to different thoughts and emotions? Some thoughts we get fascinated by. We get caught up and seduced by them. Other kinds of thoughts and emotions we might condemn or judge or try to get rid of. Just as with unpleasant sounds, can we open to unpleasant thoughts and feelings? It's very helpful to have a sense of humor about ourselves. When we see all the different reactions in the mind, and all the different ways we get caught again and again, can we smile?

Years ago I heard a yogi comment about his practice, saying that "the mind has no pride." We might have a sense of that when we watch our own minds. Once I was on a retreat with Sayadaw U Pandita in Australia. The retreat was very intense, and everyone was practicing with great diligence. I was going through the lunch line in the dining room and everything was completely silent. The person right in front of me took the cover off one of the pots of food, and as he placed it on the table, it fell to the floor, making a huge clatter. And the first thought in my mind was "It wasn't me!" As I watched my mind I wondered, where did that one come from? But all kinds of thoughts do come, as we all know. Can we smile at this? Can we lighten up a little bit?

What is our relationship to the practice itself? Are we caught up in expectations disguised as right effort? Do we think we are making right effort when it is actually just expectation in disguise, our wanting something to happen? Please remember that we are not practicing for some experience. We are practicing the mind of no-clinging. Whatever experience arises is also going to pass away, so why practice for that? It is much simpler, much easier, when we free ourselves, when we disengage the gears of attachment. Instead of leaning forward with expectation in our practice, with that strain or struggle of wanting some special experience, we settle back with ease. Rest in the awareness of whatever it is that is arising. Sometimes pleasant, sometimes unpleasant. Let it all come and go.

This nonattachment is expressed in one line of the *Diamond Sutra*: "Develop a mind that does not cling to anything." As you are sitting with the breath, with sensations, with thoughts, remember that nonattachment is what you are practicing. The practice is not about changing this experience into something else. It is very freeing to settle back into awareness in that way. When you feel you are struggling or straining in the practice, sit back and ask yourself the question, "What is happening here?" The sense of struggle means that something is going on in the mind or body that we are not accepting. What we want to do is sit back, open up, and just see what is there. In that moment of seeing, of acceptance, the struggle ends.

As we bring together the science and art of meditation, coming into an exact and open relationship with whatever arises, we begin to discover the nature of the subtlest elements of our experience. What is a thought? Do we ever stop to investigate, to see what it is? What is this phenomenon that has so much power in our lives—that drives our lives—when we are unaware of it? And yet, when we are aware of a thought, it is seen to be as insubstantial as a puff of wind. Something that is totally empty of substance is the master of our lives. What is this phenomenon that so rules us? The practice is just to discover, to look again and again until we come to see the emptiness of it all.

What is the nature of awareness, the basic process of consciousness? It is a tremendous mystery, because when we look for awareness, there is nothing to find. And yet it ceaselessly and spontaneously knows, cognizes, everything that is arising. It is quite amazing. Through the development of the science and art of practice, through the balance of precise investigation and open receptivity, we cut through to the essential nature of our minds, of our bodies, of our awareness. We begin to touch the truth of our lives. This is the great voyage of discovery that we are on, discovering ourselves.

W. H. Murray, the leader of a Scottish Himalayan expedition, observed something about mountain climbing that is very relevant to the practice of meditation:

> Until one is committed, there is hesitancy, the chance to draw back, always ineffectiveness. Concerning all acts of initiative, there is one elementary truth, the ignorance of which kills countless ideas and splendid plans: that the moment one definitely commits oneself, then providence moves too. All sorts of things occur to help one that would never otherwise have occurred. A whole stream of events issues from the decision, raising in one's favor all unforeseen incidents and meetings and material assistance, which no one could have dreamed would have come their way. I have learned a deep respect for one of Goethe's couplets. "Whatever you can do, or dream you can, begin it. Boldness has genius, power, and magic in it."

MINDFULNESS

Bhante Gunaratana

"MINDFULNESS" IS THE ENGLISH TRANSLA-
TION of the Pali word *sati*. Sati is an activity. What exactly is that? There can be no precise answer, at least not
in words. Words are devised by the symbolic levels of the mind,
and they describe those realities with which symbolic thinking deals.
Mindfulness is pre-symbolic. It is not shackled to logic. Nevertheless,
mindfulness can be experienced—rather easily—and it can be described, as long as you keep in mind that the words are only fingers
pointing at the moon. They are not the thing itself. The actual experience lies beyond the words and above the symbols. Mindfulness
could be described in completely different terms than will be used
here, and each description could still be correct.

Mindfulness is a subtle process that you are using at this very
moment. The fact that this process lies above and beyond words does
not make it unreal—quite the reverse. Mindfulness is the reality that
gives rise to words; the words that follow are simply pale shadows
of reality. So, it is important to understand that everything that follows here is analogy. It is not going to make perfect sense. It will
always remain beyond verbal logic. But you can experience it. The

meditation technique called *vipassana* (insight) that was introduced by the Buddha about twenty-five centuries ago is a set of mental activities specifically aimed at experiencing a state of uninterrupted mindfulness.

When you first become aware of something, there is a fleeting instant of pure awareness just before you conceptualize the thing, before you identify it. That is a state of awareness. Ordinarily, this state is short-lived. It is that flashing split second just as you focus your eyes on the thing, just as you focus your mind on the thing, just before you objectify it, clamp down on it mentally, and segregate it from the rest of existence. It takes place just before you start thinking about it—before your mind says, "Oh, it's a dog." That flowing, soft-focused moment of pure awareness is mindfulness. In that brief flashing mind-moment you experience a thing as an un-thing. You experience a softly flowing moment of pure experience that is inter-locked with the rest of reality, not separate from it. Mindfulness is very much like what you see with your peripheral vision as opposed to the hard focus of normal or central vision. Yet this moment of soft, unfocused awareness contains a very deep sort of knowing that is lost as soon as you focus your mind and objectify the object into a thing. In the process of ordinary perception, the mindfulness step is so fleeting as to be unobservable. We have developed the habit of squandering our attention on all the remaining steps, focusing on the perception, cognizing the perception, labeling it, and most of all, getting involved in a long string of symbolic thought about it. That original moment of mindfulness is rapidly passed over. It is the pur-pose of vipassana meditation to train us to prolong that moment of awareness.

When this mindfulness is prolonged by using proper techniques, you find that this experience is profound, and it changes your entire view of the universe. This state of perception has to be learned, how-ever, and it takes regular practice. Once you learn the technique, you will find that mindfulness has many interesting aspects.

THE CHARACTERISTICS OF MINDFULNESS

Mindfulness is mirror-thought. It reflects only what is presently hap-pening and in exactly the way it is happening. There are no biases.

Mindfulness is nonjudgmental observation. It is that ability of the mind to observe without criticism. With this ability, one sees things without condemnation or judgment. One is surprised by nothing. One simply takes a balanced interest in things exactly as they are in their natural states. One does not decide and does not judge. One just observes. Please note that when we say, "One does not decide and does not judge," what we mean is that the meditator observes experiences very much like a scientist observing an object under a microscope without any preconceived notions, only to see the object exactly as it is. In the same way, the meditator notices impermanence, unsatisfactoriness, and selflessness.

It is psychologically impossible for us to objectively observe what is going on within us if we do not at the same time accept the occurrence of our various states of mind. This is especially true with unpleasant states of mind. In order to observe our own fear, we must accept the fact that we are afraid. We can't examine our own depression without accepting it fully. The same is true for irritation and agitation, frustration, and all those other uncomfortable emotional states. You can't examine something fully if you are busy rejecting its existence. Whatever experience we may be having, mindfulness just accepts it. It is simply another of life's occurrences, just another thing to be aware of. No pride, no shame, nothing personal at stake—what is there, is there.

Mindfulness is an impartial watchfulness. It does not take sides. It does not get hung up in what is perceived. It just perceives. Mindfulness does not get infatuated with the good mental states. It does not try to sidestep the bad mental states. There is no clinging to the pleasant, no fleeing from the unpleasant. Mindfulness treats all experiences equally, all thoughts equally, all feelings equally. Nothing is suppressed. Nothing is repressed. Mindfulness does not play favorites.

Mindfulness is nonconceptual awareness. Another English term for *sati* is "bare attention." It is not thinking. It does not get involved with thought or concepts. It does not get hung up on ideas or opinions or memories. It just looks. Mindfulness registers experiences, but it does not compare them. It does not label them or categorize them. It just observes everything as if it were occurring for the first time. It is not analysis, which is based on reflection and memory. It is, rather, the direct and immediate experiencing of whatever is happening, without the medium of thought. It comes before thought in the perceptual process.

Mindfulness is present-time awareness. It takes place in the here and now. It is the observance of what is happening right now, in the present moment. It stays forever in the present, perpetually on the crest of the ongoing wave of passing time. If you are remembering your second-grade teacher, that is memory. When you then become aware that you are remembering your second-grade teacher, that is mindfulness. If you then conceptualize the process and say to yourself, "Oh, I am remembering," that is thinking.

Mindfulness is non-egotistic alertness. It takes place without reference to self. With mindfulness one sees all phenomena without references to concepts like "me," "my," or "mine." For example, suppose there is pain in your left leg. Ordinary consciousness would say, "I have a pain." Using mindfulness, one would simply note the sensation as a sensation. One would not tack on that extra concept "I." Mindfulness stops one from adding anything to perception, or subtracting anything from it. One does not enhance anything. One does not emphasize anything. One just observes exactly what is there without distortion.

Mindfulness is awareness of change. It is observing the passing flow of experience. It is watching things as they are changing. It is seeing the birth, growth, and maturity of all phenomena. It is watching phenomena decay and die. Mindfulness is watching things moment by moment, continuously. It is observing all phenomena—physical, mental, or emotional—whatever is presently taking place in the mind. One just sits back and watches the show. Mindfulness is the observance of the basic nature of each passing phenomenon. It is watching the thing arising and passing away. It is seeing how that thing makes us feel and how we react to it. It is observing how it affects others. In mindfulness, one is an unbiased observer whose sole job is to keep track of the constantly passing show of the universe within. *Please note that last point.* In mindfulness, one watches the universe within. The meditator who is developing mindfulness is not concerned with the external universe. It is there, but in meditation one's field of study is one's own experience, one's thoughts, one's feelings, and one's perceptions. In meditation, one is one's own laboratory. The universe within has an enormous fund of information containing the reflection of the external world and much more. An examination of this material leads to total freedom.

Mindfulness is participatory observation. The meditator is both participant and observer at one and the same time. If one watches one's emotions or physical sensations, one is feeling them at that very same moment. Mindfulness is not an intellectual awareness. It is just awareness. The mirror-thought metaphor breaks down here. Mindfulness is objective, but it is not cold or unfeeling. It is the wakeful experience of life, an alert participation in the ongoing process of living. Mindfulness is extremely difficult to define in words—not because it is complex, but because it is too simple and open. The same problem crops up in every area of human experience. The most basic concept is always the most difficult to pin down. Look at a dictionary and you will see a clear example. Long words generally have concise definitions, but for short basic words like *the* and *is*, definitions can be a page long. And in physics, the most difficult functions to describe are the most basic—those that deal with the most fundamental realities of quantum mechanics. Mindfulness is a pre-symbolic function. You can play with word symbols all day long and you will never pin it down completely. We can never fully express what it is. However, we can say what it does.

Three Fundamental Activities

There are three fundamental activities of mindfulness. We can use these activities as functional definitions of the term: (1) mindfulness reminds us of what we are supposed to be doing; (2) it sees things as they really are; and (3) it sees the true nature of all phenomena. Let's examine these definitions in greater detail.

1. *Mindfulness reminds you of what you are supposed to be doing.* In meditation, you put your attention on one item. When your mind wanders from this focus, it is mindfulness that reminds you that

your mind is wandering and what you are supposed to be doing. It is mindfulness that brings your mind back to the object of meditation. All of this occurs instantaneously and without internal dialogue. Mindfulness is not thinking. Repeated practice in meditation establishes this function as a mental habit, which then carries over into the rest of your life. A serious meditator pays bare attention to occurrences all the time, day in, day out, whether formally sitting in meditation or not. This is a very lofty ideal toward which those who meditate may be working for a period of years or even decades. Our habit of getting stuck in thought is years old, and that habit will hang on in the most tenacious manner. The only way out is to be equally persistent in the cultivation of constant mindfulness. When mindfulness is present, you will notice when you become stuck in your thought patterns. It is that very noticing which allows you to back out of the thought process and free yourself from it. Mindfulness then returns your attention to its proper focus. If you are meditating at that moment, then your focus will be the formal object of meditation. If you are not in formal meditation, it will be just a pure application of bare attention itself, just a pure noticing of whatever comes up without getting involved—"Ah, this comes up . . . and now this, and now this . . . and now this."

Mindfulness is at one and the same time both bare attention itself and the function of reminding us to pay bare attention if we have ceased to do so. Bare attention is noticing. It reestablishes itself simply by noticing that it has not been present. As soon as you are noticing that you have not been noticing, then by definition you are noticing and then you are back again to paying bare attention.

Mindfulness creates its own distinct feeling in consciousness. It has a flavor—a light, clear, energetic flavor. By comparison, conscious thought is heavy, ponderous, and picky.

But here again, these are just words. Your own practice will show you the difference. Then you will probably come up with your own words, and the words used here will become superfluous. Remember, practice is the thing.

2. *Mindfulness sees things as they really are.* Mindfulness adds nothing to perception and it subtracts nothing. It distorts nothing. It

is bare attention and just looks at whatever comes up. Conscious thought pastes things over our experience, loads us down with concepts and ideas, immerses us in a churning vortex of plans and worries, fears and fantasies. When mindful, you don't play that game. You just notice exactly what arises in the mind, then you notice the next thing. "Ah, this . . . and this . . . and now this." It is really very simple.

3. *Mindfulness sees the true nature of phenomena.* Mindfulness and only mindfulness can perceive that the three prime characteristics that Buddhism teaches are the deepest truths of existence. In Pali these three are called *anicca* (impermanence), *dukkha* (unsatisfactoriness), and *anatta* (selflessness—the absence of a permanent, unchanging entity that we call soul or self). These truths are not presented in Buddhist teaching as dogmas demanding blind faith. The Buddhists feel that these truths are universal and self-evident to anyone who cares to investigate in a proper way. Mindfulness is that method of investigation. Mindfulness alone has the power to reveal the deepest level of reality available to human observation. At this level of inspection, one sees the following: (a) all conditioned things are inherently transitory; (b) every worldly thing is, in the end, unsatisfying; and (c) there are really no entities that are unchanging or permanent, only processes.

Mindfulness works like an electron microscope. That is, it operates on so fine a level that one can actually directly perceive those realities which are at best theoretical constructs to the conscious thought process. Mindfulness actually sees the impermanent character of every perception. It sees the transitory and passing nature of everything that is perceived. It also sees the inherently unsatisfactory nature of all conditioned things. It sees that there is no sense grabbing onto any of these passing shows. Peace and happiness cannot be found that way. And finally, mindfulness sees the inherent selflessness of all phenomena. It sees the way that we have arbitrarily selected a certain bundle of perceptions, chopped them off from the rest of the surging flow of experience, and then conceptualized them as separate, enduring entities. Mindfulness actually sees these things. It does not think about them; it sees them directly.

When it is fully developed, mindfulness sees these three attributes of existence directly, instantaneously, and without the intervening medium of conscious thought. In fact, even the attributes that we just covered are inherently unified. They don't really exist as separate items. They are purely the result of our struggle to take this fundamentally simple process called mindfulness and express it in the cumbersome and inadequate thought symbols of the conscious level. Mindfulness is a process, but it does not take place in steps. It is a holistic process that occurs as a unit: you notice your own lack of mindfulness; and that noticing itself is a result of mindfulness; and mindfulness is bare attention; and bare attention is noticing things exactly as they are without distortion; and the way they are is impermanent (anicca), unsatisfactory (dukkha), and selfless (anatta). It all takes place in the space of a few mind-moments. This does not mean, however, that you will instantly attain liberation (freedom from all human weaknesses) as a result of your first moment of mindfulness. Learning to integrate this material into your conscious life is quite another process. And learning to prolong this state of mindfulness is still another. They are joyous processes, however, and they are well worth the effort.

MINDFULNESS (SATI) AND INSIGHT (VIPASSANA) MEDITATION

Mindfulness is the center of vipassana meditation and the key to the whole process. It is both the goal of this meditation and the means to that end. You reach mindfulness by being ever more mindful. One other Pali word that is translated into English as "mindfulness" is *apparnada*, which means non-negligence or absence of madness. One who attends constantly to what is really going on in his or her mind achieves the state of ultimate sanity.

The Pali term *sati* also bears the connotation of remembering. It is not memory in the sense of ideas and pictures from the past, but rather clear, direct, wordless knowing of what is and what is not, of what is correct and what is incorrect, of what we are doing and how we should go about it. Mindfulness reminds the meditator to apply his attention to the proper object at the proper time and to exert precisely the amount of energy needed to do that job. When this energy is properly applied, the meditator stays constantly in a state of calm and alertness. As long as this condition is maintained, those mind-states called "hindrances" or "psychic irritants" cannot arise—there is no greed, no hatred, no lust or laziness. But we all are human and we all err. Most of us err repeatedly. Despite honest effort, the meditator lets mindfulness slip now and then and finds him- or herself stuck in some regrettable but normal human failure. It is mindfulness that notices that change. And it is mindfulness that reminds us to apply the energy required to pull ourselves out. These slips happen over and over, but their frequency decreases with practice. Once mindfulness has pushed these mental defilements aside, more wholesome states of mind can take their place. Hatred makes way for lovingkindness, lust is replaced by detachment. It is mindfulness that notices this change, too, and that reminds the vipassana meditator to maintain that extra little mental sharpness needed to retain these more desirable states of mind. Mindfulness makes possible the growth of wisdom and compassion. Without mindfulness they cannot develop to full maturity.

Deeply buried in the mind, there lies a mental mechanism that accepts what the mind perceives as beautiful and pleasant experiences, and rejects those experiences that are perceived as ugly and painful. This mechanism gives rise to those states of mind which we are training ourselves to avoid—things like greed, lust, hatred, aversion, and jealousy. We choose to avoid these hindrances, not because they are evil in the normal sense of the word, but because they are compulsive; because they take the mind over and capture the attention completely; because they keep going round and round in tight little circles of thought; and because they seal us off from living reality.

These hindrances cannot arise when mindfulness is present. Mindfulness is attention to present-time reality and therefore directly antithetical to the dazed state of mind that characterizes impediments. As meditators, it is only when we let our mindfulness slip that the deep mechanisms of our mind take over—grasping, clinging, and rejecting. Then resistance emerges and obscures our awareness. We do not notice that the change is taking place—we are too busy with a thought of revenge, or greed, whatever it may be. While an untrained person will continue in this state indefinitely, a trained meditator will soon realize what is happening. It is mindfulness that notices the change. It is mindfulness that remembers the training received and that focuses our attention so that the confusion fades away. And it is mindfulness that then attempts to maintain itself indefinitely so that the resistance cannot arise again. Thus, mindfulness is the specific antidote for hindrances. It is both the cure and the preventive measure.

Fully developed mindfulness is a state of total nonattachment and utter absence of clinging to anything in the world. If we can maintain this state, no other means or device is needed to keep ourselves free of obstructions, to achieve liberation from our human weaknesses. Mindfulness is nonsuperficial awareness. It sees things deeply, down below the level of concepts and opinions. This sort of deep observation leads to total certainty, a complete absence of confusion. It manifests itself primarily as a constant and unwavering attention that never flags and never turns away.

This pure and unstained investigative awareness not only holds mental hindrances at bay, it lays bare their very mechanism and destroys them. Mindfulness neutralizes defilements in the mind. The result is a mind that remains unstained and invulnerable, completely unaffected by the ups and downs of life.

BEING A
GUEST HOUSE

Michele McDonald-Smith

O NE OF THE CORE TEACHINGS of the Buddha is that
when we investigate life with wise attention, we see clearly
that change is an inherent characteristic of our existence.
Life is a changing stream of experience, with each moment of consciousness having either a corresponding unpleasant, pleasant, or
neutral feeling. This is a profound teaching. We might say, "Yes, I
know that," but we tend to avoid investigating the implications of
change. Continual change means that we cannot control much of
anything that appears in our life. We never know what's going to
happen next. Everything that takes birth in the universe shares this
kind of vulnerability due to change.

There is a way that we can learn to be at home in this world, in
our life that is a stream of change. The foundation of peace and happiness in the world is our ability to accept that our life is changing
and not to take this personally.

Rumi, the thirteenth-century Sufi mystic, wrote a poem called

"The Guest House" that describes what life is like when we can fully experience and accept whatever is happening.

> This being human is a guest house.
> Every morning a new arrival.
>
> A joy, a depression, a meanness,
> some momentary awareness comes
> as an unexpected visitor.
>
> Welcome and entertain them all!
> Even if they're a crowd of sorrows,
> who violently sweep your house
> empty of its furniture,
> still treat each guest honorably.
> He may be clearing you out
> for some new delight.
>
> The dark thought, the shame, the malice,
> meet them at the door laughing,
> and invite them in.
>
> Be grateful for whoever comes,
> because each has been sent
> as a guide from beyond.*

Being a guest house is a beautiful, poignant image. Yet it is very difficult to do. We tend not to relate to each experience, each feeling, that comes our way as a guest we can welcome. Or, if we invite them in, maybe we think that they stay too long or should never come back. How many guests did we put in the basement today? Or in the attic? Or did we lock the doors and not let any in? We tend to sort through and judge each experience, get rid of some, keep others.

---

*"The Guest House" by Jelaluddin Rumi, translated by Coleman Barks with John Moyne, *The Essential Rumi* (San Francisco: HarperSanFrancisco, 1995), p. 109.

However, life changes, the guests come, uninvited, and our practice is to accept them, to accept our experience without getting lost in it, and to see that it is an impersonal, ever-changing process.

A friend of mine decided to go on a long silent meditation retreat after not doing one for some years. Afterward he called me, and the first thing he said was, "Nothing compares to knee pain." I said, "What?" He answered, "Well, I thought I was having great difficulty in my life, but after this last week I've realized that nothing compares to knee pain." I appreciated him saying this so much, especially for those of us who have meditated a lot. We can sometimes forget how basic and straightforward our practice is. This ability to accept pain is essential to experiencing freedom in this world. Not as an endurance test, but as a way to learn how to relate to physical pain with wisdom. The insight that comes from accepting pain in the body prepares us to relate to any pain that appears at our door with wisdom and compassion.

Our life and our meditation practice are filled with really wonderful times and really hard times. Sometimes physical, mental, or emotional pain becomes our unexpected and uninvited guest. We might not have the attitude of being a guest house—in fact, we may have been expecting something different. But, even when it's very difficult, we try to have the courage to be mindful. In mindfulness practice we look more closely and intensely at how life really is within our own direct experience, to develop the strength of intuitive wisdom. The challenges in our formal sitting practice prepare us for the challenges of daily life.

In developing awareness, we gradually learn to give attention to more and more of our experience and to treat each experience equally. After drinking tea, we dip our hands in warm water to wash our dishes, then go outside to fill the bird feeder. We may think those experiences aren't as important as being aware of the breath. But they are. The moments of fear, the moments when we lie down to go to sleep—all are equally important, because we can see clearly and develop wisdom in any moment. In our practice the story around each experience is not important; what is important is how we are relating to that experience. But treating each moment equally can be difficult to remember to do.

When my husband, Steve Smith, and I are getting ready to leave home to teach some extended retreats, I make long lists of things I have to do. Sometimes, even when I just look at these lists, stress arises. Once, on the day before we had to leave home, I had an unpleasant, and seemingly impossible, list of things to get done. One of our teachers from Burma, Sayadaw U Pandita, had been leading a retreat near where we live in Honolulu. The course was ending that day, so there were many responsibilities for us. I had a tiny window of time in which to buy a present for him and for the translator. I had it planned to the second, and there was no space for anything to get in the way.

I pulled into a mall in Honolulu, got out of the car, and started to put my sandals on, leaving the door open. I had borrowed Steve's mother's car, which would lock all doors with the press of one button. While I was putting my first sandal on, I glanced over at that button and decided to lock the car right then so that I wouldn't forget. I pressed the button down and went back to my sandal. Just as I was ready to reach for the other sandal, some people rushed past me to their car, which was right next to mine. They were in such a hurry that they pushed me out of the way and, in the process, shut the door of my car! I looked in and there was my other sandal, the keys to the car, and my bag with all my money in it. My mind exploded into complete aversion and resistance. "I don't have time for this!" I was so upset.

It was twelve noon, and the pavement was burning hot. So I hopped in total aversion to the security center in the mall and begged them to assist me. The security guard announced that they had a new policy of not opening car doors, even though they can, because they're afraid that people will sue if they damage the car. He said I could get a tow truck to come for thirty dollars. I was fast running out of time to get my gift for U Pandita, but I thought that maybe I would call Steve instead of the tow truck. "Do you have a quarter?" I asked the guard. He actually put his hand in his pocket and jiggled some coins around, but he pulled it out and said, "No." That's when

I lost it. I started crying and said, "Order the tow truck." I was so stressed about not having enough time that I could see no other options.

The tow truck eventually came, and they opened the door. I got my other sandal and my money, and I rushed to the store. Then, when I found the gifts, I had to get into a long line at the checkout counter. I kept looking at my watch every two seconds. I'd really gone over the edge. Finally I got up to the counter and handed the lady the stationery I had found. She asked me, "Oh, do you know that this stationery is made out of tobacco?" At that point I could have cared less how interesting the stationery was, and it must have showed. Just then the man behind me in line said, "You know, if your day gets any more nerve-wracking, you can always smoke it." This comment was so funny that instead of struggling with the uninvited guest of stress and hurry, I laughed and relaxed. It allowed me to keep going even though the situation had not changed. Afterward I was grateful to that man for helping me wake up.

How do we become more like a guest house—in our mind and in our body? Sometimes we have to gently wait until that moment arrives when enough spacious attention appears and we can let the resistance to our uninvited guests be, and even feel "grateful for whoever comes." Sometimes we can approach the experience with the nonjudging acceptance of mindfulness, bringing to each experience the quality called beginner's mind—an attitude of pure exploration that sees clearly that each moment is truly new.

Mindfulness has four aspects that make it possible for us to pay full attention to our direct experience: recognition, acceptance, interest, and nonidentification. When those four aspects of mindfulness are present, we can be aware of the momentariness of experience.

Recognition is waking up rather than being on automatic pilot. It's knowing what our direct experience is with present-time awareness. When we can recognize our experience, we have won half the battle.

Acceptance is allowing our experience to naturally take its course without controlling it. We let each experience take birth, live, and pass away because that is the truth of life at this moment. We can tell the degree to which we are resisting by the level of our suffering.

With acceptance we don't have to fiddle with our experience or try to fix it. We just let it be.

Interest is taking the time to investigate our experience, free from any past ideas about it and without any resistance whatsoever. We can't fake interest. Interest makes it possible to greet each experience as a new and welcome guest.

Nonidentification is understanding that our experience isn't personal. Instead of relating to each experience as "me" or "I" or "mine," we can see it as insubstantial conditions arising. This perspective allows us to see that immediate experience is like ephemeral clouds floating through the vast sky of mind, rather than referring back to a permanent self-centered person having an experience.

When these four aspects of mindfulness are present, we realize that no experience is worth holding on to, and at the same time we can experience each moment fully and completely.

So when we notice the breath, it could be light pressure coming and going, or just movement. Recognition is just noticing that. When there is recognition, there is some direct experience of the sensations themselves. Then acceptance is just allowing this movement, this light pressure or air element, to come and go by itself. When the acceptance isn't there, we might want it to be different—we want more refinement or less refinement, a deeper breath or a more shallow breath. Acceptance is letting it happen exactly the way it is happening. It is actually not that easy to let the breath be just as it is. Interest is taking the time to be fully aware of the movement in that moment—there is no past and no future; we see it as if for the first time. Without interest, we think that it is just another breath. With nonidentification there is a deep understanding with the experience that there is no one who breathes, only breathing—that this breath is air element coming and going, not "mine."

Mindfulness allows us to develop a relationship of wise attention with all of life. If we can learn to explore the breath, then when we experience something difficult, such as loneliness, we may have some ability to explore that experience as well. We may think that we know what loneliness is, but thinking about the experience of loneliness is getting lost in the experience of loneliness. When mindfulness is present we learn how not to be a victim of the experience. The breath just comes and goes by itself: there's nothing we have to do with it; we only have to notice it. If we can let a breath come and go by itself, then maybe we can let loneliness come and go by itself. We can recognize it as an experience of sensations in the body, or a quality of our mind. We can accept its presence and realize that we don't have to do anything with it, but take the time to see what happens to it. We can take an interest in it, not just push it away reflexively as something unpleasant. And, perhaps most important, we can understand that this is not "our" loneliness; it is simply the experience of loneliness.

Gratefulness for whatever guests appear at our door can arise when we remember to take the time to be present with what comes into our lives. The comet Hayakutake appeared in the sky in Honolulu in 1996 at a busy period in my life. I read about this celestial visitor in the newspaper, but I didn't really make an effort to find out where in the sky it was. Finally, just before it moved out of sight, one of my neighbors said to me, "Have you seen the comet?" Only then, when he practically took me by the hand, did I look. And I was so happy that somebody had taken the time to show me this ancient presence. Maybe what is present is not a comet. Maybe it's a friend or a flower or a bird or the breath. Or knee pain, busyness, or loneliness. Cultivating mindfulness allows us to appreciate each moment. There is an Osage Native American women's initiation song about planting corn in a sacred way that reveals a way of being mindful with each step. As you read it, think of walking mindfully, taking time with each step.

I have made a footprint.
A sacred one.
I have made a footprint.
Through it the blades push upward.
I have made a footprint.
Through it the blades radiate.
I have made a footprint.
Over it the blades float in the wind.

I have made a footprint.
Over it I bend the stalk to pluck the ears.
I have made a footprint.
Over it the blossoms lie gray.
I have made a footprint.
Smoke arises from my house.
I have made a footprint.
There is cheer in my house.
I have made a footprint.
I live in the light of day.

Every time we notice a step or a breath with awareness, every time we notice anger or joy with mindfulness, we are planting the seeds of wisdom. Walking with mindfulness is being the sacred center of the world. When we are fully attentive to the experience of taking a step, in that moment we're totally free from any mental torment. We are truly at peace. That step has an effect on us that then radiates throughout the world. The peace inside reflects as peace outside.

At times, when we attempt to be mindful, our attention isn't refined enough to be with the movement of a step or with the movement of the breath. We're usually bombarded with so much stimulation in our daily lives that to be aware of the breath is very difficult, and the mind tends to wander a lot. At this time we need to refine our awareness by establishing the intention to be awake and interested in our experience.

To do this, we can ask ourselves some questions to activate the interest. In walking meditation you might ask a question as simple as "What is the experience of a leg, free from my idea about it?" Or, if you are experiencing sadness, you might ask, "What is the experience of sadness, free from any concepts or idea about it?" This is the practice of investigation. Again, if we think we know the answer, we are not really alive to the moment. Wise investigation allows us to bring the attention to the actual experience in the present moment rather than thinking about an experience. This deep delight in investigating the truth allows us to not be lost in the past or the future. Present-time awareness occurs in the truth of every moment related to as a new arrival. The truth is found in our own body and mind, when we are being like a guest house.

If asking the questions doesn't awaken interest, it may be that we don't have enough energy to be interested in our guests. We may need to rest the mind for a while. This doesn't have to be done out of aversion to our guests. We can anchor our attention to something neutral, such as the experience of the sensations within the movement of the breath. Resting the attention in an uncomplicated way strengthens us by renewing our energy. With patience, interest arises naturally.

Another word for this type of rest is *concentration* or *seclusion*. Sometimes when we are not able to be like a guest house, it is more skillful not to investigate physical pain or emotions. It's time to be more secluded. Being in the present moment with a certain lightness, the attention anchored on a neutral object, is the great art of meditation practice. In that "seclusion" one can be protected from difficult experiences that we are identified with and resistant to. Then when the energy is renewed and the mind is rested, we can open up the guest house again.

If we react with aversion to having no interest, we tend to use up whatever energy we have in struggling, rather than opening to it with acceptance and choosing skillfully to seclude ourselves. We start to realize that we suffer precisely because we don't understand how we suffer, and so we don't see how we can be free of that suffering. In fact, we suffer when we resist the uncontrollable changes of life and we are unable to bring interest to our suffering.

There's a deep stream behind a meditation center in Honolulu that our meditation group rents for retreats. Once in a while during a course there, I have the chance to go to the stream. Year after year, I do the same thing. I head upstream, walking on top of the little rocks that are showing through the swiftly moving water. I try to keep from falling in because I don't want to get wet, but invariably at some point I do. There's always that moment of fear: "Oh, no, I'm falling in." Then I fall in, and it's fine. It's really fun, and I have a good time.

Many times we respond to emotions and mind-states in the same way. As Rumi says in his poem, we might be experiencing unhappiness, shame, or a mean thought. When we finally allow ourselves to recognize, "Oh, it's simply fear," or "It's simply shame," falling into the stream of unpleasantness, we might find that the experience is actually not so bad. Falling in doesn't mean drowning; it doesn't mean that we are lost in thinking about the experience. Falling in means that the additional suffering of resistance disappears, allowing interest to appear in an experience that we were previously unable to accept.

I had been looking forward to doing a self-retreat for a long time before I finally had the opportunity in my own little cottage. I was sitting the first day, so happy to be on retreat, when a big flatbed truck pulled up beside the cottage. It turned out that the center where the cottage was located had decided to expand their dining room during my retreat. The carpenters were there every morning at seven o'clock, hammering, sawing, and playing the AM radio really loud. My first thoughts were, "Oh, no! I wanted peace and quiet—not AM radio!" It took some time before I could accept the particular sound that was happening, drop my resistance, and just be present with that unpleasant experience. It turned out to be a very wonderful retreat with "no 'I,' no AM radio, just sound." This is the realization that there is the concept of a hammer or a saw or AM radio music, and there is the direct experience of the vibration of hearing itself. The key is not to try to get rid of the concepts, but to be interested in life enough to not get trapped in the prison of concepts. Then life doesn't become narrow so that we grow weary of it and miss our experience of our life. That freedom of seeing clearly is what we practice for.

Real peace and quiet occur when we can let a sound just come and go by itself. It may be unpleasant, but we understand that it isn't a personal attack. Our practice is being able to open up to the unpleasantness of life as well as the aversion to the unpleasantness—to welcome these guests into our house. When we let all of our experiences come and go by themselves, there is a deeper joy, a deeper delight in the truth of life. As Rumi says, "Even if they're a crowd of sorrows, / who violently sweep your house / empty of its furniture, / still treat each guest honorably. / He may be clearing you out / for some new delight."

Whatever arrives as our guest is sure to change, like the weather in a New England springtime. First it's cold and then it's warm and then it's cold again. There are clouds, then rain, then sunlight and clear sky, and then thunder, hail, and lightning. It's a good metaphor for what happens to us in life. The weather isn't personal. There's good weather, there's bad weather, and it just keeps changing. Sometimes we're lost. Sometimes we're identified with experience. Sometimes we're not. There's birth, aging, and death. There are all kinds of change on a moment-to-moment level and on a broad level. Can we be interested in all the different aspects of the change? Can we be interested in what is happening when we take a shower? Can we be interested in the birth of a wildflower, in the experience of fear, interested in mosquitoes and what it feels like when they bite?

We become more like a guest house when we develop mindfulness. We learn how to seclude ourselves at times, focusing simply on the experience of the movement of one breath, or taking just one step at a time. Being that simple and uncomplicated rests the mind so that we can understand the guests as they arrive. Ultimately, we develop a much deeper and broader ability to treat each moment of our life equally and with wisdom, compassion, and gratitude. We can welcome each moment—whether it is pleasant, unpleasant, or neutral—into our guest house as our teacher, as an opportunity for awakening.

BEYOND LETTING GO

Moving into Deep Silence

Larry Rosenberg

A T THE HEART OF OUR PRACTICE, behind everything else, surrounding everything else, within everything else—such spatial metaphors are inevitably inadequate—is silence. We have little experience of silence in our world today, and the culture as a whole seems to value only more and more elaborate kinds of sound. Yet our sitting practice is silent, and retreats are profoundly so. Enlightenment has been called the great silence. In that way, Buddhist practice is at odds with the culture. It is at odds with every culture.

Most of us appreciate certain kinds of silence. We have all been in a room where the air conditioning is on, or a refrigerator is running, and it suddenly shuts off, and we breathe a sigh of relief. Parents of small children speak of the exquisite (and often short-lived) silence at the end of the day, with the children finally in bed, the television off, the house still. Some of us take vacations in quiet places, and even in our own houses we value moments when we can get off to a room by ourselves, to read a book or write a letter.

The silence I'm talking about is deeper than any of those and is sometimes—though not exclusively—reached in profound states of meditation. It extends all the way to the deepest stillness that human beings are capable of experiencing.

I became interested in this subject several years ago. One reason was that I had a number of students who had progressed quite far in their meditation practice, had reached the threshold of a deep silence, but had encountered a profound fear and pulled back. With the goal of seeing students progress as far as they could, I asked myself how to deal with what was holding them back.

At roughly the same time, I saw an article in a news magazine about exploration of the oceans, saying that they were the last frontier left open to us. I couldn't help thinking there was one frontier the writer was ignoring: human consciousness.

We have explored certain parts of the mind, of course, and done intricate analyses of them. But there are vast realms that we have yet to touch, in all the millennia that human beings have been around. A few brave individuals have made inroads and have come back to tell us what they've seen. But most people don't even know these places exist. Meditators are psychonauts, to use Robert Thurman's term. We're explorers in the most fascinating realm of all.

For most people in the world today, life has much to do with verbalization. Talking. Reading. Writing. Thinking. Imagining. Language is a magnificent human invention (though other species seem to have done all right without it), but it is so embedded in our consciousness that we don't realize how much revolves around it. It wouldn't be too much to say that we worship language or that we're addicted to it. We equate it with living itself.

Another aspect of life for most people—related to language, obviously—is some form of action. Doing things. Creating. Moving things around, piling them up, arranging them. Engaging the body in physical activity, even just to enjoy ourselves in recreation.

In those two forms of endeavor, our culture—compared with others today, and especially compared with cultures from the past—is rich. We have more things, and more things to do, more varied uses of thought and language, than at any other time in human history. We're beyond rich. We're opulent.

Inwardly, however, we are paupers. Our throats are parched, and our spiritual bodies are gaunt. That is probably why we have so many outer things. We keep using them to satisfy a hunger that never gets any better. It seems insatiable.

We have a similarly vast craving for relationship. I know someone, for instance, with a great interest in mountain climbing who was recently extolling the wonders of the Internet. The night before, he had been talking to a fellow mountain climber in Siberia. That's wonderful, I said. But have you talked to your wife lately? Your children? We have this marvelous technology, but it doesn't seem to be helping with the life right in front of us. I have no doubt that if the Siberian mountain climber had shown up at my friend's door, he would have dialed 911. He wanted to know him on a screen, not face to face.

I don't mean to make light of our technology. The computer—like language—is a marvelous human invention. I'm writing this chapter on one. I have no doubt that the Internet is a wonderful resource, like having the greatest library in the world at your fingertips. But if accumulating information were going to save us, we'd have made it a long time ago.

The shortcomings of that kind of knowledge were brought home to me more than twenty years ago, when I was in Korea and studied with a monk named Byok Jo Sunim, one of the most memorable people I've ever encountered. He almost visibly glowed, radiating the joy that the practice brought him. He was extremely loving, had a wonderful sense of humor. He was also completely illiterate. He couldn't sign his name.

While talking with him through an interpreter one day, I discovered that he thought the world was flat. I was absolutely astounded, and naturally decided to straighten him out. I went back to grade-school science, brought out all the classic arguments: if the world is flat, how can we sail around it? How come a ship doesn't just fall off the edge? He just laughed. He was adamant. I got nowhere.

Finally, he said, "Okay. Maybe you Westerners are right. I'm just an illiterate old man. The world is round, and you know that, and I'm too stupid to grasp it.

"But has knowing that made you any happier? Has it helped you solve your problems of living?"

It hadn't, as a matter of fact. It hadn't helped us with our problems at all. None of our knowledge has.

With all that we've learned, we human beings have not solved even the simple problem of living together. We have incredible technology, which can put us in touch with people on the other side of the world, but we don't know how to get along with the people in our own neighborhood, even in our own house.

One part of our culture is soaring, and another part is barely crawling. We are caught up in an illusion, a marvelous conjuring trick that has convinced us that the things we produce will make us happy. Not only are we the audience for this trick, we are also the magician. We have convinced ourselves.

We need to go much deeper into the mind. It's as if we are surrounded by vast fields, fertile soil as far as we can see, but we've only cultivated a tiny patch of it. We've done a wonderful job with that patch, but we need to explore the fields all around it. We need to get away from all the building and doing, coming and going, all the talking and thinking and reading and writing.

Silence is not a perfect word for what I'm trying to describe. There are no perfect words for it. In a sense I am using words to describe something that is the antithesis of speech (though it is also accurate to say that all speech comes out of it). Other teachers and other cultures have used words like *void* and *emptiness*, though those words have their own shortcomings.

Silence, as I am using the term, is a dimension of existence. You can live in it. It is what spiritual life is all about. It is quite literally unfathomable, limitless space permeated by a vast stillness. In a way it is inside us—that is where we seek it—though at some point in our exploration words like *inside* and *outside*, all the spatial terms I've been forced to use, don't mean a thing.

All of the accumulated history of human civilization—language, culture, thought, commerce—is relatively small compared with what is behind it. Silence is a dimension of existence, and for some people—throughout history, probably—it has been the primary dimension. They have been our most extraordinary individuals. They have learned to inhabit the world of silence, and to move out of it into the world of action.

It isn't really that I am criticizing the other dimension of existence, the one we are all so familiar with. My point is just that things have gotten out of balance. I have to sound critical just to let people know there is more to life than they have realized. We have such strong conditioning toward the world of thought and action that we need to weaken it, diminish its hold on us, before we can taste the vast richness of silence.

The first help I got in that direction was from my first Buddhist teacher, Venerable Seung Sahn. He had come to this country from Korea and seemed to know only ten or fifteen English phrases when he got here. But he was extraordinarily skillful at using those phrases, a master of the Dharmic sound bite. He repaired washing machines for laundromats to support himself when he first arrived, and seemed to get by with just two phrases. "That broke? I fix." But before long he had a reputation as a Zen master, and on Friday nights as many as a hundred people, many of them university-educated, would come to hear him give talks with those fifteen phrases.

In the tradition in which I now teach, interviews are quite informal, but in his Zen tradition they were formal, and every time I came to him, no matter what I said, he always responded in the same way. "Too much thinking!" He would ring the bell, and I would have to leave. It was extremely humiliating. Finally one day I had a quiet sitting—given enough time, we all tap into silence—and came to him quite excited with the news. In that whole sitting, I told him, I had had only a few weak thoughts. He looked at me with utter disbelief. "What's wrong with thinking?" he said.

It isn't thinking that is the problem, he was letting me know. It is our misuse of it, our addiction to it.

Eventually I went with him to Korea for a year, and I vividly remember our flight over. I pulled out a sack of books, all my cherished Dharma books, which had been so important in leading me into the practice. "What's that?" he said. Those are my books, I said. "Oh no," he said. "You don't read any books all this year." No books! All year! He didn't understand whom he was saying this to. A Jewish intellectual junkie from Brooklyn!

"That's the whole problem," he said. "You know too much already. You merely know everything."

It was extremely difficult for me. I sometimes found myself reading the labels of ketchup bottles, I was so hungry for English words. But I followed his advice and didn't read a book all year. It was very liberating. Reading has been very different for me ever since, much lighter, with less attachment.

Similarly, when we have retreats at the Insight Meditation Society, we ask that meditators not read (not even Buddhist texts) or write (not even a journal of their experiences). Eliminating these two activities is another way of diminishing the incessant hum of thought and language, of penetrating deeper into silence.

Silence is extremely shy. It appears when it wants to and comes only to those who love it for itself. It doesn't respond to calculation, grasping, or demands; it won't respond if you have designs on it or if there is something you want to do with it. It also doesn't respond to commands. You can no more command silence than you can command someone to love you.

There are concentration practices that achieve silence, but that silence is relatively coarse, willed, provisional, and brittle, very much subject to conditions. The silence I'm talking about is much deeper. It awaits us; it can't be grasped for. We don't create it; we find our way into it. But we have to approach it with gentleness, humility, and innocence.

The road to silence is filled with obstacles. The major obstacle is ignorance. We don't experience silence because we don't know it exists. And though I am emphasizing the difficulties, it is important to understand that silence is an accessible state for all human beings. It isn't just for hermits who live in caves in the heights of the Himalayas. It is available to everyone.

The first part of the journey is through the practice of breath awareness. Typically, when beginners sit down to follow the breathing, what they notice is a tremendous amount of noise, which seems pretty far from the exquisite stillness I'm talking about. The Tibetans have an expression for this stage of practice, "attaining the cascading mind." That doesn't sound like much of an attainment. You notice that your mind is like a cascading waterfall, noisy and flowing all the time.

But the fact is that everyone's mind is like that, and most people don't know it. It is a major step to see that. Our world is very probably being run by people who don't realize their minds are like Grand Central Station at rush hour. Is it any wonder we're in the shape we're in and that things look and sound the way they do?

There is an old Jewish joke about a man who has gotten his hands on a beautiful piece of cloth and decides that he wants to make a suit out of it. He visits an expert tailor, who makes a number of measurements, says everything will be fine, and tells the man to come back in a couple of days. But when he returns, the tailor says, "No, I'm not done. Come back in a couple more days."

This happens four or five times, and the customer grows quite concerned, but finally one day he shows up and finds that the tailor has created an absolutely beautiful suit. "This is exquisite," the man says. "But do you realize that it took you longer to make this suit than it took God to create the world?"

"Maybe so," the tailor said. "But you see my suit. Have you taken a look at the world lately?"

We don't wonder at the shape of the world once we see our cascading mind and realize that it is running the show. But there is no need to be impatient with it. Impatience doesn't help anyway. As you sit over a period of time and try to stay with the in-breath and out-breath, the mind will eventually quiet down, and you will notice moments when the breath is silky and soft and you are just with it. You may also notice the stillness of the pause between breaths.

That is a taste of silence, and you may find a certain refreshment even in that. It is an encounter with a very pure kind of energy. There is much more to come. But such early brief encounters give you faith to continue. And in dealing with silence, a certain amount of faith is extremely important.

Much deeper kinds of silence are available, but not through striving to attain them. Once you've achieved a certain calm with *samatha* practice (giving *exclusive* attention to breathing in order to develop serenity of mind), the way to silence is by making friends with your noise, really coming to know it. The biggest noisemaker is your ego, your tendency to attach to things as "me" or "mine." The ego knows that there is no place for it in the world of silence, because silence belongs to no one. There will be nothing for it to appropriate. Silence is where the ego isn't.

In approaching deep silence, therefore, a much better approach—when you are ready for it—is choiceless awareness. A certain amount of silence is available through concentration, but a different quality of silence comes through understanding, which does not create silence but discovers what is already there. You are more likely to encounter such silence on a long retreat, when your mind has an extended period in which to slow down.

You sit with the breathing and allow everything to come and go—thoughts, feelings, sounds, sensations, mental and physical states. At first your attention will not be choiceless; you'll be directing it at this or that. But in time that tendency will fall away, even the breath won't be especially featured, and you'll be noticing whatever is, in an utterly undirected way, sitting with undivided presence in a state of total receptivity. You're not for or against anything that comes up; you just take a friendly, interested, accepting attitude toward it.

When the mind is allowed to roam freely in that way, it eventually gets tired of itself. It is, after all, just saying the same things again and again. It grows tired of all the noise and begins to settle down. As it does, you stand on the threshold of the vast world of silence.

Sometimes on retreats, meditators who have just been introduced to choiceless awareness will come to interviews and say, "Nothing's happening." We are so used to having things *happen* in our lives that we don't know the value of this nothing. But it is extremely valuable, the first step into the realm of silence. There is no need to do anything but just stay with it.

Another way to think of the approach to silence is that it grows out of true vipassana practice. You allow whatever arises to come into your mind, and what you see about all of it is that it is impermanent. In that seeing, there is a letting go, and past that letting go is silence. From the clarity of a silent mind, one sees impermanence much more clearly. That clear seeing allows more letting go, and a deeper penetration into silence. The two things feed on each other, what I'm calling wisdom and what I'm calling silence. Each deepens the other.

It is true that on the threshold of silence we often experience fear. It is the ego that is afraid. In the panoramic attention that you devote to choiceless awareness, the ego is not allowed to occupy center stage, where it thinks it belongs, and it begins to wonder what it will be like in silence, where it won't be present at all. This fear resembles the fear of death, because entering into silence is a temporary death for the ego. The great silence would be its permanent death. Naturally it is afraid.

When this fear comes up, it isn't an obstacle or hindrance. It is just one more aspect of the noise. Your encounter with that fear is very valuable, and the skill called for is just to stay with it. In time, like every other phenomenon, it will pass away. When it does, what is left is silence.

I have noticed in my own practice and teaching that the attainment of silence is somewhat related to the ability to handle loneliness, and also to the acceptance of death. Especially for the ego, those things are closely related. We are afraid of being alone, and afraid to die, so we create company for ourselves with our thoughts, and they keep us from getting to silence.

It is therefore often helpful for a contemplative to do a certain amount of practice with death awareness. Apart from its inherent value, it helps us enter the realm of silence, which we fear because—like death—it is unknown. Actually, this realm is quite wonderful, an immense relief, but the mind doesn't know that. It might also be helpful, when a meditator feels ready, to go on prolonged self-retreats, where one may encounter loneliness in a profound way.

Once we have made friends with our loneliness, silence will be much more accessible.

I might in this connection tell a rather personal story. My father died recently, after a long illness. We had been close all my life, and I had a great deal of grieving to do. At times I thought I was doing well with it, at other times not so well. I'm human, just like everyone, and not exempt from the tendency to deny, repress, run away from, and intellectualize.

I took his ashes to Newburyport, Massachusetts, where I frequently do self-retreats, and floated them out to the Atlantic Ocean (which he loved) by way of the Parker River. Afterward I went to the house where I do my retreats. I had already sat with my grief a great deal, but at some level, apparently, I hadn't even begun, because that day I encountered more sorrow than I had thought was possible.

There had previously been elements of self-pity in my grieving, also elements of pity for my father. My self-centeredness was there, not allowing sorrow fully to flower. But now there was a direct experience of sorrow without any holding back, direct penetration of it for an extended period of time, real intimacy with it. Finally the sorrow ended. Beyond it was an immense silence.

I learned a great deal that day about the way that elements of the self keep us from fully feeling, and what is available to us if we let them go. Another term for such silence is absolute presence, which is only possible if there is absolute absence of the self.

Meditators often ask what to do when they get to silence. We typically have various agendas. Sometimes we are still basically afraid of it, want to taste it briefly and get out. Other times we sit in silence full of anticipation, waiting for something to happen. We view the silence as a door to something else. It is a door to the unconditioned, but if we attempt to use this door to get there, it stays shut.

If we are looking too hard for something special to happen, silence will collapse. We can also cause it to disappear by making it into a personal experience, naming it, weighing it, evaluating it, comparing it to other experiences we've had, wondering what we will tell our friends about it, or how we will shape it into a poem.

What we need to do instead is just surrender to it. Allow it to be there. It sounds like it must be just emptiness, a break from real living, but that is a failure of language. Silence is much more than that

So what I advise meditators to do when they encounter silence is: absolutely nothing. Bathe in it. Let it work on you. The experience will make you realize what an inadequate word *silence* is for what I'm talking about. It is actually a highly charged state, full of life. It couldn't be more alive. The energy in it is subtle and refined but extremely powerful. It doesn't have to apologize to action.

Silence is also full of love and compassion. After you have been intimately embraced by silence, you come out feeling much more open to the world. You also come out—and this sounds strange, but it's true—more intelligent. You haven't acquired any information, of course. I'm speaking of another kind of intelligence, an intrinsic one. You're kinder, more sensitive, more compassionate. You can't achieve these things by trying, but if you value silence for itself, you will find them there.

Anyone who practices meditation has probably had some taste of silence. Maybe you've had ten seconds during a sitting when you were suddenly quiet and calm—you had no idea why—and you got up refreshed, infused with a new energy. Maybe you've come out of a sitting and noticed that the world looks different, or feels different, perhaps just for a little while. Meditators often report after a retreat that they feel more compassionate. They weren't trying to develop that quality; it just happened.

But the silence I'm talking about does not happen just on the cushion, and it is not something that you have to leave there. It is not actually damaged by noise. This is not the silence that is the opposite of noise. It is a quality that is intrinsic to us, an inexhaustible energy. It is not dependent on the approval of others, on what happens to us out in the world. It is not an experience that we have now and then. It is inherent fulfillment, which can permeate our lives. We can take it into the world and act from it

Silence in action is the doerless doing that we've spoken of before, in which you just wash the dishes, just vacuum the floor. The ego is not present. Typically, whatever we do, we bring an "I" to it, attach to it as me or mine. But silence is the place where there is no ego, and silence in action involves acting in the world without making the action "me" or "mine." In the process of uniting with the particular activity, we at least temporarily forget the self and are intimate with the vividness of what is there.

Various traditions come at this truth in different ways. In China, one answer to the question "What is enlightenment?" was "Eating rice and drinking tea." Actually, you can eat and drink anything, but just eat and drink. The preoccupation with self goes into abeyance, and you are manifesting the depths of silence in the ordinary world. You can do the same thing with any action. That is what Zen means by No Mind, or Clear Mind. You step away from your past conditioning and are fresh, alive, and innocent in the moment.

Another answer to that age-old question is: the grass is green, the sky is blue. We all know that, of course, but when the mind comes out of the experience of being bathed in silence, it really sees it. It is an incomparable experience.

Early in my practice I had been sitting one afternoon in my apartment in Cambridge, Massachusetts, then came out into the street and saw a Yellow Cab parked at the corner. I was waiting for a friend, in touch with my breathing, and focused on the cab. And I really saw it—I saw yellow. (I understood why they called it Yellow Cab.) It brought me to tears. In that state, anything could have had the same effect. A squashed beer can might have done it.

When the mind is clear of all obsession with "me" and "mine," life is just there. Words can't describe it. It has an enormous impact on us, and we experience it much more deeply. Trying and striving do not get us to that point. An open, clear seeing does.

So the point of all I'm saying is not to throw out culture, or abandon our involvement in the world. It is just to put things in better balance. I have not found any way to come into touch with silence except by going on extended retreats, with other meditators or by myself. I need a period without responsibilities in which the mind can exhaust its preoccupation with itself and settle into its inherent nature. But I don't regard these retreats as the only worthwhile—or even the most worthwhile—moments in my life. That would reduce my life to just a month or so per year, or even worse, to just a few moments of special insight. I have a very active life outside of retreats, and the key thing for me is to take what I learn on the cushion out into the world. The Dharma quest is to grow more and more into the large mind that leaves me and the story of my life behind. What is left is clarity.

We can't hanker after this state. We're all learning to be free, and the only way to do that is to see the ways in which we're enslaved. Occasionally we have big insights, but more often just small ones. Moments of self-preoccupation become moments of freedom when we see into and through them.

In some ways, all of these truths are expressed in one of the most famous stories in Buddhism, the meeting between Bodhidharma and the emperor Wu. Bodhidharma was a great Indian teacher who is credited with having brought Zen to China. The Chinese, when he arrived, had already been exposed to the doctrines of Buddhism and had done some remarkable things with them, but their interest was largely theoretical and scholarly. They were great with translations and commentaries, but no one was getting free. Bodhidharma, on the other hand, was a great master of the practice; following this encounter he would spend nine years in solitary sitting.

The emperor had been anxious to meet him, and immediately posed a question.

"I've contributed huge amounts of money for the building of temples, the financing of monks and nuns, the health of the Sangha in general. How much merit do I get for all that?"

Bodhidharma could see that the emperor was speaking out of his attachment to "me" or "mine." If he had done those things in another spirit, the results might have been different.

"No merit whatsoever," Bodhidharma said.

The emperor was stunned. He wasn't familiar with this kind of thinking (or nonthinking). He tried another approach. "What can you tell me about the holy Dharma?" he said. He was asking for Bodhidharma's exposition of Buddhist theory, a subject about which Chinese scholars could have gone on forever.

"Nothing holy," Bodhidharma said. "Just vast space." This was a man who had spent some time in the abode of silence.

The emperor was exasperated. He was getting nowhere. He felt personally insulted.

"Who is it who is standing before me making these statements?" he said.

Bodhidharma looked him straight in the eye. "I have no idea," he said.

It is when we finally have no idea that we see things as they are.

Nothing Is Left Out

The Practice of Lovingkindness

Ajahn Sumedho

LIBERATION COMES FROM LETTING GO of our attachments. When this is our only concentration, however, we may develop an attitude that is excluding, almost annihilistic. We may tend to see conditions only in terms of not being attached to them, or even try to get rid of them. *Metta*, or lovingkindness, on the other hand, is an all-inclusive practice. With metta we are relating to all conditioned experience with an attitude of kindness and accepting things as they are. Metta includes the totality of our world and experience. It includes every possibility—the born and the unborn, the created and the uncreated, those who are present and those who are absent. With metta we contemplate all phenomena, all sentient beings, in terms of lovingkindness and inclusiveness rather than in the divisive terms of which is best, which is worst, what we like, what we don't like. Metta, then, is the way we relate to the totality.

Initially we need to deliberately adopt this attitude of lovingkindness. There's no need to make it sentimental just because of the word *love*. Instead, we can emphasize the word *kindness*. Kindness is our ability to accept people and situations for what they are, without hating them or getting caught up in what we don't like about them. This is not an attempt to dismiss the dark side while pretending that every person is nice and every situation is beautiful; it's not a goody-goody type of practice. It is a way of training ourselves to not get entangled in our judgments about ourselves, or our neighbors, our society, or even mosquitoes, spiders, and flies. With metta there is a sense of embracing everything with an attitude of patience, nonaversion, and kindness, without singling out one experience as deserving of more or less love. This love is unconditional.

Our society, in general, is highly critical. We are brought up to emphasize what's wrong with ourselves, our family and friends, the government, the country, the world at large—and so we become very conscious of the negative. We can only see the faults in people and things, and we become obsessed with that to the degree that we are no longer able to see what's right about them. In practicing metta, however, we deliberately avoid clinging to faults and weaknesses. We are not blind to them, and we are not promoting them; rather we maintain an attitude of kindness and patience toward defects in ourselves and in others. In this way, we develop a sense of well-being, recognizing that everything belongs in the totality, that there is nothing we can think of or imagine, nothing that has ever happened to us, that doesn't belong.

The discriminatory mind, on the other hand, thinks that life should be one particular way; it is clear about which things belong and which don't. It knows which actions are "right" and which are "wrong." We have plenty of ideals of how life ought to be, and when we come up against the ugly side of ourselves or others—criminality, atrocities, or just bad thoughts—we think it shouldn't be like that. But with metta we are contemplating the whole, no matter how corrupt or perverted, evil or good. Everything belongs in this totality. We begin to recognize that things are as they are, and our relationship to them can be not one of approving or disapproving, but of being patient, being willing to experience life in all its aspects with kindness and acceptance.

Metta can be a very inspiring, positive practice that uplifts the mind. If we constantly dwell on what's wrong with ourselves and the world, our mind becomes weighed down. This negative state can lead to depression. The more we obsess our minds with negativity, the more we get weighed down, and pretty soon we're stuck in a realm of ongoing, seemingly unmitigated negativity.

In contemplating victims and victimizers, for instance, it is easy to side with the victim and want to harm the victimizer. We see examples every time we read a newspaper. People get upset when the amount of punishment served on the victimizer doesn't seem great enough for the crime. In every war there is ongoing revengefulness, each side seeking out increasingly horrendous ways of harming the other. The most terrible things have been done, just out of revenge. When I reflect on this, I'd rather be the victim than the victimizer; even if I weren't punished by the justice system, I'd hate to live the rest of my life with such an enormous amount of fear.

In contemplating the law of karma, we realize that it is not a matter of seeking revenge, but of having this sense of metta and forgiveness. The victimizer is truly the most unfortunate of all because there *is* justice in the world. People who do wrong may not be discovered and punished by society, but no one gets away with harmful actions. We must be reborn again and again until we do resolve our karma. We don't know how many lifetimes we have had so far, but here we are in this incarnation, with our own particular character and karmic tendencies. We have had the good fortune to come across the Dharma, and so we have been given great gifts with which to resolve things. But how many people have such opportunities? Considering the billions who now live on this planet, there really are very few who have that chance.

In my lifetime there has always been some kind of violence taking place. I was a child in the Second World War, and I was in the U.S. Navy in the Korean War. Then there was the Vietnam War and the ongoing Cold War. I remember the destruction of Cambodia and, more recently, Yugoslavia and Rwanda. There is always terrible news of slaughter, of torture, and yet for me it has never been a direct experience. Somehow I have existed for over sixty years and escaped it all! I am grateful that I haven't had to see my parents murdered or had to endure any of the appalling things that have happened to others. In getting to know several exiled Cambodian communities, I have witnessed the anguish and anxiety these people feel, for they have all experienced horrifying losses.

Even without having had a lot of war and unpleasantness in my life, without being involved in murder, pillaging, rape, or destruction, I can still find within myself the tendency to seek revenge; it is a common human emotion. In terms of the law of karma, however, we can contemplate whether that is really how we want to conduct our lives—or would it be more beneficial to cultivate forgiveness and compassion toward all sentient beings, even those who have harmed us? In developing lovingkindness, it is important to recognize that the practice begins with ourselves. This means accepting everything in us: the dark side, the selfish side, the proud, conceited side, as well as the virtuous and good. Metta isn't about finding fault with ourselves but about accepting our meanness of heart, our desire for revenge, the pettiness or stupidity we might feel at times. Having metta for our own moods, our own emotional habits, enables us to let them be what they are, to neither indulge in them nor reject them, but to recognize: "This is my mood; this is how it feels." The attitude is one of patience, nonaversion, and kindness.

What often confuses us is our idealistic concepts of what we should be; for example, some of you might think: "I shouldn't want revenge for the victimizers; Ajahn Sumedho says I should have metta for them!" and then you might feel, "No, I can't include everyone; it's too hard. I can have metta for everyone else, but not that totally hateful person." What can be done in that moment is to have metta for that very feeling; finding an attitude of kindness rather than criticism, knowing it for what it is, not indulging or repressing it but simply being patient with that particular state as it is in the present moment.

If we actually practice this, what is the result? In my experience, I find I'm no longer making problems around my faults and weaknesses, I'm not hating myself continuously for not being able to live up to my high ideals of what I should be. I'm able to bear with some of the emotions and reactions I have, rather than just being caught up in aversion to myself. When we do this, those negative reactions fade out. We are no longer making a karmic connection to them; we are letting them go rather than getting entangled in them, so there is a feeling of greater ease. We are developing a proper attitude toward ourselves.

People sometimes say, "Before you can practice *anatta* (nonself), before you can let go of self, you need a good sense of self." They think that we should develop a proper ego in order to let go of it later on. But in reality, it's not a question of developing one before another. It is more integrated than that. As we move through life, a lot is going on simultaneously, though we may not always be aware of it. With the proper practice of metta, even toward our very worst side, we're developing a mature and patient frame of mind in which our sense of self is positive, rather than neurotic and negative.

It can be helpful to see the practice of metta within the container of the whole Buddhist path. The core of practice in Theravadin Buddhism is *dana* (generosity), *sila* (morality), and *bhavana* (meditation). Simply to be a generous person, one who is not selfish and who is able to share what he or she has with others, is the basis for being a good human being. Generosity is quite naturally better than mean-heartedness. There is joyfulness in it, for sharing brings gladness into our lives. With the practice of sila, or morality, there are precepts to keep and actions to refrain from. When we practice sila we learn to take responsibility for our actions and speech. The two together, dana and sila, bring us a sense of self-respect. Then there is meditation, bhavana, through which we begin to relinquish all the delusions we have about the self.

This whole process is one of purification. In practice we can begin to release the negative emotions and impurities we hold within us. As they start to rise up into our consciousness, if we are simply mindful of these unpleasant states and we can see them with kindness and acceptance, they begin to move away. But as long as we take the view that something is wrong with us, as long as we identify with them, we will push them down again, saying, "Oh, I mustn't think like that!" Then the purification process cannot take place; because of our aversion and refusal to accept them, the negativities stay with us and begin to accumulate.

So we can actually be glad when unpleasant states keep coming up in our meditation practice. By having metta for the wretched creatures we lock away inside us, we're opening the door of the prison. We are letting them go, and we release them out of compassion rather than the desire to be rid of them. If we contemplate the difficulties in this way, they can be borne more easily, because we are looking at them with wisdom rather seeing them as "me and my problems." As long as they are "mine," I can only hate myself for thinking or feeling a particular way. The spurious logic is: only a bad person would think such bad thoughts, so therefore I'm a bad person! Then we feel tremendous guilt and self-aversion.

Once we change our relationship to these negativities by moving from ignorance to wisdom, then whatever horrible thought or feeling may enter our mind is simply what it is. We are not denying it; instead, with metta, we allow it to be. We're willing to be with it and, as its nature is impermanent, it does not stay. In that willingness to let things be what they are, we liberate ourselves from them. As we become increasingly skillful at releasing these habits, there is a sense of lightness, because the heart isn't burdened by guilt, self-dislike, blame, and all the rest. Clinging to negative states, identifying with them, only creates endless neurotic problems about what we're feeling or thinking.

The practice of metta must always start with ourselves, because that's where we feel life most directly. It's easy to have lovingkindness for a billion Chinese who are distant and absolutely no threat to us at this moment. But to have metta for what is close and may threaten us, from our own bad thoughts to our husband, wife, child, or neighbor, is much more difficult. We can be quite grand on one level by saying, "May all beings be well and free from suffering," but nearer to home we may be feeling a lot of aversion to others or ourselves. In the Western world it is especially important to develop this attitude of patience and nonaversion to everything within ourselves. This includes our fears and desires, emotional habits, sicknesses, physical aches and pains, arthritis, cancer, crumbling bones, old age—all the mental and physical phenomena we experience. It doesn't mean we don't try to heal the body—this impulse comes quite naturally, and we do the best we can. Trying to make the body feel well can be lovingkindness toward it. But to hate the body because it's sick or painful or old only leads to misery and is an obstruction to spiritual development.

So we can begin metta practice with lovingkindness toward our own body, all its organs, its functions, its mental habits. This metta then spreads out toward relatives, friends, those living far away, all human beings, those born and not born, all animals, insects, birds, fish, reptiles, all angels and demons, gods and goddesses, in the whole universe. Nothing is left out. We have a sense of a totality of being, which we can then let go of, not out of aversion but because we see it for what it is and are no longer caught up in preferring this, resenting that, the endless struggle with the conditions. Instead, there is much more a sense of *upekkha*, or equanimity, toward the whole conditioned realm. Because we are no longer so fascinated and bound by this realm, we are able to let it go, and in that letting-go and nonattachment is the liberation, the realization of the Deathless, enlightenment.

The danger of description is that it makes things sound very complicated. Reading this last paragraph, someone might say, "Well, to develop all that, to get as far as the totality and be able to let go of it, would take the rest of my life! I'd never have time to do it." But descriptions and explanations are really for reflection only. The practice is always in the present. Noting our experience, seeing it clearly, is in the present. We begin where we are now, and we need to trust more the liberation in the present.

Say, for example, that obsessive thoughts keep coming up in our meditation, or we are obsessed by certain emotions in our daily life, or something deeply upsets us and we dislike the feeling of being taken over by it. We can look at that obsession as a sign that something is saying, "I want out!" Perhaps our reaction to this particular state has always been to ignore or reject it, but now we can see it is a sign demanding our attention. Perhaps we don't want to be bothered with it. We would like to have a nice, calm day and be able to just listen to the sound of the birds and the wind in the trees, and instead we have this insistent clamoring from our mind. But rather than trying to get rid of it, the attitude can be simply one of metta, being patient with it, being willing to feel it.

I used to have a lot of difficulty with anxiety. I didn't want to feel anxious, so I was always resisting it. To distract myself from it, I'd read a book or do some task. Or I'd try analyzing it: "I'm anxious because . . ." and end up concluding that something was wrong with me. This turned the anxiety into a problem, which then had to be dealt with and solved. But when I reminded myself to have metta for this feeling, not to think about it or analyze it, but to go to the place in the body itself, to the mental quality, and really embrace it, really be willing to feel that particular emotion, it became bearable. By changing my attitude to acceptance rather than rejection, to interest rather than just wanting to get rid of it, I found it was something I was able to tolerate. Then it ceased all on its own, for all conditions are impermanent.

So our anxieties about ourselves, our fears of our own emotional habits, are nothing to worry about, really. Using the approach of lovingkindness, we are able to reflect skillfully and wisely on these things for what they are, rather than speculating about what they might be or where they come from: "Does this mean there's something bad about me? Maybe it's because my great-grandmother was schizophrenic!" and so on. In the monastery we have people who have been in the drug scene, who have mentally ill parents, or who have done all kinds of things, and this can sometimes cause them enormous anxiety. They fear that they'll never be okay, maybe that they have ruined their minds with drugs and can never be enlightened. Once we get into that mode, anything seems possible. "Maybe I'll be the first in my family to have a breakdown!" Or we begin to see ourselves as flawed from birth: "God didn't give me a complete set of everything!" Of course there are some of us with real physical handicaps or mental problems, but even then we can have metta for these things, and develop trust and nonaversion, a sense of well-being.

This is a process of changing our attitude from "I don't like this in myself; I want to get rid of it," to "Oh, so this is what I'm feeling," and having patience and a willingness to experience what *is*, in the present moment. This is being willing to feel jealousy or anxiety, and taking an interest in it as experience. Because that which is aware is not worried, is not angry, and is not the condition that is present. We start to develop confidence in this state of pure awareness. Awareness is like light: it has no color, it is not a "thing" you can objectify. You can't *see* awareness, but you can be aware. It is awareness that allows you to see, to know the conditions, to know that your experiences are the way they are, that anxiety, fear, worry, are "like this." Through that patient attitude the conditioned realm stops being an endless struggle to control or get rid of things.

Then, as our practice develops, there is a sense of resting more and more in the silence of the mind, in that pure state of being in the present. You are investigating, finding out for yourself what really works, not just believing somebody else or being inspired by the theory of it all, but actually practicing. It is direct knowledge—not speculation or "knowing about" Dharma, but knowing Dharma.

LIBERATION FROM SUFFERING

Christopher Titmuss

I REMEMBER THE FIRST MEETING I had with Venerable Ajahn Buddhadasa, Abbot of Wat Suanmoke Monastery (Monastery of the Garden of Liberation) in Chai Ya, Thailand, in early 1970. I asked him what was necessary for liberation. He said: "Nothing is worth being attached to. Nothing whatsoever. To know liberation is to know complete nonattachment." Ajahn Buddhadasa, who lived in the forest for more than sixty years, then took hold of his monk's robe and pulled it to expose his shoulder. "It is not worth being attached to anything to do with this," he added. This proved to be a breathtaking moment in my life.

The truth of what he said stood out as clearly as color to a person with good eyesight. Within a few months, I took full ordination as a Buddhist monk for six years. He unwaveringly emphasized seeing through clinging as the way to liberation. To know liberation is to know an enlightened life.

THE THIRD NOBLE TRUTH

Liberation from all manner of suffering, anguish, and dissatisfaction through the elimination of clinging is the Third Noble Truth taught by the Buddha. Although this goal may seem inconceivable to the ordinary, everyday mind unexposed to the Dharma, that does not put it out of reach. Even those who practice the Dharma may harbor the view that the task lies beyond human capacity. It is not unusual for profound teachings to get watered down to popularize them. There are a few sins in teaching the Dharma, and one of them must surely be reducing the teachings to the overcoming of stress. A life totally dedicated to the Dharma embraces more than meditation and mindful exercises for coping calmly with daily life. While appreciating calmness and clarity of mind—features of the last two links of the Noble Eightfold Path—one must know that they can never serve as a substitute for liberation.

The Third Noble Truth speaks of an authentically enlightened existence, not a cool response to it. We should never forget that discovering a truly liberated life is much harder than we think. In these teachings, those who have realized liberation are called Noble Ones. They have found the way out of problematic existence. They have not generated a new construction but simply have ceased believing in and giving substance to the modes of the constructed self and its various standpoints. They have realized liberation. This is nirvana. It is unformed, unmade, and not dependent on conditions for its presence. Nirvana does not belong to an unconscious state arising in meditation that fluctuates. Nor is it a condition of absolute detachment from the world or a state of annihilation.

In essence, liberation is the realization of the end of suffering, the full emancipation of the human spirit and the joyful understanding of the nature of things. Cessation of suffering removes the struggle born of greed, hate, and self-delusion. It eradicates that compelling need to pursue or gain things as an ultimately satisfying way of life. The emptiness of the ego, of any substance to "I" and "my," is obvious.

Dharma teachings encourage us to resolve the force of wanting, to extinguish the problems, confusions, and conflicts associated with it. This reveals the completion of the path to enlightenment. The cessation of dissatisfaction around wanting and not wanting points to the essence of the Third Noble Truth. We may think that our mind expresses only wanting or not wanting, and every action would appear to confirm this. All this is true for ordinary mind with ordinary consciousness, but it cannot be said that this is how it is for everybody. We are then closing the door to enlightenment, preferring to take shelter within our fixed views.

Nirvana is knowing an emancipated life; it is not merely a clarity of mind. There is a danger that in making nirvana into just clarity of mind, we substitute the unconditioned, unborn, unmade, for the conditioned, born, and made. All states of mind, pleasant and unpleasant, shallow and deep, calm or confused, arise owing to the presence of causes and conditions that enable them to arise. We use our perceptions and experiences to fix cause and effect. We live in a world that assumes the relationship and impact of things and events upon each other, and the truth of our perceptions. It is not through piling one effort on to another, nor through acts of will, that our natural freedom shines through.

The Noble Ones know that this remarkable liberation shines through states of mind—without dependency upon them. Knowing this releases much joy for the Noble Ones and also releases much love for others caught up in states of mind. This liberating discovery takes the grip of events out of one's life—not through detachment but through clarity, insight, and an incomprehensible intimacy. The grip of the perception that we are born and that we die also loses substantiality. Birth and death only have real significance for those who identify the activities of "I" and "my" with mind and body.

In enlightenment there is no notion of wandering from one thing to another; there is nothing for the self to gain or achieve. There is no further evolution for the self, and desire and becoming have lost all relevance. Liberated people neither cherish self-existence nor withdraw from it; neither cling to others nor reject them. They have done what has to be done. They have reached the top of the mountain that was always there in front of them. They know that the path is not the condition for the mountain. The mountain—that is, the nature of things—stands firm and steady whether there is a path to it or not.

The "world's" interactions with our "perceptions" deceive us into thinking we live in touch with reality. We invest substance and reality in our perceptions even though our experience of the world keeps changing. It is these changing experiences and views that naturally refute any standpoint that the mind makes. We assume that we are an agent who acts upon the world and a recipient of other people's actions, who also act as agents. Infatuated with this way of thinking, we cannot see a way out of it. It seems as though we keep switching our identities. One minute we are the agent, next minute others are. We live in a kind of bubble that produces suffering and dissatisfaction. The final delusion is believing that this is the way things really are. Morality, depths of meditation, and wisdom shake out of us the complacency of such a view. They open out our whole field of awareness. The constructions of the self collapse. Everything is in place without beginning, middle, or end. Wanting and not wanting, existence and nonexistence, produce a distorted world upon which all anguish comes to rely. There is nothing to grasp or possess or cling to. An enlightened life breaks us out of the spell of self-deception. We are free. Utterly free.

THE FOUR NOBLE ONES

Among the Nobles Ones who have become free, there are four types: (1) the Stream-enterer, (2) the Once-returner, (3) the Nonreturner, and (4) the Arahat (fully enlightened being).

Nobility emerges out of realization, not from birth, marriage, or titles. The Noble Ones all share something in common—they are grounded in the Dharma of the Unshakable. They know profound friendship toward all forms of life. They have ceased to live in the duality of hungering for victory over defeat, success over failure. They do not cling to yesterday, today, or tomorrow. They know a freedom that is indestructible.

Noble Ones do not rely upon a savior, a sacred book, or a transcendent God for their illumination. They do not grasp on to the view that such nobility arises solely through association with a teacher, personal effort, or meditation.

Noble Ones remain reluctant to make claims about their realizations. For the "I" to make such claims can put into question liberation and its natural connection with the vast web of life. Life does not belong to self, to "I" and "my." It belongs to the nature of things. Knowing this brings joy. Noble Ones know a profound sense of fulfillment through life's journey.

We recognize Noble Ones through their way of being in the world and their steadfastness in times of trouble. There may be still some signs or outbursts of selfishness, negativity, and fear for the Stream-enterer and to a much lesser extent for the Once-returner. The Non-returner knows the conceited "I" and restlessness, and gets attached to formless experiences. But Noble Ones have lost any appetite to feed unwholesome patterns. The Arahat remains unfettered to anything anywhere.

The personality of a Noble One varies. The personality of one may appear strict. Another may appear as the embodiment of kindness and humility. Yet another may have a sharpened mind that cuts through superficiality. They regard opinions about personality as empty.

Noble Ones know they have no life of their own. The notion of *having* a mind and body seems superficial in the extreme. Noble Ones pay respect to life while remaining free from giving value to selfishness.

The Stream-enterer

The Dharma offers a practical and direct approach to a fully enlightened life; it is a resource pointing directly to the full and unexcelled enlightenment of a human being. The Dharma is not something to cling to.

Stream-enterers are enlightened since they know authentic liberation, but they still have work to do on themselves. Their realizations and way of living make them Noble Ones. There is a knowing for Stream-enterers of this immeasurable and indestructible freedom in daily life. Unwelcome and unwanted states of mind may arise and may well need clear attention, but these mind-states have no power to eradicate the discovery of freedom. The sun shines whether clouds drift across it or not. Stream-enterers know the sweetness of living with the truth of things, the emptiness of the ego, and the joy of freedom. Some will speak the language of finding God. Their sustained practices destine them for complete enlightenment, free from any remaining fetters or obstructions. Stream-entry indicates the first major turning point toward a fully enlightened life.

There are practical signs of such realization. The knowing of liberation does not exist in a vacuum. This means that any inner change that takes place remains relatively steady. It is not easily overcome by the changing circumstances of day-to-day life. The signs are:

1. *There is commitment to ethical principles; there is no wish to harm or exploit.* The quality and level of awareness regarding this are deeply significant. The nature of dependent-arising circumstances is understood, and the gap between "us" and "them" has dissolved dramatically. In a very real way, one often perceives others as oneself. This view affects one's heart, mind, and activities—true morality belongs to realization. There is an effortless acknowledgment and appreciation of the Five Precepts: they are not commandments nor pressures to define oneself in a particular way. The Stream-enterer understands the interconnectedness of things.

2. *There is no doubt.* Conflict and uncertainty no longer torture the mind. In sudden transformation, one may wonder what happened, what that was all about. The Stream-enterer may not be able to put such realizations into language or description. Thoughts may arise about the significance of the change, or one may have some doubts about its long-term impact, but here there is freedom from doubt about freedom itself. One has tasted pure, fresh water. There is no doubt about it.

3. *There is the end of clinging, attachment, and identification with rites and rituals.* It is not unusual for teachings and practices to deteriorate into clinging to religious observances. Ceremonies, rituals, methods, and techniques become a substitute for opening the heart, depths of *samadhi* (calm and concentrated attention), and insight into liberation. We begin to imagine that our particular methodology guarantees the highest wisdom. The method and techniques then matter more than the liberation from clinging to such forms. There are countless numbers of sincere people who become stuck with their

particular form. They cannot see through it. The problem is over for the Stream-enterer.

4. *There is no more clinging to personality belief.* It is easy to become obsessed with our personality, our self. Our personality becomes an area of major attention. There is the desire to impress and please. We think that our personality has an inherent existence to it. Through preoccupation with it we become narcissistic. Self-infatuated, we only want to talk about ourselves. Everyone and everything else becomes secondary. Seeing through this, the Stream-enterer does not give great significance to personality. One has seen much more deeply than that. Others may speak of our personality in various ways. They will isolate different aspects of the mind and make that a description of who we are, but in clarity and realization there comes natural happiness and contentment. One is no longer thinking in terms of "me and my personality" and all the ego that involves.

5. *There is no falling into hell.* Hell is an acutely painful state of mind. There are far too many people living a tortured inner life. There is much despair, depression, and evidence of abnormal psychology. It becomes hell when a person no longer has the inner resources to resolve a situation. Falling into the pits of unhappiness is hell. The Stream-enterer cannot fall into such a hell. There is a sufficient degree of inner well-being to stop that from ever happening. Clarity and freedom become one's refuge. Consciousness is steadfast and supported with wisdom, and this brings confidence and understanding, diminishing the chance for any descent into hell.

6. *The Stream-enterer can still experience unresolved issues.* There is no hiding behind roles or acting through large layers of ego. Faults and failings do not remain hidden. The questions often arise, "How then can I know a liberated person? How do I know that there are such people on this earth?" It is easy to draw conclusions, favorable and unfavorable, about the realizations and attainments of certain people. Sometimes we measure people by the amount of good they do, their warmth and kindness or their clarity of mind. We cannot draw quick conclusions.

We must have a long-term association with somebody we regard as liberated. It is folly to ignore the wisdom of such a person. We may become impressed with a guru or charismatic figure and with very little contact build up a picture of this person. Time and close contact will tell whether he or she lives a noble life or not.

How does that person deal with a difficult situation or crisis? With personal health or life-and-death issues? Stream-enterers know the sweetness of the nonduality of life and death, presence and absence, coming and going. Stream-entry reveals the knowing of inner freedom and any patterns and inner conditions to work on. Awareness reveals this without producing a conflict. The mind is truly vast, deep, and immeasurable. The waves belong to the ocean. The Stream-enterer knows what is what. It is this clarity and its practice that bring complete fulfillment in the journey to Arahatship.

The Once-returner

We recognize the value of making outer changes in our life. We rarely give the same consideration to the significance of genuine and profound inner change.

Authentic inner change means the fading of the ego. The degree to which the ego dissolves is the degree to which the joy of emancipation reveals itself. The Stream-enterer knows freedom as an authentic statement of fulfillment. There is a dramatic reduction in the grip of problematic existence upon consciousness. There is knowing of the Immeasurable. But there is still some residue of greed, anger, and self-deception. The Once-returner has reduced this residue significantly compared with the Stream-enterer.

Some will imagine that the major change occurs in realization of Stream-entry. They believe that once realization has occurred, the rest is effortless change until the ego is totally exhausted. For the Noble Ones, the shifts from Stream-enterer to Once-returner and from Once-returner to Nonreturner, and from Nonreturner to Arahat are equally important. There is no sense of complacency. Just as a log flows downriver to the sea, if it does not get washed up on the bank, so the Stream-enterer flows to final freedom, but it still requires vigilance not to get caught on the bank of extremism. Stream-enterers retain a keen sense of liberating wisdom and insights. There is a passion and love of discovery, and of not returning to the forces of wanting and denying. The Once-returner has almost exhausted greed, anger, and self-deception.

The Once-returner continues his or her dedication to the dissolution of all that is unsatisfactory within. The potency of each of the Five Hindrances (sense desire, anger, boredom, worry, and doubt) gets challenged when any one of them, or combination of them, arises. This is not an obsessive attempt to make oneself perfect. It is a wise outlook. There is an understanding that these hindrances influence the inner life and have an impact upon the world.

The work to dissolve them provides real support for others as much as ourselves. It is hardly surprising that one of the outstanding features of Noble Ones is their unfailing compassion, known as the *bodhisattva* mind. Such a mind shows itself in the solitary forest-dweller who takes care of every creature or plant. It also shows in the Noble Ones' dedication to lifelong service to others.

The Once-returner has no interest in blindly accepting the corrupting influence of unpleasant mind-states. For one who has known and tasted the sweetness of great liberation, there is no enthusiasm to fall back into the grip of unwelcome states of mind. The Noble Ones develop and explore the wide range of resources available for complete emancipation. There is use of meditation, reflection, practices, and teachings for the resolution of all that may arise. The fading of anger and negativity does not take away constructive criticism. There is the freedom to express concerns clearly and directly. Others may misunderstand. They may think that criticism is negativity, moral concerns are self-righteousness, and accountability means revenge, but these confusions do not apply to the perceptions of the Once-returner.

There is nothing passive about the Noble Ones' relationship to life. The dissolution of selfishness enhances the natural enjoyment of seeing, hearing, smelling, tasting, touching, and what arises in consciousness. There is a depth of receptivity to joy rather than pursuit of personal pleasure. The heart and mind of the Once-returner stand steady like the truth itself. Such a person expresses immeasurable wisdom.

The Nonreturner

The Nonreturner never returns to greed and anger. There is no more living with such expressions of self-deception. This brings a clear release from such matters, leaving only traces of ignorance, conceit, subtle clinging, and restlessness for the Nonreturner to dissolve to reach utter fulfillment of the teachings and practices.

By the time one reaches this stage, unwelcome states of mind have diminished considerably. These useless forces spring from the blindness of expectations and the excess of demands that we put upon ourselves and others. The Nonreturner has negated such an unsatisfactory flow of conditioning. Even the ability to be in the subtle grip of a tendency is virtually exhausted for the Nonreturner. There is very little left in the way of unsatisfactory conditioning of "I" and "my." Wisdom prevents expectations leading to disappointment.

The concepts *Stream-enterer, Once-returner, Nonreturner,* and *Arahat* will appear awkward to those unfamiliar with them. They serve as definitions of states of realization. They enable us to break away from the major problem associated with spiritual practices—the idea that one must become perfect. The Noble Ones live an enlightened life. They cling neither to notions of imperfection nor to perfection. They have abandoned these viewpoints. The Nonreturner works with the ignorance and conceit involved in any views. His or her primary interest is full realization, free from such unsatisfactory influences.

For example, there is the religious view that one can be saved. "God has saved me" easily expresses a conceit of the self. For the realized ones, there is nothing to be saved or lost. The self experiences the pointlessness of building itself up on such standpoints or reacting against them. There is nothing to pursue or hold on to. Liberation is here and now. Grace is not an occasional handout from a selective transpersonal force. The Nonreturner is one step away from complete, unexcelled liberation.

The Noble Ones know who they are. They may or may not place themselves into one of these four categories. Labels are not important to them. What is important is the wisdom of knowing the truth of things. Nonreturners bring the light of awareness and insight to the last traces of the ego. Their compassion is all-embracing because they understand how states of mind bewitch people.

The Noble Ones barely concern themselves with personal desires. There is only a little significance in "I" for the Nonreturner. The Nonreturner's ignorance manifests as blind spots in understanding. He or she can cling to the identity of being a Noble One. This shows conceit.

Nonreturners regard experiences of ignorance and conceit as clouds obscuring bright sunlight shining through to the earth. Through insight, there is less momentum for the ego to rise again. It is this expansive and steady sense of great liberation that makes all the ardor of the teachings, disciplines, and practices worthwhile.

The Buddha teaches seven factors for enlightenment: awareness, Dharma inquiry, vitality, happiness, tranquillity, *samadhi*, and equanimity. The Noble Ones know the liberating fruits of the Dharma life. The Nonreturner has one stage left before Arahatship and the complete fulfillment of the teachings.

The Noble Ones reveal the full potential of human existence. We should never underestimate the extraordinary significance of the Noble Ones in this world.

The Arahat

To fulfill our capacity to see into life sets us free, utterly free, once and for all. Then there is no more grief and anguish, no more fear and indifference, no more confusion about the way things are. We have seen through the world of birth, change, and death. Our mind is not a problem to us. We know that "I am" is a conceit. Such a one is an Arahat, who is fully liberated.

Yet our mind finds itself trapped in greed, negativity, fear, and confusion. These psychological patterns distort our lives, actively preventing us from seeing clearly. What we have contact with are unsatisfactory states of mind. Wisdom only becomes available as we free the mind from such influential inner forces. The Arahat has ceased projecting all sorts of qualities and attributes onto objects and stands free from the conceit of a substantial self. The world of ego and all of its investments and compounded ideas has lost any significance. Unlike his noble predecessors—Stream-enterer, Once-returner, and Nonreturner—the Arahat has nothing more left to work on. He or she is free from living in a state of mental agitation, including longing for subtle experiences.

The Arahat knows a freedom that goes beyond any kind of measurement. Nothing whatsoever can take this sublime liberation away. The comprehensive nature of such understanding shows itself in timeless understanding, natural joy, and love. To see and know things as they truly are is to know liberation. To know liberation is to see and know things as they are. The so-called problems of life have gone for good.

When an old Thai monk in our monastery was dying, there was a quiet acknowledgment among some of those around him that he was an Arahat. He had led a selfless existence, and when he spoke, other monks listened with rapt attention. A few weeks before he died, I said to him, "It won't be long before King Yama [the Lord of Death] comes looking for you. How do you feel about that?"

The old monk turned to me with a smile and said, "King Yama has searched all over this earth looking for me. But he cannot find me anywhere. This monk is not to be found here nor there nor in between." On the morning he died I was on the alms round in the nearby village. He sent a monk to fetch me. I lay beside him on the mat on the floor in his hut while he died. At the end, he said: "Seeing gone. Listening gone. All complete." Then consciousness dissolved. Being enlightened, the Arahat has broken through the world of life and death. This awakening triggers extraordinary realizations and a generosity of spirit that remains undiminished. Death loses its sting. The notion of becoming, and fear of the end of it, gets swept away in these realizations. The "I" has as much significance as a line drawn on water with your finger.

There is the ordinary view and the trans-ordinary view. The ordinary view says that we never stop evolving. There are some who will proclaim that there is no end, that we are always changing and evolving as a human being. What is important here is understanding the difference between the need to grow and develop and knowing the end of the Dharma journey.

There is always much to learn. We believe we ought to cultivate and sustain this attitude right until the last breath of our life. It would seem conceited to claim that one has come to the end of the evolutionary process, reached the completion of all becoming. Others may say of the Arahat, "Oh, he is growing. He has changed over the years. He has greater insights / is a more loving person / has a strengthening presence." But this is the perception of others. It has little or no meaning for the liberated one.

Any apparent developments of heart and mind occur through the impulses of life rather than through having to make an effort to be a better person. From a conventional perspective, an Arahat also grows, changes his or her mind, and becomes receptive to new areas of life. Apparent modifications of the inner life are of little importance to the Arahat.

Liberation ends becoming, ends clinging to views, ends comparing past to present, ends notions of personal survival or otherwise after death. Issues of self lose all their meaning. The picture we carry of the self in the world belongs not to reality but to the determinations of the mind. The picture we carry of the world does not belong to the world.

The Arahat sees through the debate of one life or many lives since he or she is free from location in or outside any of the Five Aggregates (body, feelings, perceptions, thoughts, and consciousness). In this there is no location anywhere for "I and my life" or "I and my death." The Arahat is untraceable here and now, and he or she knows it. The Arahat knows intimately a trans-ordinary understanding.

The Arahat has done what has to be done, laid down the difficulties and burdens. There is an indestructible freedom. The Arahat has exhausted all karma, the unsatisfactory influences from the past. Victory and defeat, success and failure, have no inherent significance. The truth, namely that which sets us free, neither expands nor contracts, neither stands still nor moves. It remains unaffected by the fluctuating circumstances of events between birth and death, including them both. The Arahat knows this. Arahats rest in the timeless Dharma of all things.

It doesn't matter whether one believes complete liberation is possible or not. It is not a subject for dogma or speculation. It is a matter of realization. The end of suffering reveals the end of all clinging. Liberation is incomparable.

May all beings live in peace.
May all beings be liberated.
May all beings realize a fully enlightened life.

PART THREE

The Sangha and
Practice in Daily Life

INTRODUCTION
TO PART THREE

W HEN THE BUDDHA'S first group of disciples reached enlightenment, he said to them, "Go forth, go out, for the good of the many, for the welfare of the many, out of compassion for the world, for the benefit, for the welfare, for the happiness of beings." By saying this, the Buddha made it clear that freedom should be expressed and shared in the world.

People who put the teachings of the Buddha into practice are known as the Sangha. The Sangha is the third of the three traditional refuges in Buddhism; it is said that if we look at the Buddha, we will automatically see the Dharma, and if we look at the Dharma, we will automatically see the Sangha. One meaning of *Sangha* is the ordained community of monks and nuns. One meaning is the community of those who, from beginningless time, have realized the truth. One meaning is the community of all who are dedicated to lives of truth and good-heartedness, who live with the benefit of all beings in their hearts and minds.

The Buddha's teaching, as expressed in the lives of the Sangha, is never removed from a sense of humanity. The Buddha was a human being who talked about what it ultimately means to be a human being and to be happy. The teachings guide us to go beyond our ordinary sense of limitation, to know liberation, and to relate to others with generosity and an open heart. Our daily life is a revelation of what we care about and value, because we express this in all that we do. Our ordinary activities are a mark of what we are dedicated to.

When we explore Sangha, we explore what supports us, clears our vision, and inspires us, and what protects us in a life committed to wisdom and good-heartedness. The chapters in this section are about this journey, and they reflect the tremendous pragmatism and integration of the Buddha's teaching. To explore the meaning of community, and the exhortation to go forth "for the good of the many," is to explore a quality of compassion that isn't lofty or abstract or removed from the concerns of people, but is very present and available. When the Buddha was asked about the different experiences of life—about being a parent, a renunciate, a friend, being sick, being the one who gives, being the one who receives—he said, "Any life at all may be lived well or may be lived wrongly. If it is lived well, it will bring great results, but if it is lived wrongly, it will bring very poor results." Whatever the particular circumstance of our lives, our potential is great when we honor our own sense of purpose, when we bring wakefulness into the different aspects of our day, and when we remember a heartfelt commitment to the welfare of all beings.

REFUGE
IN THE SANGHA

Narayan Liebenson Grady

A LL BEINGS NEED A REFUGE, a place where they can find ease or peace. In our day-to-day existence, we are constantly trying to find relief from the torments of the heart—refuge from fear, refuge from loneliness, refuge from anger, refuge from boredom. However, we tend to seek this refuge in outer things, which ultimately prove unreliable.

This yearning for relief takes many different forms. At times, we try to find refuge in accumulating possessions or through success in our career. We sometimes try to find refuge in memories or fantasies. Some of us try to find refuge in alcohol or drugs. We often try to find refuge in entertainment or in sleeping and eating—ice cream is a favorite! But if we want to find a refuge that doesn't melt, that does not pass away or change, we need to find a more reliable one. Without awareness, we blindly seek solace where it cannot be found. And, over and over again, we find ourselves disappointed because we are trying to find happiness in that which is impermanent. Through the power of awareness, we begin to realize that a lasting source of ease and comfort can only be found within.

In Buddhism, finding an inner refuge means taking refuge in the three gems: the Buddha, the Dharma, and the Sangha. The Buddha is an example of someone who became free—a person just like you and me who awakened because of his own effort and earnestness. Thus, taking refuge in the Buddha is actually taking refuge in our own Buddha-nature and the possibility that we too can awaken out of the conditioning of the mind. *Dharma* means truth. To take refuge in the Dharma refers to the attempt to find out what is true in life and to take refuge in that truth rather than in deception, pretense, or denial. Finally, taking refuge in the Sangha can be looked at as taking refuge in the community of all those inclined toward freedom, beauty, and wholesomeness. These three refuges—refuge in the vision of awakening out of the conditioning of the mind, refuge in the truth of things, and refuge in the recognition that we have company—are common to any spiritual search, and are ultimately found within our own heart when we are open to looking.

The Buddha, the Dharma, and the Sangha are all aspects of the same process. Each refuge is powerful and essential in and of itself; at the same time they are all connected in a full and integrated path. In this way, the Buddha is vision, the Dharma is embodying that vision, and the Sangha is sharing or expressing that vision. The Buddha is wise view, the Dharma is meditation, and Sangha is wise action. The Buddha is faith or motivation, the Dharma is practice, and the Sangha is intimacy. The Buddha is enlightenment, the Dharma is actualizing of enlightenment, and the Sangha is manifesting enlightenment. The Buddha is wisdom, the Dharma is the truth, and the Sangha is harmonious action. Taking refuge in the Sangha means embracing a seamless view of practice that integrates how we are meditating with how we are in the world and then expressing our understanding through wise action and speech. It is living our meditation, and allowing our lives to express the truth. Sangha reveals the gap between ideals and actuality. It allows us to see when we are lost in wonderful ideals that have little to do with our daily life.

There are many different ways to look at what Sangha as community means, however. Communities have many shapes and forms. Some communities may even seem formless and fluid. Taking refuge in community does not necessarily mean that we are taking refuge in a specific group of practitioners. We need to hold a more inclusive vision of what community is.

In the Buddhist community one way to take refuge in the Sangha is to remember that we come out of an ancient tradition of awakening. The fact that for over two thousand five hundred years people just like us have been walking this path can help to give us a sense of direction, protection, and confidence in our own capacity to awaken. It can be comforting to remember that everything that we think is so unique and personal to our own experience has been very well documented in the discourses (*suttas*) of the Buddha. When we read what was written down so very long ago and see that it is our own experience that is being written about, we may gain a sense of strength and unity.

In the time of the Buddha, practitioners had to work with the very same difficulties, hindrances, and obstacles that we meet in our minds today. There are descriptions in the suttas of yearning and longing and anger and agitation and restlessness and doubt and sleepiness and dullness and boredom. The Buddha spoke about these states of mind because they are possible to see through, to let go of, and to transmute into the essence of joy and freedom. We can recognize, not just as a concept but as an actuality, that we are on a path together and that we are part of an ancient tradition. To remember this can be a refuge. To recognize that we are part of something so vast can help with our confidence. It can be a place where we can nourish ourselves when we hit dry or difficult spots.

Historically, the Buddha's teachings have been preserved by the monastic tradition, and the term *sangha* has referred to the community of monks and nuns. Sangha can, as well, be seen in a much more inclusive way to mean all like-minded spiritual seekers. The Buddha, when asked whether anyone who had not ordained as a monk had become fully awakened, replied, "There has not been just one person. There have been many people who have awakened, who have lived a householder life." In the original discourses of the Buddha we see that there were all kinds of people who practiced and realized the deepest freedom—people with different levels of education, people from diverse socioeconomic classes, practitioners with big families, both men and women, and even some seven-year-olds. There is a whole group of children who were said to have been enlightened at the age of seven in the Buddha's time! We can take refuge in this recognition that each one of us has the potential to awaken through diligent practice.

Practicing together gives us strength. The Zen master Dogen said that if there is just one log on a fire, the fire will be weak, whereas many logs make a fire strong and powerful. He said that people can help each other by combining their strengths as they practice. This is one reason why we get together in retreat centers. While practicing together, we might experience great difficulties and then open our eyes and realize that everyone is still sitting. This inspires us to be able to continue to sit ourselves. Whatever is going on inside of us, we see a commitment in others that can inspire us to stay still. There are so many choices. We can all help one another through the difficulties and challenges of practice. Even the most self-reliant practitioners are nourished by sitting with others at times. To sit alone for short or long periods can be invaluable, but in terms of a lifetime of practice, most of us can benefit from the support of one another. We are dependent on ourselves to practice; no one can sit for us. But at the same time, most of us need support.

Because the practice of insight meditation goes against the grain of the culture, we in the West especially need the strength that practicing together brings. The values of the culture in the world at large differ greatly from the values that we uncover and strengthen in our meditation practice. One example is that in the culture we are generally encouraged to have strong opinions. Having strong views is seen as making one more stable and productive, whereas if we don't have firmly held dogmatic views, we are seen as wishy-washy. When we look deeply, however, we see that attachment to views and opinions narrows our world and limits creative possibilities. Opinions and views are very subjective and are not something to cling to too tightly.

In spiritual practice we begin to question what is defined as success. The dominant culture encourages us to be as busy and frantic as possible, telling us that if we are doing something, we are on the way to becoming someone. The more crowded one's life is, the more successful. The culture urges us to live for the future and values greed and accumulation. But our practice invites us to be aware and present, while letting go of our attachment to fantasy and preoccupation with external things. It is a radical act to do nothing and to sit in stillness. In a conventional way doing nothing means being passive or lazy. Doing nothing in a meditative sense means keeping the heart still and being completely present with whatever activity we are engaged in: it is an extremely vibrant creative activity. The art of doing nothing, however easy it may sound, requires a great deal of practice and training.

The support and encouragement that we receive from the Sangha are invaluable, given the nature and depth of our inquiry. Cultural conditioning, with its obsession with the external, keeps us searching for happiness outside of ourselves. It's easy to forget that happiness lies within. It is a refuge to absorb the environment when we are around others who are practicing; to take in the atmosphere of not trying to attain, of not trying to accumulate, and, instead, discovering the great beauty in letting go. This allows us to uncover a more reliable refuge. Through practicing together we can experience the joy of sitting quietly and touching that which is authentic and unconditional.

The spiritual path has nothing to do with achievement or attainment or becoming someone special. Because we live in such a competitive culture, we need to be especially mindful of feelings of competition when we practice together. It is almost second nature to compare our own experience with another's, and we need to be aware of how easily and chronically we bring this into the spiritual life. When we compete with one another, we reinforce the discontent that comes from feelings of separateness and incompletion.

We take refuge in the Sangha through wise friendship. Wise and compassionate friends bring the teachings to life. Sometimes we lack the inner confidence that it is possible to wake up. Sometimes we find ourselves overwhelmed by how things are. But to see the Dharma being manifested in another human being is a way of visibly touching the teachings. To have wise friends can help keep the practice alive when our motivation and confidence are faltering. We can read and study and practice, but at times we find ourselves lost. At times the teachings may not seem quite real or quite enough. Having contact with wise friends is a way to ground the practice in reality. When we see that others have changed and have grown into deepening levels of freedom through practice, we see that this path of liberation is also available to us. When we begin to recognize and let go of our competitive conditioning, others can inspire us when they share themselves and the fruits of their practice.

The Buddha clearly valued the presence of wise friends on the path. In the suttas he taught that when a particular quality of heart such as generosity, patience, or concentration needs to be developed, one should try to have contact with others who have already developed that same wholesome quality. The Buddha emphasized the importance of "noble friendship and suitable conversation." It makes sense. If we want to realize truth and freedom, it's helpful to be in the presence of those who are manifesting and expressing truth and freedom. It is more than inspiration. On some level it is transmission: we seem to absorb qualities of heart from one another and are very much influenced by one another. Although wholesome qualities of heart are developed through our own effort, we can get a clear sense of what they look like and how wonderful they are by seeing them embodied in others. Being in contact with wise friends points to and strengthens our own latent wisdom, generosity, and compassion. When we are in contact with those who are wise or free, it touches that which we already know within ourselves but have forgotten. Some part of the heart remembers a little bit more through this contact. Our own Buddha-nature gets revealed.

The people that we choose to be with in intimate ways and as friends have a strong influence on our lives. It is important to notice what we base our relationship choices on. Are we being drawn by blind desire or by wisdom? It is a true treasure in this life of attempting to awaken to find friends who will tell us the truth when we ask.

It is very easy to find people who will talk behind our backs, but to receive the truth from friends in a kind way is a wonderful gift. We can take refuge in their discernment. We can check out our assumptions and conclusions. Discerning friends can help us examine ways that we habitually cause suffering for ourselves and others. The path of freedom is a difficult one, a path that requires great effort and earnestness. To be in the company of spiritual friends who can help us recognize and transform the inevitable obstacles that we encounter along the way is invaluable. It is hard to walk on this path of awareness without friends gently pointing out our blind spots.

Though wise friendship is an essential aspect of the spiritual path, this doesn't mean to avoid or insulate ourselves from people who we think do not have the qualities that we aspire to. There's a great deal to be learned from interacting in situations that are not so protected or consciously supportive of our inner development. We certainly don't have to search too far—life is offering us such opportunities all the time. Driving in traffic is a prime example of this. We can observe our minds and awaken wherever we are and no matter whom we're with. When we are being challenged in ways that are not necessarily of our own choosing or within our control, life can continue to teach us. We can develop patience and compassion in situations that provoke impatience and aversion, if we are willing to be mindful of our own reactivity and learn to take responsibility for our response. If we can bring these situations into our practice, then we do not have to relate to ourselves as victims, subjugated to the whims of others.

While being part of the Buddhist tradition that began with the enlightenment of the Buddha, we are also part of a much larger Sangha that includes not only Buddhists but also the greater community of those who are seeking freedom and truth. We are part of this greater community simply through our commitment to being awake and choosing not to engage in harmful actions toward ourselves and others. We are immediately brought into this larger Sangha with our willingness to be openhearted and with our intention to grow in discernment. Taking refuge in the Sangha is not a matter of adhering to a particular belief system or of identifying oneself as a Buddhist. The Buddha didn't want people to follow him blindly or to identify with what he taught; his teaching is an invitation to know freedom for ourselves.

Another more expansive way of looking at taking refuge in the Sangha is taking refuge in our interconnection with all beings— whether they are engaged in a spiritual practice or not. We can be aware of our deep sense of a common bond to one another, and can take refuge in being intimate with all beings, if we see through the apparent separation of self and other. The Indian sage Neem Karoli Baba said, "Don't throw anyone out of your heart." This means not only seeing our interconnection but living it. Not to throw anyone out means to continue to practice opening our hearts to all beings, even those beings that engage in harmful actions. This doesn't mean that we approve or condone unskillful actions, or that we can't say no and set protective boundaries. Boundaries are important if we want to be able to keep everyone in our hearts. There are times when we need to protect ourselves. Situations of oppression or abuse may require throwing someone out of your house to avoid throwing them out of your heart.

When we come in contact with others, as we do every day, we are bound to be hurt from time to time, and at certain times quite a bit. Our first reaction is to cling to our hurt feelings, to our sense of being separate from one another. Instead we can bring mindfulness into our relationships with others rather than taking refuge in withdrawal or blame. If we bring mindfulness into relationship, perhaps we can take refuge in risking something different from the old familiar unworkable and unsatisfying ways that we all know so well. Taking refuge in openheartedness often means taking refuge in that which is new and unfamiliar. We can be mindful in relationship and ask: Am I acting in a habitual or mechanical way? When we are up against that which seems unworkable, what does it mean to remain openhearted? To stay open may go against every bone in the body! So taking refuge in the Sangha also means making a commitment to bringing mindfulness to this rich area of relationship in all its diverse forms.

Our relationships reflect to us those areas of our spiritual practice that we have not fully integrated. There is a story about a man coming down from a mountaintop after having practiced in a cave for many years. He finally decided that he must be enlightened—he felt a lot of bliss and joy and peace—so he thought he'd share his insight with others. He left his cave and started on his way down the narrow mountain path. When he was halfway down he saw a woman with a big burden on her back. As they passed, the woman jostled the supposedly enlightened man. He was immediately infuriated! He said, "Don't do that to me!" And then he felt very sad. He thought: Maybe I'm not as enlightened as I thought I was.

Relationship is essential on our path because it strips away our ideas about ourselves. We can be very loving while sitting alone, and then become totally angry when we come into contact with someone else. We can have great ideas about being more generous, for example, but then, when we find ourselves in a position to give, we don't. Thinking about giving can be a lot easier than the actuality, if it means that we have to extend ourselves beyond the range of what we have determined as comfortable. Practice in relationship requires us to examine ourselves with a commitment to honesty, recognizing our limitations and then gently stretching beyond them. It is important to remember that some conflict is a natural part of being in relationship with anyone. Trying to avoid conflict with others out of fear, ironically, prevents intimacy and ultimately leads to greater discontent. We need to learn how to take conflict that arises and work with it skillfully, using the conflict to be more aware of our reactivity and attachment to views and opinions. If our hearts and minds can regain balance in the midst of reactivity and conflict, faith in our practice grows and we discover a more reliable refuge than avoidance or withdrawal.

This story is told by Kosho Uchiyama Roshi in his book *Opening the Hand of Thought*: "Behind a temple there was a field where there were many squashes growing on a vine. One day a fight broke out among them and the squashes broke up into two groups and made a big racket, shouting at one another. The head priest heard the uproar and, going out to see what was going on, found the squashes quarreling. In his booming voice the priest scolded them. He said, 'Hey, squashes! What are you doing out there fighting? Everybody, meditate! Meditate right now!' The priest taught them how to meditate. 'Fold your legs like this; sit up and straighten your back and neck.' While the squashes were meditating in the way the priest had taught them, their anger subsided and they settled down. Then the priest quietly said, 'Everyone please put your hand on top of your head.' When the squashes felt the tops of their heads, they found some weird string attached there. It turned out to be a vine that connected them all together. 'Hey, this is really strange,' the squashes said. 'Here we've been arguing when actually we're all tied together and living just one life. What a mistake! It's just as the priest said.' After that, the squashes all got along with each other quite well." If a squash can do it, we can too. The inner stillness that the squashes came to through sitting quietly together allowed them to recognize their interconnection. We recognize our interconnection as well when we are willing to let go of our personal agendas in relationship and work with our attachment to having things be a particular way.

Taking refuge in our interconnection means that when we hurt another person, we recognize that we hurt ourselves as well. Similarly, when we hurt ourselves, we also hurt others. We may think that we can hurt ourselves and that no one else will be harmed. But because we are interconnected, this is never true. Unless we learn to take care of ourselves, we won't really know how to care for others. We can guess and speculate, but we won't really know. To begin with, one has to learn how to be compassionate with oneself. If we haven't learned how to be kind with ourselves, being kind to others is often merely an ideal to strive for. Taking care of oneself also means being willing to acknowledge one's suffering and then investigating its source. What I mean by investigation here is to silently observe our suffering without judging or reacting. This process takes a great deal of patience and courage, and we gradually discover an inner refuge through cultivating these qualities. By training the heart to be steady and equanimous, our confidence grows as well as our capacity to help others. When we remember to bring our mindfulness practice to the complex world of relationship, the gap between spiritual ideals and actuality dissolves.

While we try to be openhearted to everyone around us, we can practice being openhearted to all the emotions, inner voices, and thoughts in our inner environment. Taking refuge in the Sangha means being openhearted with this inner Sangha as well. If we can embrace and accept negative emotions and unpleasant states of mind when they arise, without identifying with them or acting on them, we can begin to trust ourselves and live with greater ease. The practice of meditation teaches us to face whatever is occurring, and this strength of heart and mind becomes a lasting refuge. In the words of the Buddha, "By wise effort and earnestness, find for yourself an island that no flood can overwhelm." As we find an inner refuge that no flood can overwhelm, we quite naturally become a refuge for others.

PERFECTING
THE HEART

Sylvia Boorstein

A JOURNALIST PREPARING an article for a magazine phoned me recently to ask what I thought about the fact that "people are mixing and matching religions." He said, "People seem to feel free to invent 'salad' religions. A little bit of this and a little bit of that. Do you think that's good or bad?"

I said, "I don't know if it's good or bad. But," I added, "*if* they are doing this, I have two ideas for why that might be. The first idea is that it's a very American trait (at least Erik Erikson thought so) to be a 'lone cowboy' pioneering a new frontier. (I can't think of another culture with such emphasis on Do-It-Yourself.) The second idea is that these private and singular attempts are part of a growing, widespread recognition of spiritual need. People need personal, genuine connections with a sense of meaning in their lives, a sense of something sacred. Consumerism and materialism don't work as religions. When people don't get a meaningful spirituality from their family or community—either no spirituality or one that doesn't work—they need to invent it."

"But do you think it's good or bad?" the interviewer asked again.
"I don't know," I replied.

"Is it dangerous?" he asked.

"I can see," I said, "at least one possible pitfall, one potential shortcoming."

"What is it?"

"In a solo practice," I explained, "there is no one available for feedback, no one who can encourage us, and no one to tell us that we're deluding ourselves or that nothing is happening."

"What do you mean," he said, "by 'nothing is happening'? What's *supposed* to happen?"

His question, which is really, "What is the point of spiritual practice?" is the basis for teaching the *paramis*, the perfections of the heart.

"We're supposed to be *transformed*," I replied.

The transformation, which I trust deeply, the transformation that is the goal of my spiritual practice, is the purification of the heart, our conversion to benevolence and altruism. These ten qualities, the paramis, are our birthright, present in all of us at least in seed potential. The karma of our birth circumstances, physical and mental, social and cultural, is where we start. The practice of consciously cultivating character—of having morality as a goal—is fundamental to what the Buddha taught. For myself, I have found it very useful to focus on these ten specific qualities as inspiration. Here they are, listed sequentially, although my experience has been that they are all reflections of each other and grow, simultaneously, through practice.

GENEROSITY

The Buddha said that generosity was the simplest quality to cultivate because everyone could give something away. I think it's not simple. We often think—and are strengthened in our thinking by modern advertising—that we need things and that more things make us happier. Twenty years ago I was a student at a retreat in Southern California. A group of Burmese monks, led by the Mahasi Sayadaw, were the visiting teachers for a week. The monks were housed in one of the cottages at the edge of the retreat center. One morning the students were advised, "The monks are leaving this morning. If you want to offer homage and respect, you can stand—silently, of course—outside their cottage as they depart." The monks emerged from their cottage in single file, each of them carrying his begging bowl in a string bag. I realized, as I watched them get into their bus, that the few suitcases on top of the bus, presumably carrying the second robe of each of these monks, constituted all of their worldly goods. They didn't have other belongings at home in Burma. I thought to myself, "These men understand that they have everything that they *really* need." I was touched by their apparent contentment. This image has returned to me often over the past two decades. It returns particularly at those times in which my own natural generosity has felt inhibited. It often helps me remember that my view that I need to have some *thing* or that I need to have something *my way* is itself the cause of my suffering and the cause of my unhappiness. The memory of the visible nongreed of the monks is the proximal cause of this liberating realization.

MORALITY

It has been consistently my experience that as soon as my mind and body calm down, I am presented with a spontaneous inventory even without asking for it. When this began to happen to me early in my retreat practice, I was startled. I thought I was making a mistake in how I meditated. It's not a mistake. I think the heart waits for a time when there's enough space in the mind to bring up for reflection and possible correction the errors we have made through unskillful behavior. I think the shelf-life of guilt and remorse is very long. I can remember incorrect things that I did a very long time ago. I'm sure you can, too. Even when we recognize that whatever we did, intentionally or unintentionally, was karmically determined (we couldn't have done otherwise), even when that understanding allows us to forgive ourselves, we still wish we hadn't done it.

I have felt fortunate when I've been able to right wrongs I've committed. I've had friends who, knowing that they were dying, had enough time to heal ruptured relationships. And when I've been touched by friends who have worked in this way—even until the last day of their lives—it has inspired me to try to heal what needs to be healed in my life as soon as I know about it. I don't know what the circumstances of the end of my life will be, and I cannot be sure that I'll have time for reconciliation then.

RENUNCIATION

I was walking on the treadmill at my gym, watching the news on TV. The broadcast was interrupted by a news flash of a bomb explosion on Ben Yehuda Street in Jerusalem, and, soon after, live camera coverage. It was terrible to watch. People had been killed, many people were wounded, emergency personnel were working very hard in rescue operations. I was shocked and also worried. I have many friends in Jerusalem. I left the gym for an appointment with a friend who also has relatives in Israel. When I met my friend, I could see she was disturbed even before we spoke.

"Have you heard the news?" I asked.

"I have," she answered.

"What was your first thought?" I asked.

"I'm embarrassed to tell you," she answered. "I thought, 'This is too much. Israel should bomb Damascus!' "

"I thought the same," I said.

"It's the wrong answer."

"Of course it is."

Human beings are animals, with animal nervous systems. We are easily frightened. At the moment of hearing the news of the bombing, my friend and I both felt fear and anger, and the instinctive desire for revenge. This is not a mistake. The habitual response of the body to frightening experience can sometimes be functional and self-protective. It is also true that human beings have more sophisticated response systems than other animals and can sometimes make temperate responses. We need not be victimized by our anger.

Renunciation does not mean nonresponse; it means the freedom to choose a response. As one student described it to me, she still startles when she is frightened, but she responds more gracefully. "The nervous system does whatever it does," she told me, "and then the heart does the right thing."

WISDOM

When we renounce our habitual ways of thinking—"I need this" or "I'll get revenge"—our minds clear. We become wiser. We see things as they actually are. Then we can more easily say, "This is a very attractive thing or person, but it's not really appropriately available, so I'll give it up," or "This is an unpleasant, scary moment. I need to address it with some helpful, measured response." Without sufficient clarity, the mind gets stuck in fogs of lust or aversion. To whatever extent we are able to stop struggling with what we cannot change, suffering is lessened.

ENERGY

I was talking on the phone with my friend Julie, and we were both melancholy. She was, at the time, experiencing some deep sadness in her life. So was I. We were telling each other the truth of our sadnesses. At one point Julie said, "You know, Sylvia, the trouble is that the Buddha was right. Life is *really* suffering." We both laughed. It seemed so silly—so *extra*—for two vipassana teachers who spend a lot of time talking about the First Noble Truth to need to be reminding each other of it. But the reminding, and the laughing, dispelled the melancholy. We noticed the energy in our voices had returned. We could talk about our pain without collapsing into despair or retreating into denial.

I have added a phrase to the First Noble Truth that reflects my experience. "Suffering is manageable." I'm not as frightened of pain as I used to be, and I can, more easily than before, rely on my natural energy of hopefulness to buoy me up. This is important energy. Acknowledging my own suffering has made me even more sensitive than ever before to what must be the enormous pain of the world, and I am eager to have the strength to make a difference.

PATIENCE

I heard the Dalai Lama teach the parami of patience, using as his guide Shantideva's *Guide to the Bodhisattva's Way of Life*. Over the five days of teaching, he read aloud each of the 134 verses on patience and commented on each one. Each verse describes different situations in which anger might arise in the mind. Each verse proposes a response other than retaliation. As the Dalai Lama read the last verse, he leaned over suddenly and held his head in his hands. My first response was, "Oh dear, something has happened to him." Then he looked up. I saw that he was crying. I was touched by the awareness that although he had surely studied, read, and taught that text many, many times before, the idea of responding to every possible challenging situation with patience rather than with denial or rebuttal still moved him to tears. It was a stunning lesson for me, reminding me that happiness rests in being steadfast, in considering, "How can I respond to this situation without adding more pain to the world?" I think the great respect Westerners feel for the Dalai Lama is mainly in response to his demonstrating a peaceful attitude of patience toward the Chinese at the same time that he works for independence and freedom for Tibet.

TRUTHFULNESS

On a holiday with my husband in Aspen, Colorado, I discovered an aspect of the potency of truth-telling that had never occurred to me before. My friend Elaine lives in Aspen and attends Mass at the Trappist Monastery in nearby Snowmass. Elaine said, "I'll phone up and see if you can come along with me." I knew that one of the elders in that community had done mindfulness practice at the Insight Meditation Society in Barre, Massachusetts, where I often teach. I was eager to meet him personally. Elaine arranged for our friends Stephen Mitchell and his wife, Vicki Chang, to join us, so five of us were expected, although on the day of our scheduled visit, only Seymour (my husband), Elaine, and I were able to go.

We were greeted in the entry room by the very monk I recognized as the man I had seen before in Barre. Elaine said, "Father, this is my friend Sylvia Boorstein." The monk shook my hand, saying, "I'm glad to meet you," and, turning to my husband, said, "You must be Stephen Mitchell."

"No, I'm Seymour Boorstein."

"Oh, I'm very disappointed," said the monk. "I was so looking forward to meeting Stephen Mitchell."

I was startled. I was also surprised that his spontaneous response didn't seem to embarrass him. Later, I was pleased. This same monk was the celebrant for Mass that morning. I have many friends who are Catholic monastics, and I have been their guest often enough to be familiar with the liturgy and the form of Catholic service. That morning in Aspen felt different. I realized that this monk, who had startled me with his truthfulness, was also without guile in his relationship to his prayer life and his relationship to God. As he met God, his open presence transmitted his sense of the Divine to me. I realized that when people are truthful, they convey the gift of intimacy.

DETERMINATION

Sometimes I sit down on my meditation cushion and say to myself, "I'm not getting up until I'm enlightened." Perhaps that sounds like hubris. But, I think to myself, "Why not? Why *shouldn't* I say that to myself?"

Sharon Salzberg tells about going to Burma to learn lovingkindness *(metta)* practice from Sayadaw U Pandita. At her first interview with him, U Pandita asked, "So, how do you think you're going to do with metta practice?" Sharon thought, "This must be a trick question to see if I have too much pride. I'd better answer this question carefully." So she said, "Really, I don't know how I'm going to do. Maybe I'll do okay, maybe I'll do well or maybe I won't do so well."

U Pandita said, "That's not a good way to think. Why shouldn't you think, 'I'm going to do great. I'm going to do wonderfully at this'?"

Of course! Why not? It's much more energizing to think positively. Perhaps Westerners have been conditioned to think that confidence is pride, and "pride goeth before a fall." Alas!

Whenever I've said, "I'm not getting up until I'm enlightened," I have not said it frivolously. I say it in times of distress and confusion. It feels appropriate. I trust that we can all have enlightened moments where we see clearly and behave wisely. Saying "I'm not getting up until I am clear about this, until I have the fullest possible understanding," is a declaration of faith. Why not do it?

LOVINGKINDNESS

In 1995 I was invited to go to Dharamsala, India, to meet with the Dalai Lama as part of a group of twenty-six Western teachers of Buddhism. Although a trip to India—especially a trip to Dharamsala—is very long and difficult under any circumstances, I was honored to be included and eager to go. When we arrived, all the teachers met together as a group to prepare their presentations. I knew perhaps half of the other teachers there. I realized that there were people that I knew and liked, people I had never met before, and one person whom I knew but disliked on the basis of impressions I had formed of him at previous meetings. He had made remarks critical of me at those times, and I had felt insulted. Jack Kornfield was the facilitator of our first meeting. Instead of simple introductions, Jack suggested, "Let's go around the room and each of us say our name and then describe the current greatest spiritual challenge in our personal and teaching lives." This, in my opinion, was the most intimate question that could be asked of twenty-five people, most of whom didn't know each other. I felt startled, somewhat uncomfortable, and acutely aware of being on a mountaintop, thousands of miles from home, unable to leave.

Realizing that there were no alternatives to present, balanced, alert mindfulness, I relaxed and paid attention. I listened to the stories of the people I knew and the people I did not know. All of the stories touched me with their directness. When the microphone passed to the person whom I thought I didn't like, he, too, shared his truth. I realized, as I listened to him, that I was feeling the same about him as I had felt about the person before him. At that moment he was simply a person telling the truth about his current situation, a person struggling, as I do, to be clear, to be content, to be happy, to live gracefully. What a relief it was to refrain from adding all my stored-up stories of hurtful remarks that I thought he had made about me on previous occasions. "I like you" or "I don't like you" is part of our neurological memory bank, very likely an instinctive safety device. It's very strong, but it's really not coming from our clearest level of understanding. Balanced attention, erasing fear and resentment, makes genuine appreciation and friendship possible.

Equanimity

Equanimity is the capacity of the mind to regain its balance. My experience is that I am continually being startled—something disappoints me, or angers me, or saddens me. I remember being very touched, years ago, hearing Sharon Salzberg talk about balance in the mind being like walking on a tightrope. She described what a relief it was for her to discover (after having *permanent* balance as a goal) the ease that comes with realizing that we stumble all the time, lose our balance and fall, and find there is another tightrope waiting—that mind based in equanimity has space enough to allow for a full range of emotions and space enough to see around them, or through them, so that everything becomes workable.

I recall a puzzle people were learning a few years ago. It was a set of nine dots: three rows of dots, three vertical and three horizontal, in a square. The challenge was to use a pen to connect all the dots without ever lifting the pen from the paper and never passing the same dot twice. People often struggled. There seems, at first, no way to do it. The solution, the *only* solution, is to draw a line that indeed passes through the dots but extends out past the corner dots, as if the square were larger. Equanimity in the mind depends on being able to have a broad perspective. Vaclav Havel said the definition of hope was being able to say no to whatever was right in front of you. I understand that as meaning, "I refuse to let what's right in front of me so fill my mind that I cannot see any possibility around it." If we are able to change the frightened and constricted small mind into the breathing space of spacious mind, perhaps in the space of hope we can figure out helpful responses.

One of the central teachings of the Buddha is that of a lawful cosmos, the truth that all conditioned things have causes and all actions have sequelae. Everything is happening for a reason. This understanding, for me, is both calming and energizing. I am sustained, when things are difficult, by the awareness that whatever is happening is lawful and cannot be otherwise, and although my previous actions surely conditioned part of my current experience, *everything* in the past is part of current experience. I think no one is ever guilty and everyone is always responsible. I am inspired by my faith that what I do now *matters*, that my actions now condition the outcome of current circumstance. Even nonaction is an action. Everything and everyone matters.

Obviously, when I was on the telephone with the journalist, I didn't offer a complete teaching of the paramis. When he said, "What's supposed to happen?" I replied, "We're supposed to be transformed. That's the *real* point of practice, at least for me. It's not enough for me to feel good or more relaxed, or even more connected to my experience. All of that is *great*, but it's only half the job. We relax, we connect deeply with our experience—then we see clearly and understand deeply the truth of suffering—universal suffering—and we are transformed by our wisdom from self-serving, trapped and limited by our own stories, to having compassion and kindness toward all beings."

There was a long (and, I hope, appreciative) pause, and then he said, "Very good!"

THE FIVE
PRECEPTS
Supporting Our Relationships

Steve Armstrong

WHEN WE BRING a deeply caring and respectful awareness to the way we interact with one another, we change
our social relationships from a source of confusion and
pain to a vehicle for personal and social transformation. Spiritual
awakening, in every tradition, brings this transformation of our actions from limited self-interest to a joyful, open response to all of life,
an inclusive love and appreciation.

In the Buddhist tradition, this move is described as the Five Precepts. These precepts involve training our speech and actions in
order to serve our inner and outer harmony. The precepts speak to
areas of life that are the source of our greatest pleasure, joy, and
happiness as well as our greatest fear, pain, and confusion. In brief,
the five precepts are commitments to nonharming, to sharing, to supportive relationships, to speaking carefully, and to keeping the mind
clear.

The fundamental practice of the precepts is this: by paying careful attention to how we speak and act, we notice the effect such behavior has on ourselves as well as others. If we notice that our behavior causes pain, can we gracefully give it up, or will we remain caught in an old habitual way of reacting? This is the challenge of practicing the precepts.

We are not asked to submit to an authority or any "one way" of behavior, but rather we are asked to look as carefully as we can and see for ourselves. The workhorse of this practice is attentive awareness, or mindfulness.

When we notice that pain results from something we have said or done, there is no threat of punishment or condemnation, but rather we acknowledge the unhappiness we have caused. It is then seen to be in our larger, more authentic self-interest to adjust our behavior so as to minimize the pain, confusion, or insecurity. This is not a grudging submission to an imagined authority. The restraint of our behavior is undertaken willingly, out of interest in the happiness of all.

1. A COMMITMENT TO NOT HARMING

Refraining from killing is an obvious place to start caring for other beings. The first precept asks us to look at how our behavior harms others. Can we acknowledge that we play a part in the chain of causation that leads to the death of other beings, animal as well as human? If we do not take an active interest in seeking the truth, we may live our lives believing that this suffering is just someone else's problem.

Did the war in Kuwait have anything to do with the miles per gallon of the car you prefer to drive? Does the massive use of pesticides and herbicides now polluting our environment have anything to do with what you prefer on your table for dinner?

When men and women undertake the renunciate life as Buddhist monks and nuns, they are admonished not to kill any living thing. At the time of the Buddha, the immediate and obvious effect of this rule was to prohibit them from killing animals directly as well as accepting the meat of animals that had been killed and prepared specifically for them. Less obvious implications went so far as to prohibit them from digging in the ground, or even scuffing their toes in such a way as to disturb the beings that might be living there.

Most of us have not undertaken a life of renunciation, but we still must ask ourselves if we can live our lives with care and consideration for the life around us. To the extent we do awaken to the vast web of life, we have the opportunity to contribute to less suffering in the world.

Where I grew up in central Maine, nearly every father teaches his sons and (increasingly) daughters how to handle guns and the joys of hunting. This is the cultural norm that we were all raised within. I have a close friend who grew up in this way, and he told me about his last experience hunting alone.

My friend had been a hunter for some time, and he had always appreciated the quiet time in the forest that this activity afforded. On this particular day he was hunting deer alone, walking along a deserted logging trail. As he silently came up over a small knoll, he came face to face with the object of his hunt. In the rush of recognition and excitement my friend steadied his attention on the deer and, in a flash, saw clearly. When he looked into the eyes of the deer, he saw the being within. In that moment he was unable to bring himself to shoot to kill.

In hunting, there is a term, "buck fever," which is used to describe the nervous excitement felt by a novice hunter at the first sight of game. My friend's buck fever, however, was a unique awakening, rather than the customary paralysis with the target in the gun's sights. My friend became aware of his feeling of connection, aware of his place in a larger circle of beings, and was unable to bring himself to harm the deer. This quality of heart is subtle and delicate, and very real. My friend awoke to his sense of respect and consideration.

In the Buddha's teaching, there is a quality called *hiri*, defined as modesty or fear of doing wrong by causing harm to oneself or another. The Buddha identified this as a wholesome quality of heart to be developed on the path of awakening and as one of the necessary foundations for a harmonious communal life. Cultural conditioning may obscure hiri but cannot remove it from the heart.

Modesty is a refined attunement to what makes our heart contract and tighten, or remain open and aware. When we are about to do something and we feel a sharp question of propriety, or a subtle lingering anxiety, we feel unsure of the appropriateness of such behavior. This quivering of the heart is a call to awaken, a call to acknowledge our own discomfort with our intended behavior. If it makes us feel queasy, it will surely be felt by others in the same way. This quality of heart is innate within ourselves. We need not attribute the fear of doing wrong to some omniscient deity standing in judgment over us.

It can be difficult to feel such sensitive quivering; many of us are insensitive to what behavior causes the suffering of separation, isolation, and fear, on the one hand, and what behavior brings openness, connection, and friendliness, on the other. To make it more difficult, there is often no universal agreement separating appropriate from inappropriate behavior in our culture. Therefore, it is our responsibility to make this distinction wisely. The key is mindfulness, paying very careful attention to our experience.

Undertaking the precepts as guidelines for behavior sets the stage for looking carefully at all of our life. It is only when we look that we can uncover other areas where we have not yet awakened by our own experience of "buck fever." In this discovery we awaken to the pain that habitual behavior may mask.

Even when we do see the pain, we may find it hard to restrain the habitual, even accepted behavior that has become compulsive. Self-restraint is empowering oneself to act differently. By restraining compulsive behavior, we conserve and consolidate mental and physical energy. Such consolidation allows our focus to remain steady, resulting in greater strength, cohesion, and confidence.

2. A COMMITMENT TO SHARING

We live in a culture and time awash in material goods promising to make us happy. The pressure to acquire the many items we are told we need is incessant. Often we may be tempted to resort to less than noble or honest means to acquire them.

The second precept involves refraining from taking what is not freely offered. In its most elemental form it means not stealing or taking another person's property without his or her informed consent. In order to break this precept, we must scheme to get something by deception, strength, or stealth. In the traditional texts of Buddhism this is called "having a thievish intent."

Our legal system makes a distinction between petty theft and grand larceny. The sole distinction is the magnitude of the resultant loss or harm. However, when we look carefully, we see that the thievish intent to acquire something improperly is the same in both cases. Acquiring material goods in such a way causes harm to others and creates disharmony in our neighborhood, whether it is local, national, or international.

Most of us are careful enough not to commit grand larceny even if strong desire should arise in the mind. But are we equally sensitive to our intent when the opportunity arises to take more than full legal advantage of our employer's supplies, our expense allowance, or our federal tax deductions? The material benefit we gain from such a petty action is far outweighed by the substantial damage we do to our heart. When we act against our heart's sensitive recognition of what is wrong, we sow the seeds of disharmony within and without, experiencing confusion and isolation. This makes our hearts tense and fearful.

Though we may not personally act on thievish intent, we may discover that we are the beneficiary of others' use of stealth, force, or deception. With the widespread reports of slave labor throughout the world, should we inquire if we are the recipients of any benefit from this forced labor? Was the Persian carpet in our home made by child labor in India? Did forced labor in China contribute in any way to the silk clothing we now wear?

When we ask these questions, we awaken the quality of heart that the Buddha called *ottappa*, which means conscience, or the shame of acting in such a way that brings harm to another. This conscience is the quality that respects others' sensitivities, vulnerabilities, and limits. As members of the human family, the world community, we are affected by everyone's actions. Opening to others' feelings and sensibilities puts our heart in touch with theirs. Knowing and caring how others feel helps instruct us in what we say and do to minimize pain and suffering.

When we act with a limited, personal self-interest, with an "I could care less!" attitude toward others, our heart contracts and tightens, becoming insensitive and numb in the process. This causes us and others painful feelings. When we act in such a way as to cause ourselves to feel ashamed, secretly hoping that others do not know or suspect this behavior of us, our heart also tightens and shuts down. In that movement we feel isolated and cut off from others. We do this to ourselves.

Opening our heart to acknowledge the pain, fear, and confusion conditioned in others takes a steadfast fearlessness, and it takes practice. It is a courageous process to develop the ability to feel our own fear and isolation without judging it as bad, denying it with bravado, covering it up with affirmation, or acting it out with blind blaming.

As we become familiar with the ways of our heart, our conscience awakens us to the effect of our actions on others. Exercising restraint of behavior that causes painful feelings in others requires a discipline of commitment as well as energy. By awakening our intention not to take anything away from another being, we strengthen the foundation of our community.

A commitment to this precept doesn't necessarily mean going without; it means knowing what is enough. Can we look at our busy and full lives to discover what we have in excess? Can we allow ourselves to feel the pain of those who must go without? Can we awaken to the wisdom of renouncing possession of more than enough? Can we be content with what we now have?

When we choose to work with the precepts, we look very carefully at our commitment to not harming and to sharing. In this exploration, we awaken and recognize the presence of modesty and conscience within our hearts. The Buddha called these two qualities the foundations of morality, and the guardians of the world.

3. MAKING AND KEEPING CLEAR RELATIONSHIPS

We have probably all felt the emotional sting of hurtful sexual behavior by another. In our own self-absorbed pursuit of fulfilling personal desires, many of us have also acted in ways that cause similar pain, fear, or insecurity in another.

Undertaking the third precept involves practicing restraint from acting out sexual energy in a way that causes harm to another. This is not a moralistic injunction against mature adults living a full, enjoyable, sensual life. Rather, we develop sensitivity to that personal behavior which, obviously or subtly, causes insecurity, fear, shame, humiliation, disempowerment, jealousy, or other painful feelings to arise within our own heart or the heart of another.

Undertaking this precept is not a capitulation to a moral or spiritual authority, nor is it an ego-investing, self-imposed spiritual ideal. It is a commitment of interest and energy to awaken to our choices and what conditions them. Whether we are aware of it or not, we choose the nature of our relationships with each other. We make commitments based upon shared understandings and expectations. We affirm our connection with all others by honoring our individual commitments.

A primary element of commitment is mutual knowledge. A clear basis for any agreement or commitment between individuals, or with ourselves, is essential. Clear definitions and boundaries support agreement. Vague relationships lead to confusion and undermine our ability to keep the commitment.

When there is difficulty in articulating the conditions and limits of any relationship, the difficulty must be faced. By being honest we might well expose a terrible fear roaring in our heart. To face it takes powerful strength of mind and confidence.

Every individual has different experiences informing his or her understanding and preferences, and so it is often difficult to reach consensus. In this case it is our responsibility to observe and learn from our most intimate experiences what is the source of joy and pain. When we recognize a behavior that causes ourselves pain, we can be sure that others feel pain with that behavior also. Understanding this effect of our actions encourages and supports us in making commitments to avoid it, and then choose a different behavior.

Actions taken in isolation, actions that fail to recognize our interconnection, damage the tapestry of our communal life. We then estrange ourselves from the community because we have fractured the bonds of safety upon which our community rests. Only by repairing them can we then feel the safety of the community as a whole again. This is done by openly acknowledging the behavior, forgiving the actor, and reconnecting with the love and respect necessary for trust. Then the communal tapestry is mended.

4. SPEAKING CAREFULLY: THE POWER OF INTENTION

We speak a lot. Our habits in speaking are extraordinarily strong. The fourth precept addresses the fact that a large part of the work of preserving communal harmony rests on the spoken word.

Before we make any move to speak or act, an impulse arises in the mind. Embedded within this impulse are either the roots of skillfulness that condition happiness or roots of carelessness that condition suffering. One vital factor in this impulse is our motivation, our intention. When we pay careful attention, we discover how elusive and indistinct our rationale can be. We need to open the mystery of our motivations in order to understand what fuels our actions. With that knowledge we can act to cut the deep roots of carelessness, disrespect, and self-interest, and then nourish the equally deep, though perhaps atrophied, roots of wakefulness, love, and generosity.

When we undertake to train our speech in order to create harmony, trust, and safety in our communal relationships, we also examine the resultant effect of what we say and how we say it. To help us in our exploration, the Buddha enumerated five conditions of speaking to attend to, five ways that we can awaken to the power of our words to cause pain or condition happiness.

First, when we speak with a friendly heart, what we say is more likely to be heard. When love, respect, and care are the foundation of what we say, we acknowledge our connection with others.

Acknowledging these relationships, we must not deceive, beguile, or slander. Such speech only places obstacles between individuals, separating them from one another.

By taking a moment before speaking, we can evaluate our intention so that we may choose to speak as a peacemaker rather than carelessly encouraging further agitation, tension, or division between individuals. Choosing sides in interpersonal conflicts is a habit that rarely helps to resolve the conflict. By speaking of reconciliation, resolution, and harmony, we encourage and support letting go of strong opinions and judgments. Renunciation of opinions brings immediate relief.

In a moment before speaking, we can let the impulse to articulate judgments pass. When we speak our judgments, we solidify them and make them more difficult to let go of later. By letting the judgment remain as a thought, we do not nourish it, and it will pass quickly, leaving little residue in the mind.

Second, words spoken gently are more likely to be heard and their true value felt. It is especially important that we speak in a nonthreatening, nonaggressive way when what we need to say will be difficult for another person to hear. Speaking gently allows our words to be received even in difficult circumstances. Speaking belligerently, forcefully, or loudly when we want to get our point across rarely has the intended effect. Rather, it may belittle, shame, or cause the listener to be afraid.

Careful attention to the moment when we feel the impulse to speak awakens us to the possibility of speaking so that we reach the heart of the listener. We can create intimacy and openness with our words by speaking softly in an affirming way.

The fabric of our community is as fragile as the intention of any single member. One person can create harm and division in any group by careless and malicious talk. It is our responsibility to monitor our speech so that we do no harm.

The third element of wise speech that preserves the harmony of community is truthfulness. It is said that the Bodhisattva, the being who became the Buddha, through innumerable lifetimes never broke this precept. After all, this path of awakening rests on acknowledgment of the truth.

Ask yourself, "Can I make a commitment to always tell the truth?" This may be difficult to agree to. Then ask yourself, "Am I a liar?" That is not easy to acknowledge either. So what do we do? Tell the truth when it is convenient? Refraining from false speech takes a firm commitment to the truth.

Gross lying is speech that is false, spoken with full intention to deceive others, to their emotional, physical, economic, or social detriment. This deception is an act of disloyalty to the peace of our heart. Deliberate lying out of envy, jealousy, desire for gain or respect, fear of another's judgment or position, or any other self-serving motive fuels an attachment to a sense of self that does much more harm than any temporary benefit received.

When we speak the truth, we come to be known as one who can be relied on, one who is dependable, believable, and honest. The boy who cried "Wolf!" when there was no danger left the whole community without protection and exposed to a real danger when the wolf actually did appear. We do the same with our false speech; we leave ourselves and our community exposed to the danger of deception.

It is unfortunate that we cannot look to our contemporary social or political mores to guide us in this arena of life. All around us we see deception in advertising, politics, and personal lives. This lack of integrity in speech conditions cynicism, disrespect, confusion, and disbelief. Though the truth is elusive and difficult to discover, our situation is as the Zen monk Ryokan says:

If you speak delusion, everything becomes a delusion;
If you speak the truth, everything becomes the truth. . . .
Why do you so earnestly seek the truth in distant places?
Look for delusion and truth in the bottom of your own hearts.*

Even if what we say is true, a fourth condition of wise speech is whether it will be beneficial and useful to another person. So much

*One Robe, One Bowl: The Zen Poetry of Ryokan, translated by John Stevens (New York: Weatherhill, 1990), p. 51.

of our talking is out of nervous habit, useless chit-chat for no purpose other than to fill up an uncomfortable silence. Useless, frivolous, foolish, or nonsensical chatter is called *samphappalapavada* in Pali. Included in this category is gossip, which for the most part is useless, potentially harmful, and not of benefit to anyone.

You might ask, "What is the harm in light banter and friendly talk?" To the extent that it may serve to initiate contact and connect us to another in a friendly way and leads toward other, more meaningful talk, there is no harm. But any activity may become a habit. Resorting to frivolous or useless chatter may lead others to consider what we have to say as insignificant. We may find ourselves unable or unwilling to speak openly about deeper, often more difficult heartfelt matters. The Buddha said, "Better than a thousand hollow words is one word that brings peace."

The fifth element of wise speech is speaking at the proper time. It is essential that one be prepared for the impact of one's own words, sensitive to the other's state of mind, and aware of any other attendant conditions. This may be the most challenging aspect of wise speech. It requires patience and discernment to determine the time when what we have to say for the benefit of others can be heard by them.

When I was a monk practicing in a Burmese monastery, my teacher U Pandita used to say, "Nothing is accomplished without patience." With practice we learn that wisdom is not the manipulation of conditions to get what we want—not "being in control," but rather the alert waiting for conditions to favor and support what we have to do. In this way, the restraint imposed by patience supports wise speech.

It is often not easy to forbear the heat of our anger and attendant self-righteousness. But angry speech conveys only the energetic intensity of anger. It is rarely effective communication. It is better to wait a day to let your anger cool down before expressing the cause of your hurt and the resulting anger to the apparent source. Renouncing the gratification of immediate expression and dumping of anger goes a long way toward preserving the peace and harmony within and without.

A commitment to wise speech relies on very precise attention to the impulse to speak as well as the motivation in speaking. Patience and perseverance are the keys to success. Being willing to begin over and over again with our commitment every time we discover behavior that is less than admirable means that moment by moment we are confronting and renouncing deeply rooted unskillful habits.

When, as a monk, I renounced control of my finances, an unintended consequence was that the lay supporters of the monastery became very attentive to what I might need or want. Burmese Dharma devotees are extraordinarily generous in their support of monks, nuns, meditation centers, and monasteries. I discovered that if I gave the slightest indication of needing anything, or if I even admired or appreciated another monk's umbrella or sandals, lay supporters would take that as a hint that I would appreciate similar things. They would return in a day or so and with great respect and delight offer them to me.

Within a short time I had more than enough. I became very circumspect in speaking appreciatively about anything. I became sensitively aware of the subtle, and not so subtle, ways I could get my wants satisfied. My wants became distinctly apparent as more than a need. Renunciation of financial self-support reinforced renunciation in speaking, which in turn encouraged a greater renunciation of material wants. The effect of such cumulative renunciation was a subtle joy, steady confidence, and tranquil ease for living so lightly on this earth.

5. KEEPING THE MIND CLEAR

We all have deeply rooted habits that can manifest as compulsive behavior. Perhaps we have an addiction to excitement, pleasure, numbness, thrills, or any other compelling experience. When not seen clearly, these habits then become obsessions. We often feel powerless in the face of our addictions as we struggle to escape their debilitating effects.

By undertaking the fifth precept to abstain from using intoxicants, we confront the tenacious and obsessive addictions of the mind. This precept traditionally refers to the use of physical drugs and alcohol that cloud our awareness. Some substances are determined to be physically addictive and harmful, such as alcohol, drugs, and nicotine. When we look carefully at what affects our judgment, we can then broaden our understanding of the domain of the fifth precept to include our attempts to free the mind from all compelling, obsessive behavior, whatever the source.

To the degree we act obsessively, we are not free. The joy of freedom is undeniable. It is also fragile. Therefore, it is important to see that a broader application of this precept includes confronting all obsessively addictive behaviors.

We limit ourselves through addictive behaviors and thought patterns. We can change. A commitment to grow, rooted in knowledge, sincerely and repeatedly remembered, gets real when we arouse confidence and energy. Activating the body and mind to at least try is the first step. You will never know what can be accomplished if you never try.

This process also draws on the power of wisdom and determination. A considered decision to abstain from some harmful behavior has tremendous power when made with awareness of the consequences and with a sincere commitment. It steadies the mind when the opportunity to indulge is presented. The commitment allows a moment's pause in which alternatives can be considered. It is a turning away not out of fear or spiritual guilt, but from a decision that we reaffirm each time conditions present the choice. With practice, confidence in our ability to make consistently wise choices begins to stabilize.

When our daughter was at the age of exposure to new behaviors such as smoking, drugs, and sex, she behaved like any normal, healthy teenager following her curiosity about the world, searching for meaning and discovering her personal boundaries. It was not our parental responsibility to somehow try to keep her unaware or naive of the conditions in the world. Our task was to encourage her to act responsibly and to let her know what we considered reasonable limits at her age.

She was determined to discover what her world looked like. We encouraged her to consider what she could make of the innumerable opportunities available to her. We could not support all of her choices. In time, however, when she saw that some behaviors were foolish, reckless, or dangerous, she outgrew interest in those activities.

Of course, we tried to guide her and explain to her the dangers of these behaviors and the benefits of our preferences. At times we pointed out what we saw as the dangers, the limitations, and the pain her behaviors caused. She listened patiently and acknowledged that she had to explore and ultimately decide for herself which path she would take. We all have to decide for ourselves which path we take. With that selection we say yes to some and no to others. There is no shame in stating our decision when it comes from wise choice. Recognizing the truth for ourselves, and then having the integrity, energy, and fortitude to walk our talk, strengthens our commitment to awaken from the bondage of blinding habits.

On a recent month-long retreat, one participant was celebrating her twentieth anniversary in Alcoholics Anonymous, twenty years of renouncing harmful behavior. She said that even though her momentum of renunciation was strong, it was still a day-to-day challenge. A commitment is not a one-time event. Commitment requires repeated affirmation of intention, the diligent application of mindfulness, determination, energy, and wisdom.

While living as a monk in a Burmese monastery, I once, out of carelessness, broke one of the major rules, a rule that required a confession, penance, and lengthy probation and readmittance to the monkhood. I was ashamed of my behavior, but more than that, the feeling of being separate from the other monks was painfully isolating.

Because I so much appreciated the opportunity the monkhood afforded me for practice, I wanted to remain a monk in good standing. When I felt how isolated I was and how agitating my behavior was to my practice, I resolved to repair my relationship with the other monks by renewing my commitment to the rules of monkhood. But I was afraid that when I confessed my misdeed, I would be ridiculed, judged, humiliated, and shamed by the other monks. I was most afraid of what I imagined would be the fierce condemnation of my preceptor, Sayadaw U Pandita.

When I gathered the courage to go see him and tell him about my behavior, he received my confession without any display of judgment or condemnation. He matter-of-factly told me what procedure of penance and probation I would have to go through. The procedure for reconciliation was explicit. It was clear what I would have to do.

When I arrived at the appointed time and place, I was met by three other monks who were also going through a similar penance and probation. I immediately did not feel so alone, but, more important, I recognized that I was not the only one who took commitment to monastic vows seriously. I went through a week of isolation and separation from the other monks, and then I was readmitted in a very formal ceremony. The formality of the process in no way diminished the humility I felt undertaking it.

What I discovered in this experience was that having a clear understanding of my agreement with the other monks allowed me to fulfill my commitment to them and myself. Instead of being a humiliating, shaming, and guilt-inducing requirement, the combined confession, penance, probation, and ceremony of readmittance was an empowering act of reconciliation, reconnection, and recommitment.

Equally important, my public expression of regret with my behavior indicated to the whole community of monks how much I valued the opportunity to live among them. I reaffirmed that I would sincerely try in the future to act in ways conducive to the preservation of harmony and faith among us.

I felt not only relieved but exhilarated and buoyed by the love, acceptance, and goodwill wishes of the other monks. This was a vital lesson in how the fabric of community is woven, rent, and repaired. By respecting and reaffirming our personal commitment to our individual and communal agreements, we preserve the foundation of safety and harmony so necessary for the opening of the heart.

SERVICE
Expressing Our Practice

Rodney Smith

WHENEVER YOU FIND yourself yearning to lead a more nourishing spiritual life, what kinds of activities do you imagine yourself doing? If you're like most people, you may have specific practices and environments that you define as spiritual. They might include going to a house of worship, a meditation hall, or a quiet spot in nature, and engaging in prayer, meditation, solitude, and self-reflection. These spiritual pursuits seem to foster a simpler, more peaceful life in which we might experience greater intimacy and self-worth. But with the many responsibilities of life in the world, we often have precious little time to devote to such practices. When time does permit them, our spiritual yearning is momentarily satisfied and we feel aligned with the needs of our hearts; but generally our spiritual practice remains secondary to our more pressing daily activities.

Is it possible that we are defining our spiritual practice in too

This chapter is excerpted from a book in progress entitled *From the Marketplace.*

narrow a way? Perhaps we have become too attached to a particular *form* of spirituality—to a specific practice or set of circumstances. If we return to the *intention* behind our practices rather than adhering strictly to a form that supports the intention, we may discover a new approach to spirituality, one that truly feeds our hearts.

For me, that discovery has led to serving others as a practice of the heart. Service work is a form that seems to be common to all the sacred traditions of the world. It cuts through all artificial divisions between "spirituality" and "life." Through it we find that service can actually be an expression of prayer, an ongoing engaged meditation.

Elisabeth Kübler-Ross once said that she never meditated and never wanted to—she found it too dry. But when working with the dying, being intimately present with that person, listening fully and learning constantly, she was as focused as any meditator sitting on the floor and attending to the breath. She *was* in fact meditating, but her meditation arose naturally from her concern for the dying, not through formal sitting practice. For her, meditation was an expression of her service to the dying.

Service has a way of transforming our daily life into a spiritual practice. If service work is defined as breaking through the artificial barriers that seem to isolate us from the rest of life, then washing the dishes, dressing, cooking, eating, and showering are not separate from our prayer or meditation. When our daily activities teach us about our relationship to all things, our life becomes an unceasing prayer of the heart. We become less dependent upon specific practices because we are more aware of the interrelationship between who we are and the activity we are involved in. We may participate in prayer or meditation, but we no longer find that these are the only ways to access a spiritual dimension. Our heart becomes as available through a variety of contacts and relationships as it does through sitting meditation. We start being fed from life itself.

My own discovery occurred after spending several years on retreat, including a few years in Asia as a forest monk, when I began feeling that my practice was becoming dry. I was not sure why. My life was very serene and simple, but it did not feel complete. I felt in some undefined way that I needed to connect with people and work with my heart. I had always thought that the monastic life would fulfill my spiritual needs, and it did for a while, but I soon began to realize that the longing in my heart was not about to obey my spiritual design. So I decided to leave the monkhood and return to the West.

Coming out of the forest was difficult because there was nothing to fall back on for security. My old spiritual practices were no longer as vital or as relevant as they once were. There was fear of going forward, and there was no turning back. I felt very alone and exposed. I was not sure I had the strength or focus to keep walking in a spiritual direction in the face of the growing responsibilities of a layperson. I needed a focus that could be applied universally, not just within a special environment—one that included others and was not dependent upon my aloneness.

Around this time I had a conversation about service with Ram Dass. I had always admired his understanding of engaged spirituality and looked forward to his advice. I told him I felt as if all my props had been removed and I was left with the imperative "Serve everyone," as Ram Dass's guru often advised his students. The problem was that I had no idea how to do it. Serve everyone? There are too many people, and I did not feel up to the task! Ram Dass told me very compassionately that he did not know how to do it either. Somehow that helped. "Okay," I thought, "I'm on my own, with no role models, no mentors for the leap I am about to take." That freed me up to be creative and to let the path unfold in my unique way, which eventually led to hospice work.

In my search to learn how to serve, I have come upon a quotation by a writer named Harold Thurman Whitman that has been extremely helpful. I keep it on my desk and reflect on it often. It keeps pulling me deeper and deeper into its meaning. It reads:

> Do not ask yourself what the world needs. Ask yourself what makes you come alive, and then go and do that. Because what the world needs is people who have come alive.

Let us explore this quotation and see if we can understand service in light of waking up and becoming alive.

Aliveness is our birthright. To come alive, we must align ourselves with our heart's desire. We just have to rediscover how to do that. The word *aliveness* implies wakefulness, awareness, and a connected passion for life. We may notice that the *essence* of aliveness is a pure quality distinct from the actions that spring from it, such as following our desires or avoiding our fears. No matter where we start with our understanding of aliveness, however, through investigation we penetrate to new and deeper meanings of this word. We need to keep redefining the idea, allowing it to evolve beyond what we think it means. In this way, it will always be fresh and new, as our aliveness itself.

Exploring Whitman's observation takes away the enormous tension in trying to understand how to serve. It solves the problem of how to practice and fully participate in our lives at the same time. It says that service is not a burden; rather, it defines service as that which feeds our aliveness. "Helping" was always a weight to me. It was like forced Christmas shopping: I really was not into it, but I thought I should be, and people expected me to do it. When I understood that service springs from generosity, not self-discipline, I began to tap the wellspring of energy from which generosity arises. This energy cannot be depleted as long as it is connected with my heart's interests. The vital understanding for me was that if it felt like a burden, it was. If service comes out of "should," it cannot be anything but an obligation. If it is a responsibility, it is helping, not serving.

Often the shift from helping to serving is only an attitude deep. I have a friend who worked as a waitress to put herself through college. She disliked the work and complained about it often. One day I asked her what she wanted to do after she received her degree. She said she wanted to serve people. We both laughed because it instantly became obvious that in essence waiting tables is service work. We talked about what needed to change in order for her to truly serve her customers. For the next two weeks she attempted to bring a service attitude to her work by making eye contact with her patrons and working from the relationship. She served food rather than filling orders. She said it totally changed the way she perceived her job.

The difference between serving and what I call "helping" is the difference between being alive and being depleted. Helping is based on sacrifice, not strength. It is giving something to someone for a particular reason. Its intention is self-enhancement at the expense of someone whom we regard as underprivileged. The helper is rewarded by knowing that he or she is better off than the person being helped. When we help someone, subliminally we pass on a message of inequality. In doing so, we diminish that person as a human being. We hold those we help in a fixed perspective and often refuse to allow them to grow. This is because if they grew out of their role, we would lose the contact we need to help. We become as dependent upon them as they are on us.

Our minds can force another into an unequal relationship, but not our hearts. Genuine warmth cannot exist unless there is equality. Love sets no limits and harbors no judgment. When we serve, we are meeting and connecting through a reciprocal affection, not through comparison and evaluation. We are being served as much as they are. Within this profound connection, there is mutual appreciation. Our hearts naturally open in service work. How could it be otherwise? Service comes from the perception that we are not isolated beings. The joy that most of us feel in service is the joy of generosity, the joy of immediate union. The yearning of our hearts is for the union of commonality, the union of inclusion. Our quest for aliveness becomes like the arrow of a compass, always pointing in the direction of connection and service.

I was once visiting Mother Teresa's Dying Center in Calcutta. There were long rows of wooden beds with dying people lying side by side. The patients were warm and clean, and the room, though modest and simple, was filled with caring nuns and volunteers. One of the nuns was mopping up vomit from the floor. I pulled her aside when she had finished and asked what sustained her through her work. She looked at me and said, "What work?" I was about to reply, "You are standing here cleaning up vomit, and you ask, 'What work?' "—when I noticed the expression in her eyes: they were so clear and radiant. I thought to myself, *This woman is alive.* She seemed to catch my initial reaction and said, "When you change the diapers of your child, is that work?" Humbled, I just nodded.

Through my hospice training, I have noticed that the evolution of our growth into service work is often analogous to the way people die. Shortly after patients are given a terminal prognosis, there is usually a period of resolution and determination. Their attitude toward the disease is like the strategy of a military campaign. Then, after a long and heroic struggle, their aspiration changes from hope for a cure to a hope for redemption. The attitude shifts from fighting the illness to alleviating a lifetime of guilt, and forgiveness is often pursued through religious or spiritual practices. Hospice patients grapple with their historical place in the world and whether their life has been of value. The dying eventually evolve away from this struggle of fighting their disease or seeking relief from being who they are, to just living for the time remaining. Gaining or adding something is no longer the issue. Now there is just being. Quality time becomes time for honoring connections and relationships.

Similarly, we often begin our spiritual training thinking that hard work and discipline will lead to success. We may feel anything but spiritual inside, so our efforts are aimed at overcoming this deficiency, approaching our spiritual work with the same "gaining" view of life that fills our everyday intentions. We rise and fall with every pleasant and unpleasant state of mind because that is the only way we recognize success. When we try to serve from this perception, we are soon depleted because we "give so much." During this phase, we are approaching service as a penance and can never be completely fulfilled through helping others. For service work to flower, we have to die to this notion.

As with the hospice patient, our spiritual practices evolve from a philosophy of self-escape and seeking our own salvation toward a realization of the importance of relationship. We may begin by operating under the assumption that we are too impure to be holy. We are looking uphill with the motivation of self-improvement. We serve others because it gives us a little psychological relief from our own inward poverty. We are called to serve out of our hurt rather than out of health. Working with other people becomes a way to blunt the pain of our inadequacy.

The problem is that the pain of our unworthiness may be held in check temporarily through service, but it has not been resolved. Doing good things for people allows us to feel the joy of connecting with something beyond ourselves, but does little toward resolving our poor sense of self-worth. People's praise, thank-you's, and hugs cannot touch the core of our self-beliefs. Secretly we believe that people are praising us because they do not know how unworthy we are of their flattery. It is this issue that continually colors the way we serve. As long as we disown our poor self-worth, our actions are still governed by it. Burnout is inevitable because our efforts are directed toward filling a black hole of need.

Service work comes into maturity when we begin to understand that we are as worthy of the fruits of our efforts as our fellow human beings. It comes when there is no deliberation over someone else's needs taking priority over our own. More fundamentally, we realize there never has been anything wrong with us. Service imparts energy because we are attending to our own growth. We are not growing to become someone different from who we already are. We are growing to understand who we are. Self-acceptance encourages the development of a relationship—a relationship with our own inward life.

A healthy relationship with ourselves is impossible as long as there is a struggle to be different than the way we are. We cannot make a genuine connection outwardly if we are mistrusting ourselves inwardly. If we have learned to fear intimacy, we will not attempt to connect with any depth. Relating means the joining of hearts. Service work can only come from that union. It begins through our willingness to move beyond our self-imposed limitations and fears.

Most of our mental difficulties are generated through a multitude of relationships with other people, and it is through relationships that these problems can be accessed and resolved. If we are willing to learn from our reactions to others, we can begin to increase the scope and breadth of our affection. Service work provides the perfect medium to begin this process. Service is in essence connecting with other living beings. All of our self-defenses will intrude upon our relationships unless we are vigilant. Our job is to recognize their appearance and step through these mental barriers to discover the intimacy inherent in the contact.

When I was living in a forest monastery in Thailand, I felt very free. Since I did not speak Thai, I was left alone by most of the monks. When another Westerner occasionally appeared at the monastery, my heart would often slam shut. "What is he doing here!" I would think to myself. In the beginning, it felt like an invasion of my solitude. But over time, I began to use these intrusions to learn about my resistance to others. My reactivity was a cue to pay attention. I began to understand my need to protect my aloneness, and how my freedom was dependent upon conditions. It was through others that I was able to learn more about myself. This understanding would not have come if I had remained untouched and isolated.

All of us have areas of life that draw our attention, make us feel more connected, and feed our need to grow. Hospice work serves that function for me. When I left the monastery and began involving myself with the dying, after an initial period of adjustment, I felt that I had not missed a step on my spiritual journey. The texture of the path changed, but not the direction or the intensity. Working with the dying was simply another form of intense retreat. It served the same function as sitting on my pillow, by focusing my attention and providing an inexhaustible object for inquiry.

My hospice work might be seen as a metaphor for passion itself. Aliveness has no definitive expression. Anything we do with passion can be done in a spirit of service. If it feeds us, it *will* feed the world. We sometimes feel we are not deserving of being fed. We may feel we are selfishly following our interests, as if we should be out there where the action is, where the problems are, not hunching over a microscope or gazing at the stars. But the world is more connected than that. The world is crying out for aliveness, not for a specific activity. Opening our hearts through whatever means serves the greater good.

The simple question is: What interests us? It does not matter what it is; if it interests us, there is focus and absorption in the activity. If we are also willing to learn while we are engaged, then all of the ingredients of spiritual growth are present. There is no need to go anywhere or do anything other than this. One of my teachers, Ajahn Buddhadassa, would sit all day long in front of his cabin, greeting people as they came. He carved his home out of the natural surroundings of the forest because that is where his heart dwelled. When questioned about his spiritual practice, he would say, "My attention is developed naturally through the things I love."

We may first have to understand where our interests lie within our chosen lifestyle. Think for a moment why you chose to do whatever work you are now doing. Think back before financial incentives, prestige, and social status became a primary focus. If you are a physician or carpenter, why did you choose that profession? If you are a lawyer or psychologist, what was it that originally excited you? For some of us, the expression of service work may not be directly connected with people at all. We might be a computer programmer or an artist. Whatever our work or hobby, if we can rekindle that passion, our meditation and our life will begin coming together.

Service moves us from an attitude of self-defense to inclusion of others. We begin to see life not in terms of getting and achieving, but as a living experience. Relationships, not objects, become the focus. Service then feeds us because we are always growing in our relationship to what is being served. This can only occur when we hold ourselves in as high esteem as those we are serving. It is work among equals. This understanding begins to break down the boundaries between self and other. Soon we begin to recognize that a life of grasping and avoiding is circular and meaningless, and ultimately leads nowhere but to pain. As the Buddha said, "The spiritual journey is a path from happiness to greater happiness." Service work is this pilgrimage.

PATH OF PARENTING, PATH OF AWAKENING

Jack Kornfield

JUST AS THERE IS a crisis in our ecology where we suffer toxic waste, ozone depletion, deforestation, and species extinction, just as there is a crisis in homelessness and hunger where every hungry person could be fed for less than ten percent of what is spent on weapons worldwide, there is also a crisis in parenting. These are the unwitting costs of modern consumer society. The same loss of connection with nature, the same loss of community and village, the same loss of the values of the heart that creates these other crises creates the crisis in child rearing.

Some days I find it a terrible thing to go to the supermarket. I'll see a two-year-old boy walking alongside his mother or father, and the boy accidentally knocks something over. Immediately the parent turns back, smacks the kid, and yells, "Don't you dare do that!" And the poor toddler is shaken up and doesn't understand. "What do they want from me?" he wonders. "I'm just learning to walk. It was an accident." Right then, this child learns that he's bad, and he also learns that if you don't like what happens, you hit somebody else.

Or sometimes I go to the playground and see people treating children in ways that make me cringe. "If you do that again, I'll—" a parent screams, making a kind of war on children. It's not that these parents don't love their kids, but that they don't know what to do. Often Mama and Papa are tired. They've got three kids and financial troubles or a bad marriage, and they haven't been sleeping well. All those difficulties enter into the way they relate to their children.

Even when you don't actually observe instances of bad parenting, you can see the effect it's had on the children. From time to time I used to go in to help in my daughter's class at the local elementary school where nearly half the children lived in single-parent homes. When I worked in the classroom I could often sense the kids who live in the midst of family crisis or are being raised primarily by TV and on junk food. You can feel their pain, their fears, their confusion and self-doubt.

At the other extreme there is a wave of children suffering from the "hurried-child" syndrome. These are the children whose parents begin pushing them to become successful before kindergarten, so that by age eight they go to doctors suffering from stress, fatigue, and fear that they will not get into an elite university. For overachieving parents, baby magazines advertise flash cards for infants and teaching materials for children in the womb.

But no one is supposed to say anything to parents in supermarkets and playgrounds or even to the parents of your own children's classmates at school. I've found a greater taboo against commenting on how parents treat their kids than against asking about their sex life or income. It's as if children are a possession, and many parents believe, "I can do with my possession whatever I think is right." And yet most parents are also beset by vast guilt and worry, pain, and fear: "Am I doing it right? Am I doing it wrong?"

As parents we usually repeat what was done to us, acting as we were conditioned to act by our own parents as well as the popular culture around us. Our child rearing is run on automatic pilot unless we are consciously taught another way.

Our country's postindustrial culture has left us to raise our children apart from a community of neighbors and elders. There aren't many grandparents around—they all live someplace else or they're off, like most fathers and many mothers, at the office or the factory. There aren't many uncles or aunts around to take care of the kids when parents become overwhelmed, or to initiate the teenagers (so that they don't have to seek initiation on the streets), to help them discover what it is to be a man or a woman and a productive member of the community. There isn't a community of elders from whom we can hear stories and learn practices that will keep us connected with our human heritage, with our instincts and our hearts.

Instead of village elders, American parents have turned to various "experts" and whatever fad or theory they have come up with. In the 1920s an influential school of child psychology actually taught parents that it was bad to touch their children. Several decades later, parents all across America read books that insisted we bottle-feed (not breast-feed) an infant every four hours and that we should not pick up a crying baby but just let it "cry itself out."

Every wise culture in the world knows that when babies cry, they cry for a reason, and that you pick them up and feed them, or hold them and comfort them. You have to really fight against yourself not to pick up a sobbing infant. Among the less technologically developed cultures of Asia or Africa or Latin America, children are always being held, always in someone's lap. Children are valued, are included in all family activities—in work, in ceremonies, in celebrations; there's always a place for them.

When children are valued in this way, the whole society benefits. In this spirit, there's a tribe in Africa that counts the birthday of a child from the day the child is a thought in its mother's mind. On that day, a woman goes out and sits under a tree and quietly listens and waits until she can hear the song of her child. When she has heard the song, she returns to her village and teaches it to the man whom she has envisioned as the child's father, so that they can sing the song when they make love, inviting their child to join them.

The expectant mother then sings this song to the child in her womb and teaches it to the midwives, who sing it when the child is born. And the villagers all learn the child's song, so that whenever the child cries or hurts itself, they pick it up, hold it in their arms, and sing the song. The song is also sung when the young man or woman goes through a rite of passage, when he or she marries, and then, for a last time, when he or she is about to die.

What a beautiful way for human beings to listen to and to comfort other human beings. This is the spirit of conscious parenting, to listen to the song of the child in front of you and to sing that child's song to him or her. When a child is crying, we need to ask why this child is singing the crying song, what pain or frustration this child is feeling.

Yet our culture seems to be telling us to ignore our instincts, to distrust our intuition. The result is that many children growing up in our society are not bonded to an adult. One of the more painful statements about what we are collectively doing to our children came one year from a teacher named John Gatto who was voted New York City Teacher of the Year. At the awards ceremony, in front of the mayor and the school board and thousands of parents, he castigated his listeners for the "soul murder" of a million black and Latino children. He challenged the audience to consider the effects of American culture on our children: "Think of the things that are killing us as a nation: drugs and alcohol, brainless competition, recreational sex, the pornography of violence, gambling—and the worst pornography of all: lives devoted to buying things, accumulation as a philosophy, all addictions of dependent personalities, and that is what our brand of schooling will inevitably produce in the next generation."

The average American child watches eighteen thousand murders and violent acts and half a million advertisements. Violence and materialism. We are feeding the next generation of children the very suffering we're trying to undo in our spiritual practice. With the highest rate of infant mortality of any industrialized nation and millions of "latch key kids," we have given up caring for our children. An increasing number are raised by day care and TV. We will end up with a new generation of Americans more connected to TV or video games (often violent ones) than to other people. We will have more Gulf-style wars and violent crimes than successful marriages. Because these children were not held enough when they were young, were not valued enough and respected enough, were not listened to or sung to, they grow up with a hole inside, with no real sense of what it means to love, with no real capacity for intimacy.

When the Dalai Lama spoke with a group of Western psychologists, he couldn't understand why there was so much talk about self-hatred and unworthiness. He didn't understand, because in Tibetan culture children are loved and held. He was so astonished that he went around the room and asked everyone, "Do you feel unworthiness and self-hatred sometimes?" "Yes." "Do you feel it?" "Yes." Everyone in the room nodded yes. He couldn't believe it, and he couldn't believe that this was a culture where people primarily talk about their difficulty with their parents instead of honoring them.

Contrast this with the healthy childhoods of the Buddha's time. The Buddha himself was raised by his mother's sister (after his mother died) and given all the nurturance, natural respect, care, and attention that every child needs. Later, when he left home to practice as a yogi, he had the inner strength and integrity to undertake six years of intensely ascetic practice: he followed every ascetic discipline, seeking to rid himself of his desires and fears, to overcome his anger, and to master his body and mind. The rigors almost killed him, yet he did not succeed in the fight against himself. Wholly exhausted, he sat down, and a vision came to him from his childhood that led directly to the path of his enlightenment. He remembered being a young boy sitting in his father's garden under a rose apple tree. He remembered sitting there and experiencing a sense of stillness and wholeness, a state of great concentration and wonderful well-being. He realized that he had taken the wrong direction in his practice, that the basis for spiritual life was well-being, not fighting one's body, heart, and mind. From this great insight he discovered the Middle Way of neither self-denial nor indulgence. He then took nourishment and began to care for himself. His strength returned, his vision returned, his lovingkindness returned, and eventually he became enlightened.

The Buddha had this vision of well-being from his childhood to draw upon in his practice. Most of us, though, have not had such an experience of well-being as children. And so years of our spiritual practice are spent dealing with grief, unworthiness, judgment, self-hatred, abuse, addiction, rage. This has become common for meditators in our culture. Of course, spiritual practice brings us to face the deep grief and sorrow and pain of the world, but for Americans, much of our pain is a hole in our soul, an empty space in ourselves that longs to be connected, that longs for intimacy and love. We all face this to the extent we didn't get it in childhood. For the next generation this suffering will be even more pervasive unless we bring a healing wisdom to parenting.

Parenting is a labor of love. It's a path of service and surrender, and like the practice of a Buddha or a bodhisattva, it demands patience and understanding and tremendous sacrifice. It is also a way to reconnect with the mystery of life and to reconnect with ourselves.

Young children have that sense of mystery. When she turned seven, my daughter, Caroline, had reached that age when the sense of mystery was getting fainter. That Christmas she announced to us, "I don't believe in Santa Claus anymore. My friends told me. Besides which, I don't see how he could fit down our chimney. He's too big." She was beginning to trade in the mystery of things for concrete explanations. She had mostly been living in a mythological, timeless world, where reindeer fly and Santa Claus appears. Now she was beginning to take out the tape and measure the width of the chimney.

But long after a child proclaims herself "too old" to believe in Santa Claus, there will be new mysteries. Anyone who has teenage kids is reminded that no one understands the mystery of sex. Teenagers don't ask you directly about it, but you can feel it in the air. As teenagers grapple with hormones and embarrassment and love and sex, we do too. "What did you do in school today?" a father asks his teenage son. "Oh, we had lectures on sex," is the reply. "What did they tell you?" "Well, first a priest told us why we shouldn't. Then a doctor told us how we shouldn't. Finally the principal gave us a talk on where we shouldn't."

Children give us the opportunity to awaken, to look at ourselves, our lives, and the mystery around us with renewed awareness.

Suppose we look at child rearing in the spirit of the Buddha's discourses on mindfulness. We are instructed to pay attention to breathing in and out; to be aware when standing up, bending, stretching, or moving forward or backward; to be aware when eating or sitting or going to the bathroom; to be aware when the mind is contracted, fearful, or agitated; and to be aware, as we learn to let go, when the mind is balanced and filled with equanimity and understanding and peace.

To further develop our awareness, the Buddha recommends sitting in meditation, practicing by sitting up all night and contemplating the sickness of the body or aging, developing a loving empathy for the suffering of all beings, and bringing wisdom and compassion to them.

Suppose that the Buddha gave instructions in using parenting as practice. It would be a similar teaching. Be as mindful of our children's bodies as we are of our own. Be aware as they walk and eat and go to the bathroom. Then, instead of sitting up all night in meditation, sit up all night when our children are sick. Know when they're afraid and when it's time to hold them or comfort them with lovingkindness and compassion. Learn awareness and patience and surrender. Be aware of our own reactions and grasping. Learn to let go over and over and over again as our children change. Give generously to the garden of the next generation, for this giving and awareness are the path of awakening.

Along with the practice of mindfulness there are four other principles of conscious parenting: attentive listening, respect, integrity, and lovingkindness.

The principle of attentive listening means listening to the Tao of the seasons, to our human intuition and our instincts, to our children. Here's a story about listening. A five-year-old boy was watching the news with his father when the war in Kosovo was underway. The boy kept asking his father questions: How big is the war? How did it start? What is war? The father tried to explain why countries went to war, why some people thought wars were necessary and other people thought wars were wrong. But the boy kept asking the same questions night after night. Finally the father heard what his son was really asking, and he sat the little boy down and said, "You don't have to worry. We are safe here. Our house is not going to be bombed. We will be safe, and we will do whatever we can to help keep other families safe." Then the little boy became peaceful, because that was the reassurance his heart had been asking for.

This is the principle of listening. Do we hear what our children are trying to tell us? It's like listening to the Tao. How long should we nurse our babies? How late should we allow our teenagers to stay out on dates? To answer those questions, we have to listen and pay attention to the rhythms of life. Just as we learn to be aware of breathing in and breathing out, we can learn to sense how deeply children want to grow. Just as we learn in meditation to let go and trust, we can learn to develop a trust in our children so they can trust themselves.

But some of us are confused by children's needs for both dependency and independence, and instead of listening to them, we impatiently hurry them along. In an article on dependency in *Mothering* magazine, Peggy O'Mara wrote:

> We have a cultural bias against dependency, against any emotion or behavior that indicates weakness. This is nowhere more tragically evident than in the way we push our children beyond their limits and timetables. We establish outside standards as more important than inner experience when we wean our children rather than trusting that they will wean themselves, when we insist that our children sit at the table and finish their meals rather than trusting that they will eat well if healthful food is provided on a regular basis, and when we toilet-train them at an early age rather than trusting that they will learn to use the toilet when they are ready to do so.
>
> It is the nature of the child to be dependent and it is the nature of dependence to be outgrown. Dependency, insecurity and weakness are natural states for a child. They're the natural states of all of us at times, but for children, especially young ones, they are predominant conditions and they are outgrown. Just as we grow from crawling to walking, from babbling to talking, from puberty into sexuality, as humans we move from weakness to strength, from uncertainty to mastery. When we refuse to ac-

knowledge the stages prior to mastery, we teach our children to hate and distrust their weaknesses, and we start them on a journey of a lifetime of conflict, conflict with themselves, using external standards to set up an inner duality of what is immediately their experience and how they're supposed to be. Begrudging dependency because it is not independence is like begrudging winter because it is not yet spring. Dependency blossoms into independence in its own sweet time.

We need to relearn how to listen with patience and mindfulness: this is at the heart of both parenting and our spiritual practice.

A second principle for parenting is respect. All beings on earth—your plants, pets, co-workers, lovers, children—thrive on respect, bloom when treated with respect. A story: A family settled down for dinner at a restaurant. The waitress took the orders of the adults, then turned to the seven-year-old. "What will you have?" she asked. The boy looked around the table timidly and said, "I would like to have a hot dog." "No," the mother interrupted, "no hot dog. Get him meat loaf with mashed potatoes and carrots." "Do you want ketchup or mustard on your hot dog?" the waitress asked the boy. "Ketchup," he said. "Coming up," she said as she started for the kitchen. There was a stunned silence at the table. Finally, the boy looked at his family and said, "You know what? She thinks I'm real."

I saw the power of this respect in traditional cultures on our family sabbatical to Thailand and Bali some years ago. My daughter studied Balinese dance for two months with a wonderful teacher, and he proposed to stage a farewell recital for her at his school, which is also his home. When we arrived, they set out a stage, got the music ready, and then started to dress Caroline. They took a very long time dressing a six-year-old whose average attention span was about five minutes. First they draped her in a silk sarong, with a beautiful chain around her waist. Then they wrapped embroidered silk fifteen times around her chest. They put on gold armbands and bracelets. They arranged her hair and put golden flowers in it. They put on more makeup than a six-year-old could dream of.

Meanwhile I sat there getting impatient, the proud father eager to take pictures. "When are they going to finish dressing her and get on with the recital?" Thirty minutes, forty-five minutes. Finally the teacher's wife came out and took off her own golden necklace and put it around my daughter's neck. Caroline was thrilled.

When I let go of my impatience, I realized what a wonderful thing was happening. In Bali, whether a dancer is six or twenty-six, she is equally honored and respected as an artist who performs not for the audience but for the gods.

The level of respect that Caroline was given as an artist allowed her to dance beautifully. Imagine how you would feel if you were given that respect as a child. We need to learn respect for ourselves, for one another, to value our children through valuing their bodies, their feelings, their minds. Children may be limited in what they can do, but their spirit isn't limited.

Another measure of respect comes in the setting of boundaries and limits appropriate to our child. As parents, we can set limits in a respectful way, with a compassionate "no" and an explanation of why something is out of bounds.

Sometimes, if we didn't get respect ourselves when we were children, we may have such a hole in our spirit that we need therapy and spiritual practice to rebond with ourselves. We may need to re-learn self-respect before we can treat our children with respect or teach them self-respect. Children are aware of how we treat them, but they are also aware of how we treat ourselves, how we treat our bodies, how we respect our own feelings. Is it okay for us to cry, or touch one another, or to be sad or angry?

That leads me to the third principle: integrity. Children learn by example, by who we are and what we do. They watch us, what we communicate by the way we drive, the way we talk about others, and how we treat people on the street. Another story: An old sailor gave up smoking when his pet parrot developed a persistent cough. He was worried that the pipe smoke was damaging his parrot's health. He had a vet examine the bird. After a thorough checkup, the vet concluded that the parrot didn't have any respiratory disease. It had merely been imitating the cough of its pipe-smoking master.

This is how children learn. We teach them by our being. Are we at ease or agitated? Are we impatient or are we forgiving? Students used to ask the Tibetan master Kalu Rinpoche, "At what stage should we start to teach our children meditation and spiritual practice?" He said, "How do you know that you should teach it to them at all? Don't bother doing that. What your children need to learn is what you communicate from how you are. What matters is not that you give them any spiritual practice but that you do your own."

In a similar vein, Dorothy Law Noble has written a poem, "Children Learn What They Live":

If children live with criticism
they learn to condemn.
If children live with hostility
they learn to fight.
If children live with ridicule
they learn to be shy.
If children live with shame
they learn to feel guilty.
If children live with tolerance
they learn to be patient.
If children live with encouragement
they learn confidence.
If children live with praise
they learn to appreciate.
If children live with fairness
they learn justice. . . .
If children live with acceptance and friendship
they learn to find love in this world.

If we are to offer this kind of respect and integrity to our children, we have to slow down, we have to make time for our children, we have to participate in our schools. If you don't have a child of your own, befriend a neighbor's child, or help the children in a refugee family in your community. Often we think we're too busy, that we should be working longer hours to earn more money; there's great social pressure to work and produce. Let's not fall for that! Let's take the time to raise our kids, to play with them, to read to them. Let's allow our children to help each of us reclaim the child of our spirit.

The last principle of conscious child rearing is lovingkindness. The central image in the Buddha's teaching of lovingkindness is a mother holding and protecting her beloved child. Develop lovingkindness for yourself, for your own children, and for all beings in the world.

Many of us try to control kids with discipline, by shaming them, by hitting them, by blaming them. But when we come to sit in meditation, we see how much pain we carry from the blame in ourselves. We find so much judgment and shame and scolding whenever we try to sit quietly. How hard we are on ourselves. We were not born being hard on ourselves; we learned it from parents and school. "You can't draw well," so many of us were told. And we stopped doing the beautiful drawing that every child knows how to do, and we haven't drawn a picture since third grade. How sad it is when instead of receiving lovingkindness, a child is berated or shamed.

We live in a society that in many ways has forgotten how to love and support our children, that has lost the fundamental values of parenting. As traditional cultures remind us, we don't need more day-care centers or more money; we need to regain a respect and care and love for parenting. We all long to feel loving and to feel loved. To be the woman under the tree in Africa listening for the song of her child. To feel connectedness and community. To touch one another and to be held by one another. To feel that the child in each one of us is honored and respected.

Parenting gives us the chance to astonish ourselves with love. We've all heard stories of mothers and fathers doing superhuman deeds to rescue their children. I read in the newspaper about a paraplegic mother whose young daughter fell into a swimming pool. The mother rolled her wheelchair into the pool and somehow grabbed her child, dragged her over to the side of the pool, and held on for hours until someone came home to get them out.

Children can bring out this kind of love in us. They teach us that what really matters in life is love itself. As Mother Teresa said, "We cannot do great things in this life; we can only do small things with great love."

It is through our parenting of our own children and the children around us, it is in supporting other parents and supporting our schools, that we can reclaim or restore this love. The Buddha taught us that the only way we can begin to repay our own parents and all the generations before us is by bringing the Dharma—which means respect, integrity, awareness, truth, and lovingkindness—to our parents, to our children, to all of life.

If we are to be a humane society, we must feed the children who are hungry, clothe the children who are cold, and care for all our children with respect, lovingkindness, and integrity. We must care for every child as if he or she were the Buddha. Then we will understand what Ralph Waldo Emerson meant when he wrote:

To leave the world a bit better,
Whether by a healthy child,
A garden patch,
A redeemed social condition,
To know even one life has breathed easier
Because you have lived,
This is to have succeeded.

URGENCY,
CONTENTMENT, AND THE
EDGES OF LOVE

Gavin Harrison

I WAS DIAGNOSED HIV-positive on July 9, 1989. At that time, the impact of hearing that I was dealing with a very serious disease reverberated through every level of my being, and it continues to do so.

There are not many benefits of living with this virus, but perhaps the primary one has been to use its presence in my life, in my bloodstream, to enter into the greater and deeper questions of human existence—questions like, "Why the suffering in my life?" "Why the suffering around me?" "What is life?" "What truly is the meaning of death?" "Is there an end to suffering?" Living with a constant reminder of my mortality and an awareness of the changes happening in my body is a tough and direct path into these difficult questions of human life. I am convinced that true happiness and "that peace which passeth all understanding" are the birthchild and possibility of a willingness to enter into communion with a singular and indisputable fact: each and every one of us is going to die one day, and not one of us knows exactly when this will happen.

For each of us the spiritual journey is no easy endeavor. It is tough and truly challenging. If our movement toward truth is authentic, we must open to the full and complete range of what it means to be born human on this exquisite planet. We must open to places of immense lovingness within ourselves and come to know the capacity of our great hearts to care, to nurture, cherish, love, and appreciate. We know, perhaps for the first time, places of deep happiness and contentment, places of kindness, calm, and lovingkindness within ourselves.

In the natural unfolding of spiritual practice, we cultivate and strengthen qualities of mind and heart that keep us going, particularly during the hard times. These qualities or attitudes of patience, surrender, trust, forgiveness, resolve, resilience, and nonharming are all vital to spiritual awakening and are important friends as we journey. Nevertheless, until we come face to face with our mortality, until we feel the ever-present sense of death in life, our efforts might remain shallow, superficial, and limited.

It is my experience that in our willingness to grapple with the fundamental issue of life and death, difficult as this might be, a great passion and urgency are unleashed into the spiritual journey. This energy fortifies us during the hard times and serves us in precisely the same way the Buddha was served so many years ago.

I do not for a moment believe that we all need to be taken by the scruff of the neck by some wayward virus in order to face our death candidly and to know a pervading sense of urgency and resolve in our lives. However, it is clear we live in a society that strenuously avoids and denies death in every way possible. Coming closer to the reality of death is no easy endeavor in our world. It is as if the royal palace walls that surrounded Siddhartha during the first twenty-nine years of his life and protected him from the harsh realities of the wider existence outside the palace have become the walls of our hospitals, mental asylums, and nursing homes—all places where we often send people so that we ourselves might be protected from the suffering they are going through, be it the suffering of sickness, old age, or death.

Most people either see death as a harsh annihilation or deny it. This means that the vast majority of human beings either live their lives in terror of death or refute something that is absolutely certain to happen! If we define ourselves by our accumulations, by our credit cards, by our personalities, by our accomplishments, and by our appearances, then death is indeed a wrenching and harsh finality. If, on the other hand, we see the deeper truths of who we are with wisdom and care, we may come to sense that death is more like a transition, stepping from one garden into the next—no finality, no annihilation, just another step in the miracle of unfolding life.

This perspective challenges a society deeply at odds with the truth of itself. Youth, sex, power, and beauty are worshiped, while we shun and marginalize our elderly and infirm. Rather than seek out, value, and celebrate the wisdom of the aged, we largely discard people whose "useful" lives are over, and leave them to die lonely and often unloved. There have been people with AIDS who have died of starvation rather than from the ravages of the disease itself. They have simply been neglected and ignored. For many people living with AIDS, the pain of being considered an outcast is far worse than the pain of the disease itself. People with terminal illnesses are often cast aside by the mainstream, stigmatized by those who are unable to face the certainty of their own death reflected in the circumstance they see before them.

When people die, their bodies are whisked away, to reappear a couple of days later, often looking more lifelike than when alive. It is all a lie. It is not surprising that so few people talk frankly and openly about death, about what it means to die.

After the Buddha's enlightenment, he taught for the forty-five remaining years of his life, never ceasing to emphasize the certainty of death and the precariousness and preciousness of life. He implored his nuns, monks, and laypeople to embrace the fundamental fact of their mortality—not to terrorize them, not to scare the living daylights out of them, but to liberate them. He knew that people would be happier if they could face this most fundamental fear. He promised the greatest fullness in life when we find peace with the certainty of our dying. We cannot live fully in this moment if we have not let go fully of the moment that has just passed.

A few months after I was diagnosed, I participated in a meditation retreat. I truly believed that I was not going to see the end of that retreat, let alone the next spring. It felt as though my world had been pulled from under my feet. Sitting in the back of the meditation hall, looking over the heads of the people in front of me, I had an overwhelming feeling of gratitude that I knew, indisputably, that I was going to die one day. I felt privileged in that understanding and wondered, "How many of these people are actually going to die before me and have no inkling of the fragility we all share?"

In the last few years, at least five of them have died. They are gone just as the Buddha is gone, Jesus is gone, Martin Luther King, Jr., is gone, Steve Biko is gone. Death is absolutely certain to happen. Yet it is so difficult in our world for death to be the touchstone from which we live our life. Can we bring a sense of urgency to our days? Can we know an abiding appreciation for the fragility of life and breath? Can death be an advisor to the decisions of our life?

Meditation practice is one sure way of engaging the immediacy of life and death. I had no idea how much my years of meditation had prepared me for the impact of that devastating diagnosis. I now understand more deeply than ever how developing an awareness of the birth and death of sounds and sights, and an awareness of the arising and passing away of emotions and feelings in the body, brings me face to face with the transitoriness of my life and of nature. In meditation we observe the beginning, the middle, and the end—the birth, the life, and the death—of all phenomena. Imperceptibly, over time, we move away from a dream of permanence to a sense of the insecurity and the instability of life.

There are times in the unfolding of meditation practice when this transitoriness is obvious, indisputable, and quite terrifying. We find that every aspect of experience is changing rapidly and ceaselessly, even on the most subtle levels. Nothing exists statically; everything is arising and passing away. Simultaneous with this arising and passing is an awareness of consciousness. Consciousness is the knowing faculty of mind, and it arises and passes away with what is observed. Two parallel processes. Nothing more. No Gavin. Nobody. Just empty phenomena. Changing, arising, and passing away, and the knowing of it all.

From this selfless perspective, we understand that we are not our credit cards, we are not our bank accounts, we are not our personalities, we are not our bodies, our thoughts, or our careers. Rather, we are a part of the ebb and flow of all life. Just this. In my experience this insight is terrifying and difficult to accept. And at the same time, I found there was a feeling of deep exhilaration as I approached and touched these deeper truths of my life for the first time.

In the early 1980s I ordained as a monk at a Burmese forest monastery in California. There we did a meditation practice that is not commonly done in the West. The practice was taught by the Buddha and is called "a meditation on the thirty-two parts of the body." Day after day, we were instructed to focus our attention on different parts of the body. We first focused on the hair of the head, and then after a few days we added the teeth to our meditation. Next we did the hair, the skin, and the bones. Then we added the fluids of the body, the blood, pus, urine, tears, and fluid of the joints. In time, we covered all the classically designated thirty-two parts of the body.

Doing this day after day, month after month, the feeling of a solidity of self began to crumble. It became scary as the experience of the body became more one of flow than of solidity. It was frightening, and it was freeing.

After many months we were taken to the anatomy department of a local university. Under the cloak of darkness we were spirited inside, and each of us was asked to sit beside a table. Each table had a huge bag on it, at about shoulder level. After a period of lovingkindness meditation, we were told to unzip the bag. I opened mine to find the body of a woman. I looked at her. She wore a small gold stud earring. Her toenails were painted red. She did not appear to have died in a lot of pain. She looked serene and quite ordinary, except she wasn't breathing.

The head nun came to me and said, "Now I want you to go to the other side of the table." I stood up, walked around, and was shattered to discover that this woman had been sliced in half. All I saw was flesh, bones, and organs. It was shocking! In that moment there was an irrevocable shift in my mind. Instantly I realized how much I had identified with the surface of myself and the surface of everyone else. When I looked at her from this other perspective, from the other side of the table, it was completely different. I was looking at raw meat.

As I perceived the liver, the brain, the tendons, the overlapping muscles, the vertebrae before me, each with its intricate physiological interconnections, I was filled with wonder for the miracle that lay before me and within me. The idea that I might be some aspect of the myriad parts of the body laid bare in front of me seemed a ludicrous, impossible notion. The body is a vehicle, pure, awesome, simple— hers was still and mine, blessedly, was breathing for the moment. The shift in perception that occurred in that anatomy room was a gift, a further preparation, and a further alignment with the deeper truth of who I am.

Two and a half thousand years ago the Buddha gave what I think is one of his most touching sermons. All of his nuns and monks gathered around him on a mountaintop; he reached down, picked up a flower, and held it for hours. He did not say a word; he just sat, holding the flower. After many hours, a beatific smile came to the face of one of the monks who was sitting near the front. He had received the silent teaching. As the flower slowly wilted, died, and fell apart in the Buddha's hand, the monk understood that everything given birth is going to die, including the flower, including himself. Not a word was spoken. The monk pierced the delusion of stability and was completely freed from suffering. He was enlightened.

As another practice, the Buddha sent monks and nuns to the funeral or charnel grounds, where dead bodies were often placed on pyres and burnt. This is commonplace in India. The Buddha instructed them to contemplate the fate that awaits us all. In this contemplation it is difficult to separate ourselves from what is happening before us. This is not a macabre, weird, or gloomy endeavor, but rather an attempt to open us to the fact that death awaits us all. It is indisputable. There is no getting away from it.

On one trip to South Africa, where I was born, I had the privilege of teaching a retreat with a wonderful man, Godwin Samararatna. He is a Buddhist meditation teacher at a retreat center in Sri Lanka. He works a lot with people who are dying. He was shocked to hear that the first time I had been with somebody who was dying was when I was thirty-nine years old. Godwin told me that he had recently been in Cape Town teaching a retreat. Somebody died while Godwin was there, and they asked him if he would speak at the funeral. He agreed. Godwin told me, "I went to this place called a funeral parlor. Everybody was putting all their energy into not crying, not showing any emotion. Everybody was 'stiff upper lip.' It was depressing. In Sri Lanka when somebody dies, we cry, we shout, and we moan. The children are right there. The body is left in the living room, and it is there for four days. It may even start smelling a little bit. Death happens all the time, and it is a part of our life."

I have not been to India, but I am told that evidence of death is everywhere there. People wrap up the corpses of relatives to take home to villages for funeral rites and rituals. Dead bodies are visible, not hidden away. Here in the West we have a conspiracy of silence that we think is protecting us.

I told Godwin, "I have a friend in America who is a hospice worker. She was with a dying woman who was ninety-six years old. The woman was lying in bed, and all she would say was, 'Why me, why me? Why me?'"

Godwin laughed and laughed. He said, "In Sri Lanka people are dying all over the place. From the earliest age you know all about death." Nevertheless, when he sits down with people who are old and facing death, the question they ask over and over again is "Why me? Why me?" His response to them is, "And why not you?"

For most of us, the fear of death fundamentally determines how fully we are able to open to life. Our need to be in control, our need for security, our need for stability, our need for insurance, I feel, are all expressions of our fear of death and our nonacceptance of change. After my diagnosis in 1989, fear hit me like a ton of bricks. I have vivid memories of sitting in meditation, drenched in a pool of perspiration. An ever-present sense of loss permeated the cells of my body. It felt like a volcano inside of me.

At times I could only see what no longer appeared possible in my life. At that point over forty of my friends had died of AIDS. I was haunted by memories of them and all the possibilities and permutations of this disease. They sat alongside me upon my meditation pillow. Thoughts tortured me. My dreams, hopes, and aspirations lay in pieces around me. It was a difficult time. Nothing felt stable, nothing felt certain, nothing felt dependable or reliable. In meditation, I endeavored to open to the fear of death, the terrors, the sadness, the grieving, the rage, and the proliferation of thoughts arising out of these emotions.

I soon realized that I was deeply at odds with the virus. The virus felt threatening, malevolent, and vicious. It had killed my friends; now it was going to kill me. More fear of death. Several people suggested I begin a visualization that was popular at that time: I would visualize the T-cells, which are the good guys in my body, going after the bad guys, the virus. A kind of internal Pac Man game: gobble, gobble, gobble. Being a rather zealous person, I engaged in massive warfare within my bloodstream. Afterward my body felt like a battleground covered with corpses and blood. It was terrible. I soon knew that this gobble-gobble visualization was not working. Instead I sensed a deep need for some sort of peace and balance with what was going on, as difficult as it was.

I think this quest for peace is true for anyone who has been diagnosed with a physical disease. First there is the obvious physical diagnosis, then there is the mental reaction to it, and then there is the process of learning to be with both, of learning to be in relationship with the body and mind.

In my experience, being diagnosed with AIDS was accompanied by a diagnosis of fear. Along with the virus come the collective terrors and the irrational phobias of a society deeply fearful of a virus that it largely neither knows nor understands. I felt all of this fear within me and soon realized that I needed to be extremely careful about my relationship with the virus. If I related to the virus with fear and anger, if I resisted it, if I fought it, if I struggled with it, I was waging war with myself. If I allow myself to be a victim of this virus, I am a goner, for feeling victimized by anything is a certain kind of death for me. The truth is that this virus is a part of my life now and has been for the last sixteen years or so. It would be easy to relate to it in the selfsame way that our society largely relates to the tragedy of AIDS: neglectfully and with confusion.

Over the years I have cultivated a relationship with the virus, and through this relationship I feel I have been able to address significantly my fear of AIDS and also my fear of death.

When in South Africa, I spend a lot of time in Zululand, which is a place very dear to my heart. There is a Zulu name that I love: Sipho. If I were ever to change my name, I would call myself Sipho. So what I decided to do was call the virus Sipho. In the morning when I wake up, the first thing I do before I get out of bed is check in with Sipho. Our conversation unfolds rather like this:

"Hi, there, how are you doing?"

"I'm okay. It was a bit of a rough night, wasn't it?"

"Yeah."

"What are your needs?"

Sipho might say, "Gee, I'm really tired today," or "I feel sort of aggravated," or "I feel petulant today."

And then I say, "Well, now, look, we're giving a talk tonight. Don't act up today! Tomorrow you can act up. That's fine. Today we have got a lot of things to do, so let's agree on this."

So we talk, we chat, we check in. If he will lay low today, tomorrow he can do whatever he wants to do. Our relationship is based fundamentally on one simple fact: I live, he lives, I die, he dies. So each day we get clear about our relationship.

I have an image of a really strapping young guy on rollerblades moving through my body. I say to him, "Now I want you to go really quickly to the parts of my body that are susceptible to disease, the parts that are weaker." He then zooms through my stomach and up along my back. Next I say to him, "When you get close to the kidneys, please let go of all the negative HIV factors and everything that can hurt me." As he approaches, the negative factors hop, skip, and jump over the blood vessels, into the kidneys, and down to the bladder. I jump out of bed and rush to the toilet. I pee and watch all the negative HIV factors go into the toilet bowl. I say, "May all beings be happy," and flush the toilet. Off they go!

Over the years I have entered into relationship with AIDS, and within this relationship the quality of humor is vital. It would be so easy for all of the heaviness associated with the virus to constellate around Sipho. The virus, however, is not in control of my life anymore; I do not feel victimized by its presence. We respect one another now. The fear of death is not ever-present as it once was. Sipho and I are doing a dance together for as long as we possibly can. I feel that all of us who deal with difficult issues, whether they are physical, psychological, or whatever, need to grapple with whatever fear is factored into our relationship with the difficult circumstances of our lives. In this way, our life is not governed by a gridlock of fear. We deal with issues free of that limitation. Life becomes more malleable and workable when fear is not holding us in a straitjacket all the time. Humor can be a skillful way of working with fear. Sipho has certainly taught me this.

This unfolding and challenging relationship with AIDS has taught me deep and difficult lessons. I feel it is one of the most important reasons why I am alive today. I am quite sure that if I had lived my years as deeply in conflict with my illness as I was in the beginning, it would have been a much, much more difficult journey.

I recently felt stirred to prepare myself for death as much as possible, on every level. All that was unresolved, unfinished, incomplete felt increasingly painful and weighty. I decided to begin full preparation to die and to live from that preparedness. I sensed the ripening of a surrender to the realities of my life, and at the same time felt undermined by all that impeded the letting go that I sensed was possible.

On a purely practical level, I found simple and modest accommodation near my healers, spiritual community, support group, and friends. I established contact with hospice and AIDS organizations. I took care of all the legal matters—my will, my powers of attorney—and entered into discussions with my family and friends about how

I wish to die. I discussed living wills, prolongation of life, my ashes, and my estate. Taking care of these details, I experienced a surprising sense of lightness, happiness, ease, and relief.

Having died to "Gavin, the athlete" and "Gavin, the healthy and perfectly able," all dreadful losses and sadnesses, I now find myself opening to places of joy and peace that infinitely surpass the things that I have had to let go of. I once again allow myself outrageous dreams and hopes for miracles and other possibilities. I allow these indulgences in fantasy because I know they are balanced by a candid, face-to-face engagement with the harsh realities of my life at this time. I let my wings open as wide as they can unfold, for I know that I am protected by a life that has death as its advisor.

In the last years, a sense of childlike effervescence, wonder, and joy has slowly emerged into my life. This is really intoxicating, and it feels like the best medicine possible for me. I sense that the parts of me that were frozen and squashed by the impact of childhood trauma and by the AIDS diagnosis are coming forward now with great delight, spirit, and celebration. What is wondrous is that these feelings are clearly not conditional upon the absence of pain and difficulty. They are the playmates of all that is happening, pleasant and unpleasant. I am graced with interludes of the deepest peace, surrender, contentment, and calm that I have ever known.

This sweetness is the birthright of each of us, and is available in all levels of difficulty. Rainer Maria Rilke wrote, "It is true that these mysteries are dreadful, and people have always drawn away from them. But where can we find anything sweet and glorious that would never wear this mask of the dreadful? Whoever does not, sometime or other, give his full and joyous consent to the dreadfulness of life, can never take possession of the unutterable abundance and power of our existence; can only walk on its edge, and one day, when the judgment is given, will have been neither alive nor dead."

For me, it feels easier to die these days, knowing that parts of me that were dead are alive again today. In spite of the inescapable physical facts, I am happier and more at peace with myself and my circumstances than I have ever been before. Renewed passion, zeal, and interest flowers in the meditation practice where this whole journey began. The bud that felt so tight when I began this journey long ago now feels wide open and filled with color and showered with blessings for all that has been possible in my life.

BECOMING THE
ALLY OF ALL BEINGS

Sharon Salzberg

I N T H E B U D D H I S T T R A D I T I O N , *bodhisattvas* are those who, aspiring to enlightenment, make a resolve, "I vow to attain full enlightenment for the sake of all sentient beings." That is a pretty incredible vow! It means that we recognize our own liberation is intertwined with the liberation of all beings without exception. It means that, rather than seeing other beings as adversaries, we must see them as colleagues in this endeavor of freedom. Rather than viewing others with fear or contempt, which arises from a belief in separation, we see them as part of who we ourselves are. Seeing the truth of this fundamental interconnectedness is what is known in the Eightfold Path as Right View.

The Buddha said, "Just as the dawn is the forerunner and the first indication of the rising sun, so is Right View the forerunner and the first indication of wholesome states." As dawn leads to sunrise, seeing the truth of our interconnectedness leads to the mind-state of lovingkindness that characterizes the bodhisattva. With lovingkindness we become the ally of all beings everywhere. We might think,

"That's impossible. How can I be the ally of those who have hurt me personally, or of those who seem to intentionally hurt others? How can I care about countless beings?"

True, the bodhisattva aspiration does seem to be up against some insurmountable odds. A friend expressed this once to me when we were standing in Red Square in Moscow, which was teeming with people. There were exotic-looking gypsies and people who appeared to be stepping out of another century walking right alongside contemporary business people. Overwhelmed by the sheer numbers and the incredible variety of people, my friend turned to me and said, "I think I'm giving up my bodhisattva vow."

It may seem impossible to genuinely care about all beings everywhere. But developing the heart of lovingkindness is not about straining, not about gritting your teeth and, though seething with anger, somehow covering it over with a positive sentiment. Lovingkindness is a capacity we all have. We don't have to do something unnatural in order to be capable of caring. We only have to see things as they actually are.

When we take the time to be quiet, to be still, we begin to see the web of conditions, which is the force of life itself, as it comes together to produce each moment. When we look deeply, we see constant change; we look into the face of impermanence, insubstantiality, lack of solidity. As the Buddha pointed out, given this truth, trying to control that which can never be controlled will not give us security or safety, will not give us final happiness. In fact, trying to control ever-changing and insubstantial phenomena is what gives rise to our sense of isolation and fragmentation. When we try to hold on to something that is crumbling or falling apart, and we see that not only is it crumbling but we are changing in just the same way, then there's fear, terror, separation, and a lot of suffering.

If we re-vision our world and our relationship to it so that we are no longer trying to fruitlessly control but rather are connecting deeply to things as they are, then we see through the insubstantiality of all things to our fundamental interconnectedness. Being fully connected to our own experience, excluding no aspect of it, guides us right through to our connectedness with all beings. There are no

barriers; there is no separation. We are not standing apart from anything or anyone. We are never alone in our suffering, and we are not
alone in our joy, because all of life is a swirl of conditions, a swirl of
mutual influences coming together and coming apart. By going to
the heart of any one thing, we see all things. We see the very nature
of life.

There was a monk in the Buddha's time, it is said, who originally
came from an extremely wealthy aristocratic family. Because he had
lived a very pampered life, he was ignorant about some of the simplest things, which made him the object of much teasing by the other
monks. One day they asked him, "Where does rice come from,
brother?" He replied, "It comes from a golden bowl." And when
they asked him, "Where does milk come from, brother?" he answered, "It comes from a silver bowl."

In some ways, our own perceptions about the nature of existence
may be a bit like those of that monk. When we attempt to understand
how our lives work, if we do not look closely, we may see only superficial connections and relationships forming our world. Upon closer
examination, we come to understand that each aspect of our present
reality arises not from "golden and silver bowls" but rather from a
vast ocean of conditions that come together and come apart at every
moment. Seeing this is the root of compassion and lovingkindness.
All things, when seen clearly, are not independent but rather are
interdependent with all other things, with the universe, with life itself.

At the celebration of the twentieth anniversary of the Insight Meditation Society, some young adults planted a tree in the garden.
When we look at that tree, we can see it as a distinct and separate
object, standing alone, a singular thing. But on another level of perception, its existence is the consequence and the manifestation of a
subtle net of relationships. The idea to plant the tree had arisen in
someone's mind as a thought one day, and the idea for some young
people to plant it had arisen in my mind another day. The earth that
received the tree had been nurtured by a succession of people who
had lived at or visited IMS. The twentieth anniversary came to pass
because of the enthusiasm and support of so many people over so

many years. Each of the young adults who planted the tree had come to have a connection with meditation through varying life experiences.

The tree is now affected by the rain that falls upon it, by the wind that moves through and around it. It is affected by the weather and by the quality of the air. We know that pollution creates acid rain, which impacts our tree. We hear that a variable as subtle as a butterfly flapping its wings in China affects the weather pattern in Massachusetts, and so events on the other side of the planet are affecting our tree. Every individual who now sees or touches the tree has arrived at IMS as the result of many forces in the universe converging to make his or her visit possible.

In the same way, we are all part of each other's life and journey toward liberation. One of my favorite things to do when I am sitting in front of a hall full of meditation students is to sense how many beings brought us all together there in one way or another. How many friends, loved ones, people we've had difficulty with, have in some way influenced our life to be there? I think of the lineage of teachers extending from the time of the Buddha, the men, women, and even children who had the courage in life to take a risk, the willingness to be different, to look at the nature of their lives and of their minds in a way that was not conventional. I feel how many people, past and present, are in some way a part of why I am sitting in that hall at that moment, and I sense their presence there too.

I couldn't even begin to trace the number of influences, encounters, conversations, meetings, partings, times of sharing great joy, and times of pain or loss that have brought me to that particular time and place. It's not exactly like a slide show in my mind; it's almost more like a kaleidoscope—with just one turn, all of the glass moves and shifts into a new and different configuration and a different pattern.

This is a vast web of interconnectedness that doesn't seem to have a beginning, doesn't seem to have any solidity, doesn't seem to have any boundary.

Seeing this vision of vastness, of interconnectedness, gives rise to lovingkindness. We look at a tree and see it not as a seemingly solitary, singular entity but as a set of relationships—of elements and forces and contingencies all connecting in constant motion: the seed that was planted, and the quality of the soil that received the seed; the quality of the air, and the sunlight, the moonlight, the wind. That is the tree. In the same way, each of us in every moment is a set of relationships. That is lovingkindness. It is a view rather than a feeling. It is a view that arises from a radical perception of nonseparateness.

In teaching lovingkindness, I have found that people are afraid when they think of it as a sentiment—afraid that they're not capable of feeling it, afraid that they will feel hypocritical or complacent if they try. But lovingkindness is not a manufactured emotion. As soon as we define it as a certain feeling, we make it into an object, a thing, something we give or don't give, something we have or don't have, something we might have to produce on demand, like a card on Valentine's Day. Lovingkindness is not an object, it is an essential way of seeing that arises when we free ourselves from our normal mental habits that create division and boundaries and barriers, that create a sense of self and other. The practice of lovingkindness is a relinquishing, a coming back, a relaxing into our natural state of mind.

Almost from my first acquaintance with Dharma practice, I heard that lovingkindness and compassion were elements or manifestations of the natural state of mind. I would hear that and think, "No way. Look at this world—it's a mess. I'm also a mess. There's just no way that these qualities can be the natural state of the mind." But as I have continued to investigate life, what I've come to see again and again and again, without a single exception ever, is that when I see things more clearly, when I can be a little more still and not rush to judgment, when I learn something about somebody or about myself, even if it is just information, when I see a situation or a person more clearly, I am always brought to a greater sense of connection, to a greater sense of lovingkindness. Never has clearer seeing led to more separation or distance, more alienation or fear. Not once.

A friend of mine was a wonderfully empathic therapist. One day a man came to see her, beseeching her to take him as a client. She found his political views alienating, his feelings about women repugnant, and his behavior quite annoying. In short, she didn't like him at all and urged him to find another therapist. However, because he very much wanted to work with her, she finally acquiesced.

Now, because he was her client, she tried to look at his unskillful behavior, and the ways he shut himself off, with compassion instead of contempt and fear. As they worked together, she began to see all the ways in which his life was very difficult. She began to see that he longed—as she herself did—for happiness and how, like her, he suffered. Although she continued to recognize, without denial, his unpleasant behavior, she found that she did so with the feeling that she was necessarily his ally. The goal became his release from suffering. He had become "hers." Even though I don't believe she ever liked him, or approved of many of his views, she came to love him.

Love and compassion are not conceptual states, they're not things we put on as a kind of veneer or pretense, not something we are obliged to parrot, no matter what we are actually feeling. When we let go of our concepts of duality and separation, then love, which is connection, and compassion, which is kindness, arise as reflections of the mind's natural state. This is not just a nice idea; this is something very real and fundamental.

The Buddha once said, "Develop a mind so filled with love that it resembles space, which cannot be painted, cannot be marred, cannot be ruined." Imagine throwing paint around in vast, endless space. There is nowhere for the paint to land. It doesn't matter whether it was a beautiful choice of color or not. It doesn't matter, because there is nowhere that the space is going to be painted or marred or ruined by it. When we relax the divisions that we usually make, the mind becomes like space. This is not something that a fortunate few have the capacity to experience; it is the nature of the mind, which every one of us has the ability to know.

In talking about practice, Tsoknyi Rinpoche, a Tibetan teacher, said we practice in order to learn to trust ourselves more, to get confidence in what we know, to have faith rather than doubt. Lovingkindness and compassion are innate capacities that we all have. This capacity to care, to be at one with, to connect, is something that isn't destroyed, no matter what we may go through. No matter what our life experience may have been, no matter how many scars we bear, that ability remains intact. And so we practice meditation in order to return to that spaciousness and to learn to trust our ability to love.

We are all bodhisattvas, not in the sense of being saviors running around taking care of everybody's problems, but through the truth of interconnectedness. There is no separation. We all belong to each other. This, of course, can be a very difficult place to act from in the course of our daily lives. A friend of mine was once home alone when the doorbell rang. When he opened the door, he found himself facing a disheveled, wild-looking person. As my friend attempted to get this stranger to leave, the man looked at him and said sadly, "Don't you know me anymore?" They had, in fact, never before met. While it was probably wise to refuse the man entry, his words were a tremendous teaching: "Don't you know me anymore? Don't you recognize me as a part of your life?" To be a bodhisattva, to open to our capacity for lovingkindness, is more a matter of recognition of our interconnectedness than a dictum for certain kinds of actions.

We are essentially no different from each other, no matter who we are. We share the same urge toward happiness, and not one of us leaves this earth without having suffered. As the Buddha said, "All beings everywhere want to be happy." It is only due to ignorance that we do the things that create suffering or sorrow for ourselves and for others. If we take the time to slow down and see all the different forces coming together in any action, we will see this desire for happiness even in the midst of some terribly harmful action. While we can and should take a strong stand against harmful behavior, we can do so without disconnecting ourselves from anyone. This is compassion and lovingkindness based on clear seeing.

Just as the root of the Buddha's psychological teaching is that we will never find happiness in trying to control what cannot be controlled, the root of his moral teaching is empathy—understanding that all beings want to be happy and that suffering hurts others in the same way that it hurts us. We use our mindfulness practice to notice our feelings and to understand them. Through that we can see very clearly that if we are immersed in tremendous anger, it is great suffering. It is a state of burning, of contraction and isolation, of separation and fear. We see this relative nature of anger as well as its more ultimate, impermanent, insubstantial, transparent nature. On the relative level, it is painful; it hurts. We can learn not to consider anger as bad or evil. We don't have to reject the anger or reject or condemn ourselves for it, but rather we can feel compassion for the pain of it. And then we understand that when others are engulfed by anger they are suffering, just the way we suffer when we're lost in that state.

This quality of empathy is also the basis of modern psychological thought on the development of morality. We learn not to hurt others because we understand how it feels to be hurt. If others are seen as objects rather than as sensitive beings, it's quite easy to harm. But if we understand, from within, the pain that others would experience from our actions, then there arises a clear and true sense of morality.

Empathy and nonseparation are the most fundamental aspects of lovingkindness. This is what we need to recognize as lovingkindness: a radical seeing of our nonseparateness, knowing our oneness, our indivisibility. When we see through ignorance and arrive at the heart of our interconnectedness, it is as if we had been living in a bad dream, and our anguish and sorrow were born of simply not seeing. From clear seeing arises the uncontrived lovingkindness that is the truth of our bodhisattva nature.

ABOUT THE
CONTRIBUTORS

STEVE ARMSTRONG has practiced the Dhamma since 1975, including five years as a monk in Burma under the guidance of Sayadaw U Pandita. He is co-founding director of the Vipassana Metta Foundation's Hermitage on Maui. He leads retreats internationally, including the annual Month on Maui and the three-month retreat at IMS.

SYLVIA BOORSTEIN is a psychotherapist and a founding teacher of Spirit Rock Meditation Center in Woodacre, California, and a senior teacher at IMS. She is the author of *It's Easier Than You Think; Don't Just Do Something, Sit There*; and *That's Funny, You Don't Look Buddhist*.

MIRABAI BUSH is Director of the Center on Contemplative Mind in Society, which works to integrate contemplative awareness into mainstream contemporary life. She formerly directed the Seva Foundation Guatemala Project, which supports sustainable agriculture and integrated community development, and codeveloped Sustaining Compassion, Sustaining the Earth, retreats for grassroots activists. She is co-author, with Ram Dass, of *Compassion in Action: Setting Out on the Path of Service*, and a board member of Vipassana Hawaii.

273

CHRISTINA FELDMAN is a co-founder and guiding teacher of Gaia House in England and is a guiding teacher of IMS in Barre, Mass. She is the author of *Woman Awake, Quest of the Warrior Woman,* and *Principles of Meditation;* co-author of *Soul Food;* and co-editor of *Stories of the Spirit, Stories of the Heart.* She lives in Totnes, Devon.

JOSEPH GOLDSTEIN is a co-founder and guiding teacher of IMS and a co-founder of the Barre Center for Buddhist Studies. He teaches retreats worldwide and is the author of *Insight Meditation: The Practice of Freedom* and *The Experience of Insight,* and co-author of *Seeking the Heart of Wisdom.*

NARAYAN LIEBENSON GRADY is a senior teacher at IMS and a guiding teacher at Cambridge (Mass.) Insight Meditation Center, where she has taught since 1985. She is the author of *When Singing Just Sing: Life as Meditation.*

BHANTE GUNARATANA has been a Buddhist monk for over fifty years and is the founder and president of the Bhavana Society forest monastery and retreat center in West Virginia. He is a visiting teacher at IMS and teaches meditation and conducts retreats worldwide. He is the author of a number of books, including *Mindfulness in Plain English.*

GAVIN HARRISON was born in Johannesburg, South Africa, and now lives in Hawaii. He leads meditation retreats and gives talks worldwide. He is the author of *In the Lap of the Buddha.*

JACK KORNFIELD is a co-founder of IMS and Spirit Rock Meditation Center in Woodacre, California. He teaches meditation retreats worldwide and is the author of a number of books, including *A Path with Heart,* co-author of *Seeking the Heart of Wisdom,* and co-editor of *Stories of the Spirit, Stories of the Heart.*

KAMALA MASTERS has practiced intensive meditation with Anagarika Munindra and Sayadaw U Pandita. Much of her practice over the past twenty-three years has been within her home, raising four children and being a householder and community member on Maui, where she is co-director of the Vipassana Metta Foundation.

MICHELE MCDONALD-SMITH has been practicing insight meditation since 1975, is a senior teacher at IMS, and is a guiding teacher of Vipassana Hawaii and the Hawai'i Insight Meditation Center. She has been teaching at IMS and worldwide since 1982. She currently helps facilitate the MettaDana Project programs in upper Burma.

LARRY ROSENBERG practiced Zen in Korea and Japan before coming to insight meditation. He is the founder and a guiding teacher at Cambridge (Mass.) Insight Meditation Center as well as a guiding teacher at IMS. He is the author of *Breath by Breath: The Liberating Practice of Insight Meditation.*

SHARON SALZBERG is a co-founder and guiding teacher of IMS and a co-founder of the Barre Center for Buddhist Studies. She leads retreats worldwide and is the author of *Lovingkindness: The Revolutionary Art of Happiness* and *A Heart as Wide as the World: Living with Mindfulness, Wisdom, and Compassion.*

RODNEY SMITH is the guiding teacher for the Seattle Insight Meditation Society and Insight Meditation Houston. He has worked in hospice care and taught insight meditation since 1984. He is the author of *Lessons from the Dying.*

STEVEN SMITH is a guiding teacher at IMS in Barre and the Kyaswa Valley Retreat Center for Foreigners in Sagaing Hills, Burma. He was a founder of Vipassana Hawaii in 1984 and founded the MettaDana Project, an education, health, and preservation program in Burma. Steven has been the lead meditation teacher for the Center for Contemplative Mind in Society. He is currently developing an international meditation center in the Hawaiian Islands.

AJAHN SUMEDHO, born in Seattle, Washington, is an ordained Buddhist monk of the Thai forest tradition in the lineage of Ajahn Chah.

He resides at Amaravati Buddhist Monastery in Hertfordshire, England. He is the author of *The Mind and the Way* and *Teachings of a Buddhist Monk.*

CHRISTOPHER TITMUSS, co-founder and guiding teacher of Gaia House in southwestern England and a senior teacher at IMS, teaches awakening and insight meditation worldwide. A former Buddhist monk, he is the author of several books, including *Light on Enlightenment, The Power of Meditation,* and *The Green Buddha.* He lives in Totnes, Devon.

CAROL WILSON has been practicing insight meditation since 1971 and is a senior teacher at IMS. She has taught internationally since 1986, including the annual three-month retreat at IMS.

INSIGHT
MEDITATION CENTERS

Bhavana Society
Rt. 1 Box 218-3
High View, WV 26808
(304) 856-3241
www.bhavanasociety.org

Cambridge Insight Meditation Center
331 Broadway
Cambridge, MA 02139
(617) 491-5070
www.world.std.com/~cimc

Insight Meditation Society
1230 Pleasant St.
Barre, MA 01005
(978) 355-4378
www.dharma.org

Seattle Insight Meditation Society
PO Box 95817
Seattle, WA 98145
(206) 366-2111
www.seattleinsight.org

Spirit Rock Meditation Center
PO Box 169
Woodacre, CA 94973
(415) 488-0164
www.spiritrock.org

Vipassana Hawaii
PO Box 240547
Honolulu, HI 96824
(808) 396-1528
www.vipassanahawaii.org

Vipassana Metta Foundation
PO Box 1188
Kula, HI 96790-1188
(808) 573-3450
www.maui.net/~metta

Amaravati Buddhist Monastery
Great Gaddesden, Hemel Hempstead
Heartfordshire HP1 3BZ England
(44) (01442) 842455
http://carmen.umds.ac.uk/~crr/newsletter

Gaia House
West Ogwell, Newton Abbot
Devon TQ12 6EN England
(44) (01626) 333613
www.gn.apc.org/gaiahouse

SOURCES
AND CREDITS

SOURCES

"The Buddha's Sacred Journey" by Joseph Goldstein is an edited version of "The Life of the Buddha," in *Seeking the Heart of Wisdom: The Path of Insight Meditation* by Joseph Goldstein and Jack Kornfield (Boston: Shambhala Publications, 1987), pp. 78–88. Copyright ©1987 by Joseph Goldstein and Jack Kornfield. Adapted by permission of Shambhala Publications, Inc.

"Mindfulness" by Bhante Gunaratana is an edited version of "Mindfulness (Sati)," in *Mindfulness in Plain English* by Venerable Henepola Gunaratana (Boston: Wisdom, 1992), pp. 149–60. Copyright ©1992 by Henepola Gunaratana. Used courtesy of Wisdom Publications, 199 Elm Street, Somerville, MA 02144 USA.

"Path of Parenting, Path of Awakening" by Jack Kornfield is an edited version of a talk by Jack Kornfield that appeared in a different form in *Voices from Spirit Rock: Talks on Mindfulness Practice by the Spirit Rock Teaching Collective*, edited by Gil Fronsdal with Nancy Van House (Rancho Cordova: Clear & Present Graphics, 1996) and in *Inquiring Mind* 8, no. 2 (Spring 1992).

"Beyond Letting Go: Moving into Deep Silence" by Larry Rosenberg is an edited version of "Breathing into Silence" in *Breath by Breath: The Liberating Practice of Insight Meditation* by Larry Rosenberg (Boston: Shambhala Publications, 1998), pp. 183–97. Copyright ©1998 by Larry Rosenberg. Adapted by permission of Shambhala Publications, Inc.

"Nothing Is Left Out: The Practice of Lovingkindness" by Ajahn Sumedho was published in a different form in *Buddhism Now*, November 1997.

"Liberation from Suffering" by Christopher Titmuss is an edited version of "Liberation from Suffering" and "Four Noble Ones," from *Light on Enlightenment: Revolutionary Teachings on the Inner Life* by Christopher Titmuss (London: Rider, 1998; Boston: Shambhala Publications, 1999), pp. 18–21 and pp. 208–218. Copyright ©1998 by Christopher Titmuss. Used by permission of Rider, an imprint of Random House UK Ltd, and Shambhala Publications, Inc.

CREDITS

The editor thanks the following publishers and authors for permission to use material copyrighted or controlled by them:

Maypop Books for "The Guest House" by Jelaluddin Rumi, translated by Coleman Barks with John Moyne, from *The Essential Rumi* (San Francisco: HarperSanFrancisco, 1995), p. 109. Copyright ©1995 by Coleman Barks. Reprinted by permission of the publisher.

Andrew Olendzki for his translation from the Pali of "A Mother's Blessing," the words of Mahapajapati, *Therigatha*, verses 157–62.

Parallax Press for four excerpts from the *Therigatha*, reprinted from *The First Buddhist Women: Translations and Commentary on the Therigatha* (©1991) by Susan Murcott, with permission of Parallax Press, Berkeley, California.

Shambhala Publications for "Sumangala's Mother" from *Songs of the Sons and Daughters of Buddha*, translated by Andrew Shelling and Anne Waldman, ©1996. Reprinted by arrangement with Shambhala Publications, Inc., Boston.

Weatherhill, Inc., for an excerpt from a poem by Ryokan from *One Robe, One Bowl: The Zen Poetry of Ryokan*, translated by John Stevens (New York: Weatherhill, 1990), p. 51. Reprinted by permission of the publisher.

Books by Sharon Salzberg

A Heart As Wide As the World: Stories on the Path of Lovingkindness

The Buddhist teachings have the power to transform our lives for the better, says Sharon Salzberg, and all we need to bring about this transformation can be found in the ordinary events of our everyday experiences. Salzberg distills more than twenty-five years of teaching and practicing meditation into a series of short essays, rich with anecdotes and personal revelations, that offer genuine aid and comfort for anyone on the spiritual path.

Lovingkindness: The Revolutionary Art of Happiness

In this inspiring book, Sharon Salzberg shows us how the Buddhist path of lovingkindness can help us discover the radiant, joyful heart within each of us. This practice of lovingkindness is revolutionary because it has the power to radically change our lives, helping us cultivate true happiness in ourselves and genuine compassion for others. Salzberg draws on simple Buddhist teachings, wisdom stories from various traditions, guided meditation practices, and her own experience from twenty-five years of practice and teaching to illustrate how each one of us can cultivate love, compassion, joy, and equanimity—the four "heavenly abodes" of traditional Buddhism.

Voices of Insight

Here is the first collection, compiled by Sharon Salzberg, of writings by leading teachers of insight meditation who have taught at the Insight Meditation Society. In all, seventeen men and women share their intimate experiences of the practice of mindfulness and lovingkindness meditation; their understanding of the basic teachings of the Buddha; the lessons they learned from their own teachers; and advice on following the Buddha Dharma in relationships, work, and spiritual practice.